THE
MISSIONARY
AND THE
LIBERTINE

THE
MISSIONARY
AND THE
LIBERTINE

Love and War in East and West

———————— ◆ ————————

IAN BURUMA

RANDOM HOUSE

NEW YORK

Library of Congress Cataloging-in-Publication Data
Buruma, Ian.
The missionary and the libertine: love and war in East and West/Ian Buruma.
p.   cm.
Includes bibliographical references.
ISBN 0-375-50222-X
1. Social change—Asia—Cross-cultural studies.
2. International relations and culture—Asia.   3. East and West.   I. Title.
HN652.5.B87   2000   303.4'095—dc21   99-53744

Random House website address: www.atrandom.com
Printed in the United States of America on acid-free paper
24689753
First U.S. Edition

Book design by J. K. Lambert

For Donald Richie

ACKNOWLEDGMENTS

I owe thanks to one person in particular, apart from my wife, and that is the original editor of most of the material in this book: Robert Silvers of *The New York Review of Books*. Bob must have popped up over the years in more acknowledgments than any editor in the English-speaking world. That is because there is no editor like Bob. I shall not bother to rehearse the already well-rehearsed legends: the phone calls at midnight in Pyongyang to discuss the placement of a semicolon, and so forth. Suffice it to say that Bob—and his coeditor Barbara Epstein—has that particular gift that separates good from great editors, the gift to inspire the desire to please. Most writers like to have an ideal reader in mind. Bob is that ideal reader. He makes you want to write for him. When he says, "On we go to the next adventure," only seconds after the last piece has gone through the final stage of editing, on one goes, with the enthusiasm of a puppy running after a stick. On I have gone for the last ten years, in Hong Kong, Tokyo, Delhi, Seoul, Singapore, Berlin and London. This book is a record of that journey.

CONTENTS

PART III

The Missionary and the Libertine

I first saw the East in 1971. The East is of course a vague notion, for it is imaginary as much as geographical or historical. I am concerned here with the imaginary East. In 1971 a Japanese theater group called the Tenjo Sajiki came to Amsterdam, where I was living at the time. The group was led by the writer/director Terayama Shuji. He had hawkish eyes and short-cropped hair, brushed forward like Napoleon's, and he wore high-heeled ladies' slippers. The Tenjo Sajiki was playing at the Mickery Theater.

Groups from all over the world performed at the Mickery. Located in the center of Amsterdam, on a wide street that had once been a canal, the Mickery had become the headquarters of the international avant-garde, a kind of United Nations of world theater. I don't know whether it was due to the genius of its owner, a burly bald-headed man called Ritsaern ten Cate, or to the spirit of the time, but the Mickery was where the action was. In 1971 the Mickery audience was ready for anything.

Terayama's new play was called *Opium War.* It had been raining on the day I went to see it. The streets were glistening in the moonlight, and misty drizzle formed yellow cones under the old-fashioned street lamps. The Tenjo Sajiki took full advantage of the Mickery; all the rooms were used, as well as the courtyard round the back of the theater. An actor in Chinese costume stood outside, softly strumming a guitar. Another actor, with an evil leer, stood in a corner of the courtyard, stroking the blue-green feathers of a rooster. A girl in a silk dress appeared, beckoning us to come in. She had a candle in her right hand and led us through a long, dark passage, at the head of which I could hear people singing, as well as what sounded vaguely like fairground music: an electric bass guitar and an organ.

Inside was a world I had never seen before. I cannot remember what the story was, or even whether there was a story. We were swept along in Terayama's play, from room to room. Sometimes the rooms were lit, sometimes they were dark. An actor's face would be revealed quite suddenly by the light of a match, and then disappear. There was a slave market, with naked girls and handsome pimps; there was an opium den, thick with incense and smoke; there was a ritual killing of a chicken. Men were dressed as gorgeous women, and women were dressed as men. In one room a girl in a sailor suit was bent over a chair and was having her bottom spanked in slow motion by a man wearing a top hat. A ventriloquist in bone-white makeup was sticking pins into a replica of himself. There were huge pictures of Japanese comic-book figures on the walls; there were street signs in Chinese and Japanese; there were circus posters of fat ladies, snake charmers and freaks.

Weird rock music and scratchy songs from the 1930s formed a constant musical background to the actors' words, which nobody understood: the words were pure sound, just as the Chinese characters on the walls were pure design. In the end we found ourselves in one large room, which was like a fantastic brothel, filled with girls, midgets, opium smokers, dandies and drag queens. The music was delirious, the singing mesmerizing. And then, in an instant, it was over: the actors and actresses were gone, the scenery had come crashing down and lay in piles on the floor, the lights came on, and the Mickery Theater was no more than a large, messy warehouse. The smell of incense lingered a bit longer, and my ears were still ringing from the sounds of music and text. Walking home on the wet Amsterdam streets, along the rank-smelling canals, the images danced on in my mind.

Three nights later I went to the Mickery again, and then again. During the days I would drop in at the theater café, where members of Terayama's troupe hung out between rehearsals. They read comic books and fashion magazines, and played pinball, and discussed the day's shopping, and cracked jokes in a language I could not understand. I was like a child who has sneaked into the caravan park behind the circus tent, to watch the acrobats and clowns and lion tamers gossiping, cleaning up, eating and drinking, or taking naps. Even without the greasepaint and costumes, Terayama's performers had lost none of their magical attraction. If this is what Tokyo is like, I thought, I want to join the circus.

I was studying Chinese at the time. But China, still in the grip of the Cultural Revolution, with its model operas and its campaigns against capitalist roaders, was not only grim but so remote as to be almost abstract. Unless you were a Friend of the People, it was difficult to visit China, and the prospect was, in any case, not inviting. China in 1971 was so distant it did not seem of this world, yet it was not exotic. Mao's China, to me, seemed like an extreme version of something any student of European history could recognize: a state driven by uniformity, orthodoxy, puritanism.

To some people this was part of China's attraction. Mao's regime offered the promise of a purer, cleaner, better world, a vision of heaven after purgatory—or was it purgatory before heaven? Maoism was a utopian religion masquerading as politics. China under Mao appeared to its Western supporters in the way imperial China must have appeared to Voltaire, as a rational paradise on earth. China was an idea. Chinese people were statistics—variables in agricultural experiments, mass political campaigns, macroeconomic data. The appeal of China could not be sensual, because the realm of the senses had been demolished. But China did have an aesthetic appeal: to misguided enthusiasts, the Chinese order had the beauty of mathematics.

Japan, on the other hand, as I saw it in Terayama's theater, was utterly fantastic, yet closer to the world I knew and lived in. The actors wore the same clothes as we did, listened to the same music, smoked the same drugs. But at the same time their world seemed more exotic than the China I read about in the *People's Daily*. This was partly because of Terayama's style: he mixed Western and Japanese imagery in a way that made both West and East look bizarre and marvelous. His Japan was like a great, colorful souk, or like a costume party in which the guests tried on this costume and then that—old, new, Japanese, Chinese, European. They did so playfully, freely, following only the whims of their imagination. Everything in Terayama's theater was opposed to dogma, orthodoxy and puritanism. He made Japan look sexy.

If Mao's version of "Asiatic despotism" appealed to religious puritans, Terayama's Japan was the modern version of a sensual Orient that has attracted libertines and appalled missionaries for centuries. Neither puritanism nor sensuality was ever unique to East or West, yet, on the whole, it is for the latter that Westerners have looked East. There has been a sensual, even erotic, element in encounters—imaginary or real—between East and West since the ancient Greeks. The European idea of the Orient as female, voluptuous, decadent, amoral—in short, as dangerously seductive—long predates the European empires in India and Southeast Asia.

In *The Bacchae,* Euripides portrays Dionysus as a fearsome Asiatic god. And in *The Persians,* Aeschylus shows the Orient to be a dangerous place. The gist of the play is that "Rationality is undermined by Eastern excesses, those mysteriously attractive opposites to what seem to be normal values" (Edward Said, *Orientalism*). About *The Bacchae,* Said remarks that "The difference separating East and West is symbolized by the sternness with which, at first, Pentheus rejects the hysterical bacchantes."

Aphrodite was modeled after Astarte, the Whore of Babylon. Even though the Greeks worshiped Aphrodite, she never quite shed her foreign, Asiatic origins; she kept her slightly scandalous reputation as the divine patroness of temple prostitutes, which is why the Church fathers called her a whore, and Emperor Constantine, in an early instance of missionary zeal, smashed her temple at Baalbek and built a church in its stead.

In *The Lotus and the Robot,* a book about India and Japan, Arthur Koestler describes his first reaction to "Lotusland" (i.e., Japan) as one of "sensuous and sensual delight." Japan, he writes, has "an atmosphere with an erotic flicker like the crisp sparks from a comb drawn through a woman's hair—a guilt-free eroticism which Europe has not known since antiquity."

These are only perceptions, of course, not exact reflections of reality. In fact, Amsterdam, where I saw Terayama's bacchantes perform, was in many respects more of a Lotusland than Tokyo. It was certainly more "Orientalist," with its fashion, among young people, for hashish, incense, patchouli oils and Indian frou-frou. Yet Koestler's first impression of Tokyo was similar to that of many Western travelers, some of whom decided to stay. It is easy to imagine the giddy sense of freedom felt by Englishmen from rainy northern towns, or Americans from God-fearing midwestern plains, when they came to Japan, or Thailand, or Ceylon, or wherever their idea of Arcadia happened to be. Because local restraints did not apply to them, and they were far from home, everything suddenly seemed possible. The American writer Donald Richie arrived in Japan in 1945. The last words of his loving travelogue *The Inland Sea* are "I don't care if I never go home." And he never did.

For centuries the East, like the Mediterranean countries, represented the sunny, pagan, hedonistic alternative to the cold, pinched and dreary climate of the Christian, especially Protestant, West. Many British writers sought permanent or temporary refuge in India, the Middle East, China or Capri. All over Southeast Asia and Japan there are self-made Arcadias, built by European or American exiles from their native puritanism. In Bangkok, Macao or Kobe, they look curiously alike: gorgeously decorated with Asian art and antiques, fenced in by gardens of bamboo, and with handsome young men or (less often) young girls in attendance.

The purest example of an exile in Arcadia I ever came across was actually someone I never met. By the time I became aware of him, he was already dead. I found him in a university library, not long after I first went to Japan as a student, in 1975. The library was closed to Japanese students, because campus radicals had occupied it some years before, but foreign students were allowed in. I found myself browsing through the stacks with another student, an English artist. We soon noticed not only that the selection of English books reflected a very particular taste, but that virtually all the books had belonged to one man. I cannot remember his name—it was something like Edward Postlethwaite. From dates and place names inscribed in his books, it was clear that he had lived in Berlin until 1936, after which he moved to a fishing village a hundred miles south of Tokyo.

Postlethwaite had a taste for such fin-de-siècle curiosities as accounts by obscure countesses of the Oscar Wilde they had known. There were first editions of Aubrey Beardsley, J.-K. Huysmans, and Ronald Firbank. Photographic books of naked German youths, sitting on rocks or on mountaintops, squinting into the sun, abounded. He also liked Greek myths, Nordic legends (a handsome edition of *Wagner's Ring of the Nibelungen*) and Japanese folktales (the complete works of Lafcadio Hearn).

But the book that caught my particular attention was not a precious literary curio but a volume of short stories by Somerset Maugham. The reason was Postlethwaite's scribbling. He had the habit of writing remarks in the margins ("good!", or, sometimes, "absolute rot!"). He also underlined passages he particularly admired. There was one such passage in a story about a British planter in Malaya. The planter is visited by another Englishman, evidently a rare occasion, for the plantation is in a remote part of the country. The two men are having drinks on the verandah after sundown. The night is silent apart from the odd animal crying out. The visitor asks his host how he can stand the loneliness of his life, without the company of fellow white men. That, says the planter, is precisely why he likes it out there. The sentence was underlined in thick red ink. I tried to imagine Postlethwaite's house in the Japanese fishing village: the books, the bamboo fence, the young boys.

The sexual attraction of the East is, of course, a complex thing, which cannot be explained only by the attraction of "guilt-free" eroticism to men or women burdened by Christian guilt. Power and domination have much to do with it. The image of the "geisha girl"—submissive, pliable, ready to indulge any fancy—dovetails neatly with the old perception of the East as a passive, feminine receptacle of masculine Occidental vigour. It is surely not for nothing that nineteenth-century French painters of Orientalist themes were fascinated by harems and slave markets. Modern Japanese pornography is dominated (if that's the right word) by sadomasochism. When Western men—black or white—appear in this material, it is usually as brutal masters. This is for the Japanese market, of course, but the fantasies conform to the Orientalist types.

The idea of the East as being more refined, more elegant than the West, of the geisha girl as the mistress of exquisite erotic arts, fits in too. To be *raffiné* is close to being decadent. To be coarse is to be forceful and virile. But there is an alternative vision of the Oriental, which is admittedly somewhat old-fashioned these days: the child of nature. Guiltless eroticism is associated with the noble savage, the beautiful, simple, human creature whose mind is uncluttered by moral and intellectual complexity. It is still possible, in certain circles, to hear the Japanese described as "innocent." This means, of course, innocent of the Christian idea of sin. On this point, missionary and libertine would agree: the difference is that one finds deplorable what the other adores.

I first fell in love with a Japanese girl in the movies. She was a character in *Domicile conjugal,* a film by Francois Truffaut. Or rather, she was not really a character at all: she was a phantom, a fantasy, a catalyst to enable the French characters to reveal themselves. A young man in Paris is married to a young Frenchwoman. Their life is a study of bourgeois French domesticity. Then the young man meets a beautiful Japanese woman. She is mysterious and exotic—everything his life is not. The young man falls in love with her. She prepares exquisite food for him. They have sex without guilt. But he never gets to know her. They are incapable of having a meaningful conversation. She remains as silent and elusive as a ghost. Finally he realizes that life with her is unreal, in fact unbearable, and goes back to French domesticity.

The French marriage, then, as shown in Truffaut's film, is real. The Japanese girl represents a flight from reality, a dream. But, as I said, I was enchanted. This was in 1972. While writing this piece, twenty-three years later, I decided to see the film again, so I bought the video. I was still enchanted. Then, a week or so after that, I was invited to judge a program of Japanese films in France. And there, among my fellow jurors, she was: Hiroko. Although no longer young, she had hardly changed: a Japanese Parisienne, or a Parisian fantasy of Japanese womanhood. I told her my story. She smiled, and said in a soft, lilting voice, "You're not the first one, you know."

I don't know whether Truffaut believed that communication between a Frenchman and a Japanese woman was impossible beyond a superficial level, but, for the sake of the film, he had to assume so. And the same might be true of Postlethwaite and his fellow escapees from Western life—the Orientalists, the "rice queens," the romantics in search of Lotusland. It is a mark of the romantic that he or she seeks the unreal. The point of going East is not to find oneself, as so many hippie seekers thought, but to get rid of oneself—or at least those aspects of oneself one does not like.

But Lotusland exacts its price, for seekers after guilt-free sex do not always manage to shed their own sense of guilt. After the sensual charms wear off, or are taken for granted, a peculiar censoriousness sometimes sets in, and the East is denounced for its lack of universal values, its frivolousness, its amorality. All of a sudden the libertine becomes a missionary; the moralism he thought he had shed is deflected on to his hosts. In Japan, Koestler speaks of a "first phase" (of delight) and subsequent negative "phases." He notes that with some Westerners the first phase can last a lifetime, but that with others soured delight can result in permanent hatred. In fact, in my experience, many Westerners in Japan veer between the poles of love and hate so fast it can cause a kind of mental seasickness. When that happens, it is best to leave. You only need to study the letter columns in the English-language press in Tokyo to see what bitterness mental nausea can cause.

The struggle between missionary and libertine goes beyond the psychology of individuals. Or, to put it in another way, the personal and the political intersect. The very notion of an alternative world, a haven of hedonism, an amoral Arcadia, is a provocation to authoritarians anywhere. Even if that alternative world is an illusion, it must be stamped out, reformed or censored. Astarte's temple prostitutes of West Asia were an affront to the Byzantine empire, just as Indian temple dancers later shocked the missionaries of the British empire. Sexual freedom and political heterodoxy are closely linked in the authoritarian mind, for good reasons. If you believe in absolutism—political or moral—an alternative cannot be allowed to exist.

This is where the dichotomy of East and West breaks down. Every society has it missionaries and its libertines. Papuas of Irian Jaya used to dismay dignitaries from Jakarta by greeting them at the airport dressed in little but their erect and elongated penis-sheaths. They were told to dress in the future like respectable Indonesians. But the Papuans were not so easily cowed. The next time a government representative arrived in Jayapura he was greeted by a line of half-naked men with their sheaths displayed in full splendor. But on their tips fluttered the red and white colors of the Indonesian flag. Islamic, let alone Christian, morality was not what drove the Indonesian missionaries. In their view, the continuation of "primitive" Papuan customs posed a threat to order in the Javanese empire. Flags flying from penis-sheaths were a demonstration of liberty from the "normal values" of the state.

What is normal, in the eyes of officialdom, changes with time. So do perceptions of the outside world and indeed of missionaries. At the end of the sixteenth century the Japanese shogun Hideyoshi persecuted Jesuit missionaries because they were turning too many Japanese heads: the attraction of Christ was a threat to orthodoxy and public order. But the autocratic politicians who ruled Japan three hundred years later imitated aspects of European puritanism. By then Europeans ruled much of the East, as "muscular Christians" carrying the white man's burden. The hedonism of British libertines in eighteenth-century India had withered with the advent of a new breed of colonizer, particularly the memsahibs among them. By the mid–nineteenth century the images of East and West had hardened: the West was virile, dynamic, expansive, disciplined, and the East was indolent, decadent, pleasure-loving, passive. In 1885 the editors of a Japanese newspaper wrote, "If a Japanese be compared with an Englishman or an American, it is not necessary to go very deep into the subject to discover who is the more industrious, better educated, more courageous and more intelligent. What a difference there is between Japan and either England or the United States in strength, wealth and civilization."

Some Japanese in the nineteenth century believed that Christianity was the unifying force that gave Europeans their vigor and discipline. This inspired them to come up with a muscular creed of their own: state Shinto. It was designed to promote absolute obedience to the emperor, as the divine embodiment of ancient Japanese values. Its official promoters were the new missionaries, who appealed to tradition while at the same time purging Japan of its supposedly decadent past. Their efforts were cultural as well as political. The Kabuki theater and other arts of the old world of licensed hedonism were cleaned up and became academic expressions of national tradition. Public nudity was to be discouraged—even the "sacred nudity" in traditional Shinto ceremonies of nature worship. State Shinto had to be clean and patriotic, just like muscular Christianity.

In the introduction to a book of photographs of Shinto festivals, called *Naked Festival,* Mishima Yukio once wrote that in the Meiji era of so-called Civilization and Enlightenment (1868–1912)

Japan tried to deny her past completely, or at least to hide from Western eyes any of the old ways that might persist despite all efforts to eradicate them. The Japanese were like an anxious housewife preparing to receive guests, hiding away in closets common articles of daily use and laying aside comfortable everyday clothes, hoping to impress the guests with an immaculate, idealized life of her household, without so much as a speck of dust in view.

It was not only to impress the guests, however, that the Meiji patriarchs behaved like puritanical housewives: it was also because they thought that, for Japan to be as powerful as the West, Japanese had to behave like Westerners—or at least like Westernized Japanese. Similar ideas arose in other parts of Asia. In India, Swami Vivekananda (1863–1902) believed that Hindus should reinvigorate themselves through the three Bs: beef, biceps and Bhagavad-Gita. This was *his* answer to muscular Christianity. King Rama VI of Thailand, who was educated at Sandhurst, led a Boy Scout movement, promoted European dress for women, designed a national flag, introduced the Gregorian calendar and wrote poems to promote a vigorous nation:

Let us unite our state, unite our hearts, into a great whole.
Thai—do not harm, or destroy Thai,
But combine your spirit, and your strength to preserve the state
So that all foreign peoples
Will give an increasing respect.

The extreme phase of Occidentalism did not last very long in Thailand or Japan, nor was its effect as deep or pervasive as some of its boosters might have hoped. And not all Western ideas were puritanical. During a brief period in the Roaring Twenties, Japan not only came close to democratic government, but an East–West cocktail of libertinism, characterized as *ero, guro, nansensu* (erotic, grotesque, nonsense), set the tone in metropolitan cultural life.

Missionary zeal, nonetheless, had not disappeared. The creed of muscular Japaneseness returned with the authoritarian regimes of the 1930s and early 1940s. And, just as conquest of the East by European nations had gone hand in hand with a *mission civilisatrice,* undertaken by promoters of "universal" Western values, the Japanese conquest of Asia came with a mission to spread Japanese imperialist values. This time Asia was to be civilized by missionaries from the East. The pattern of

East–West imagery had not changed: Japan had simply become an honorary member of the West. Japan was full of masculine energy, while China was regarded as a supine, decadent, indolent, passive country, waiting to be disciplined by a more vigorous race.

The Japanese mission failed, but it helped to bring the European empires to a speedier end. Once the weakness of Western powers had been exposed, the elaborate façade of their muscular invincibility began to crumble. The European *mission civilisatrice* did not outlast the Japanese empire for long. It was replaced by the Pax Americana, which in its early postwar stage was still driven by vigorous optimism, only to droop badly after the war in Vietnam. That war, which sapped so much American energy, inspired a whole new generation of missionaries and libertines. "Saigon . . . shit," the first two words of Francis Ford Coppola's *Apocalypse Now,* summed up the ancient view of the East as a wicked swamp of iniquity, waiting to suck Westerners into its rotting depths. Saigon was glamorous and corrupt, destroyed by the white man, and destroyer of white men. It might have been shit, but it was seductive shit.

Roughly since the fall of Saigon, however, an astonishing reversal has taken place in Asia. From the official point of view of China, Singapore, Malaysia, South Korea and Japan, Europe and the United States are now models not of masculine vim but, on the contrary, of decadence, libertinism and sloth. Spokesmen for so-called Asian values extol the superior discipline, vigor and industriousness of the East. Now it is the turn for individual Asians to seek liberty and pleasure in the West. And, just as Asian nationalists once copied the muscular virtues of Western imperialism, some conservatives in the West today dream of cracking Occidental libertines with an Oriental whip.

There is in fact nothing peculiarly Asian about Asian values. What the likes of Lee Kuan Yew call Asian values are more or less the values they were taught by their colonial schoolmasters in the days when Kuan Yew was still called Harry. The white man's burden has been covered with a Confucian sauce. When George Brown visited Singapore in the 1960s as British foreign secretary, he was harangued by Lee Kuan Yew about the rotten state of Britain. When Lee had finished, Brown said (or is said to have said), "Harry, you're the finest Englishman east of Suez."

Mahathir Mohamad, the prime minister of Malaysia, is quite open about the provenance of his Asianist propaganda. He has recalled how the Englishmen of his youth wore their collars and ties even in the sticky heat of a Malayan summer. To him this was a sign of superior discipline and propriety—what made the British great. Now in Britain he sees only sloppy permissiveness, which, if Eastern leaders such as himself are not careful, will sap the vigor of the more youthful East. He writes in his book, entitled *The Challenge* (a whiff of Newbolt or Baden-Powell here), "Just as copying proper attire once led to the East adopting Western values regarding discipline, copying improper attire has infected the East with the values behind the change in attire."

The missionaries, then, have taken post in Kuala Lumpur, and the whores of Babylon have moved to London and New York. This is how promoters of Asian values explain the rise of East Asia and the decline of the West. Now it would be foolish to deny that many parts of East Asia are fizzing with economic energy, and that many Western nations are hampered by complacency. But does this mean that the missionaries are right? Is the West being corrupted by too much individual liberty? And are collective discipline and individual repression the keys to the East Asian renaissance?

Not necessarily. Hard work and discipline are vital conditions for human achievement. But the energy that produced the Western empires had to do less with puritanical values than with political and economic liberties. The weakness of Asia in the nineteenth century was less a matter of lax morals and too much freedom than of archaic political institutions and too little freedom. Empires were not built on muscular Christianity, but they were later justified by it. The promoters of Asian values today are doing what missionaries, whether "Asian" or "Japanese" or "Christian," have always done: they use values to justify their masters' power.

I arrived in the East as a libertine, beckoned by Terayama's theater from Tokyo. I have tried to resist the enticements of the missionaries, from East or West, though not always with success: the role of the moralist can be a satisfying one. Yet the life of the libertine has its pitfalls too. For the whole point of Arcadia is to cut oneself off from the world. Those who get stuck in Arthur Koestler's "first phase" of delight are blind to the dark sides of their East, wherever it may be, for Arcadia, by definition, has no shadows. I have never renounced the sensual delights of the first phase—indeed, some of my writing was done in a spirit of celebration of them. At the same time I have tried to write, as a critic, not only of the books and films at hand but also of the ideas and events that were current at the time.

I can't claim to have been completely consistent. I changed my mind on several things. When I lived in Japan I tended to agree with Japanese cultural experts that much about Japan was unique. Experience in the rest of Asia, and, later, back in Europe, taught me otherwise. I turned out to be wrong about other things too: Cory Aquino did better than I thought she would; Japanese politics proved to be less rigid than I thought it was. Yet, apart from some pruning and the correction of factual errors, I have not revised these texts, since I did not want to kill the freshness of impressions and observations with the questionable wisdom of hindsight. For only a missionary can believe that once the correct line has been revealed the truth is established forever.

PART I

Mishima Yukio

THE SUICIDAL DANDY

A startling article appeared in 1984 in the Japanese edition of *Penthouse* magazine. In between photographs of half-undressed Japanese starlets and fully nude Western models (pubic hair carefully airbrushed away) was a story about Mishima Yukio. A housewife named Ota claimed to have been in close touch with Mishima's spirit for the last seven years. He had dictated to her messages, manuscripts and plans, one of which was to stage a musical of the Kojiki, an eighth-century chronicle of ancient myths. It is unlikely that even Mishima would have stooped to quite that level of bad taste. But the article and its presentation are typical of the way Mishima is regarded by many Japanese: a combination of ridicule and unease, of reverence and titillation.

Perhaps it is this feeling of ambivalence, of not quite knowing what to make of the man, that has made Mishima a nonsubject in Japan. Not much is written about him anymore. Few people talk about him. Sales of his books are slow. It is hard to say whether the Japanese are truly uninterested or whether there is a kind of national conspiracy of silence, to blot out an embarrassing memory. The fuss caused by Paul Schrader's film *Mishima,* even before it was screened in Japan, makes one suspect the latter, but one cannot be sure.

How different is Mishima's legacy in the West. He is the most translated Japanese author, and certainly the best known, despite being, as Gore Vidal put it in *The New York Review of Books* in June 1971, "a minor artist": minor in the sense that he had only one subject—himself.

Mishima himself would no doubt have been pleased. He was desperate for recognition in the West. Much of his grandstanding was aimed at Westerners, especially when it looked most "Japanese." One of his most bizarre creations, a film called *Patriotism,* which he wrote, directed and starred in, about a young army officer who commits ritual suicide with his wife, had its premiere in Paris. (Typically, this quintessentially "Japanese" piece, staged like a Noh play, was set to Wagner's *Liebestod* from *Tristan und Isolde.*) His "Western" dandyism—shades, aloha shirts, his claimed affinities with Thomas Mann and Elvis Presley—were more for home consumption, to shock the locals. Mishima was like those Japanese society ladies who dress in evening gowns in Tokyo but in kimonos abroad.

Mishima was an extreme mythomaniac. Any assessment of his life would have to start with a close scrutiny of the myths, to sort out what was real and what mere posing. This is an almost impossible task, as Mishima probably took at least some of his poses seriously and, as Marguerite Yourcenar rightly says in her book *Mishima ou la vision du vide* on the man and his death (which she calls his chef-d'œuvre), "the elements of his own culture and those of the West, which he had absorbed avidly, elements both banal and strange to us, are mixed in all his works." It is a necessary task nonetheless, for otherwise one is forced to take his myths at face value. And this seems to be what the Schraders (Paul wrote the script with his brother, Leonard) and Yourcenar have done.

The film shows Mishima as he presented himself. The myths are not debunked, analyzed or explained, but dramatized. The narration is drawn from Mishima's works. Scenes from three of his novels are staged in highly stylized settings to explain his actions in real life, which is presented as a series of his more spectacular poses. Mishima compulsively posed for pictures, as if he hoped to become immortal by freezing time often enough. He even requested that a picture be taken of his corpse, dressed up in his private-army uniform, so people could see that he died as a warrior. The sequences about his own life in *Mishima,* shot in black and white, unlike the scenes from the novels, are almost all based on famous photographs: Mishima in black T-shirt speaking to radical students; Mishima in loincloth photographed as Saint Sebastian, hands tied, arrows sticking in his flesh; Mishima in combat gear at boot camp; Mishima in shorts at the body-building gym; Mishima in shades on holiday in Greece. In the final scene, life and art come together: Mishima in dress uniform, white gloves and headband, moments before his death, screaming at Self-Defense Forces soldiers to rise and save the glorious Japanese spirit from Western materialism. Mishima's "real life," as shown in the film, is his carefully stage-managed public life. And the filmmakers further oblige the great poseur by adding a heavy-breathing score by Philip Glass to make his actions seem even more portentous.

Mishima's myth invites pretentiousness. In the extraordinary book of Hosoe Eikoh's photographs of Mishima, *Barakei: Ordeal by Roses,* the author is shown mostly in loincloth or tied up with a garden hose, accompanied by quotes from the Upanishads. Schrader, too, cannot take his subject lightly, presenting us with a Mishima utterly without charm, a pompous bore, unbending once in a while to crack some embarrassingly dumb joke. From the film it is unclear why so many people were captivated by him to the point that even today certain old hands in Tokyo claim a kind of hallowed status because "I knew Mishima."

Unfortunately, those aspects that might explain his poses, such as his sexual life, his family, his politics, are hinted at in the film but not shown. This may not be entirely the fault of the filmmakers. Mishima's widow will not allow anything to sully her image of Mishima, the Great Healthy Heterosexual Artist, and since she holds the rights to most of his novels she can pull a string or two. But if one cannot seriously address the sexuality of a man who was so obviously obsessed and driven by sex, then why bother making a film of his life at all?

Both Henry Scott Stokes and John Nathan in their biographies of Mishima consider sex to have been the main motive for his suicide. Scott Stokes believes that Mishima "was having an affair with Morita Masakatsu [Mishima's favorite protégé in his private army] and that the two committed a lovers' suicide." And both Scott Stokes and John Nathan see the seppuku as a culmination or a climax of Mishima's erotic fantasies. There is also a more banal explanation, which an old friend of Mishima's gave me: "He was simply terrified of getting old, and dressed his suicide up in such a way to make his motives seem grander than they were." This seems in keeping with Mishima's dandyism, about which more later.

Schrader's main interest is not lovers' suicide, the fear of old age, or homosexual fantasy. He has the romantic fascination for the artist who goes too far. The idea of actually acting out one's fantasies instead of putting them on paper or on the screen appeals to bookish intellectuals, burdened with inhibitions. Schrader tends to wear the inhibitions of his Calvinist upbringing on his sleeve—he has certainly discussed them a lot with the press—and seems to have projected his condition on Mishima. He has, as it were, painted a portrait of the artist as an existential Rambo. It is a slightly outdated idea, harking back to the days of Byron and D'Annunzio, both much admired by Mishima. It is hard to imagine a modern American director making a completely serious film about Hemingway as the great white hunter, Philip Glass music pounding away in the background. Perhaps the only way for the modern Western romantic to escape ridicule is to seek heroes in more exotic places.

The artist who goes too far is a fantasy shared by many bookish Japanese. A minor cult has developed around a Japanese student called Sagawa Issei who shot his Dutch girlfriend in Paris and ate her, after cooking her flesh in a sukiyaki pot. Sagawa, too, is a literary type. He wrote a book about the murder, entitled *In the Fog,* a pretentious work describing the author's erotic obsessions, mostly to do with cannibalism. A prizewinning book and play have been written about him. A well-known magazine editor has hailed him as a great literary taboo-breaker.

It is also true that many Japanese writers (the young Tanizaki, for example) have been drawn, as Mishima was, to the Romantic Agony of a nineteenth-century Europe precisely because it fits in with a Japanese tradition of grotesque and morbid beauty. Mishima was not the only one of his generation to see parallels between Kabuki and the Elizabethan thirst for theatrical blood, between Wagnerism and Japanese spiritualism, between Baudelaire and teahouse decadence, or between Byron and Japanese artists of action. Japanese writers created modern literature from Western models, but they chose the models most congenial to their own tradition. Among Mishima's closest friends in the 1960s were such people as Shibusawa Tatsuhiko, translator of de Sade, and Hijikata Tatsumi, father of buto dance. Buto, like Mishima's works and poses, is full of superficial Western images—freely borrowed from Christianity, Nietzsche, Wagner, even Hitlerism. Mishima once explained his attraction to seppuku and honorable death on the battlefield as the result of "my reading of Nietzsche during the war, and my fellow feeling for the philosopher Georges Bataille, the 'Nietzsche of eroticism.' " Although much of this was name-dropping kitsch, it was also a genuine search for synthesis between Japanese aesthetics and Western modernism.

So Schrader may not be entirely off track in identifying his Calvinist hang-ups with Mishima's neuroses (although the only Calvinist thing about Mishima was his deeply held conviction that if it hurts it must be good for you). Schrader sees both himself and Mishima as artists trapped in the plastic cages of modern ennui and spiritual emptiness; men who must act ever more violently, in fantasy and/or real life, to feel real. There is one big difference, though: while the Calvinist may desperately try to jettison his religion, or at least those taboos and superstitions deemed no longer valid in modern life, Mishima did the opposite: he tried to find his way back to religion. He wanted to believe in a mythical Japanese past when spirits were pure and values unsullied. The emperor in this religion, often called "Japanism," is not a fascist dictator, as some think, but both pope and the God on our side. This religion, perhaps like Oscar Wilde's Catholicism, was not just Mishima's answer to modern materialism, but also a part of his erotic fantasies. He blew up his personal problems into something of at least national scale. And Schrader took them seriously enough to blow them up to international proportions: the twentieth-century artist—a lofty concept indeed.

To find out why Mishima chose the Japanist religion to die for, so out of step with most of his countrymen, one must know the psychology of the man and the relatively short history of this religion. Marguerite Yourcenar gives up on the first, wishing to avoid what she calls "drug-store psychology," and, I think, misunderstands the second. If Schrader interprets Mishima from the perspective of an American artist fighting to be free from the suffocating grip of old-world taboos, Yourcenar speaks as an old-world intellectual applauding an Asian struggling for traditional values against American cultural "imperialism." She sees Mishima as "the witness and, in the etymological sense of the word, the martyr of a heroic Japan, which he had rejoined, as it were, against the stream."

Yourcenar does at least try to disentangle and classify some of the myths. She points out parallels with European literature, seeing shades of Bernanos here, of Huysmans there. Since Mishima borrowed so much from European romanticism it would have been interesting if Yourcenar could have gone more deeply into the differences between Mishima and his models.

But the main problem is her sometimes shaky grasp of Japanese cultural history. She presents the tension between Japanese tradition and Western modernity as mostly a postwar phenomenon, as if 1945 was the end of traditional Japan:

> One could almost say that this man, who was hardly touched by the war—that, at any rate, is what he thought—accomplished in himself the evolution of his entire country: the swift transition from battle-ground heroism to a passive acceptance of the occupation, and the subsequent channeling of energies into that other form of imperialism, namely extreme Westernization and ruthless economic development. Those photographs of Mishima in tuxedo or morning coat, cutting the first slice of his wedding cake at the International House in Tokyo, sanctuary of an Americanized Japan, or of Mishima making speeches in impeccable businessman's suits, convinced that an intellectual should be like a banker, are characteristic of his times.

Well, they were perhaps particularly characteristic of Mishima. Few Japanese writers go around in tuxedos hobnobbing with foreigners the way Mishima did. The more famous ones tend to stay aloof from Westerners, affecting a kind of shy arrogance. Even fewer Japanese writers—in fact, none that I can think of—become body-building samurai and end up as martyrs of a heroic Japan. Mishima was in almost every respect an oddity, and it is dangerous to see him as typical of anything.

Yourcenar's sketch of postwar Japan is superficial, though not entirely inaccurate. It is also, I think, beside the point. Like Schrader, though in a different way, she takes Mishima's mythology at face value. She describes Mishima's conversion to Japanism as follows: the shocks of war were not perceived or "were refused by the mind and the conscious sensibility of a young man of twenty." But later, "the voices of young kamikaze pilots, after twenty years, became what Montherlant called 'voices from another world' to a writer revolted by the flabbiness of his times." In fact, Mishima was probably at least as much concerned with the inevitable flabbiness of his own body in old age. Still, lured by the kamikaze voices, Mishima followed Byron and D'Annunzio, became a man of action, and formed his private army, the Shield Society.

The army, according to Yourcenar, may have seemed to people at the time

> insignificant, if not anodyne, a ridiculous nonsense, but it is by no means certain that we can still judge it that way. We have seen too often how countries which are roughly Westernized, . . . and apparently happy to be so, have surprises in store for us, and how in every case the consequent upheavals begin with small groups, at first disdained or treated with irony. If ever a nationalist revolution succeeds, however temporarily, in Japan, as it has in certain Islamic countries, the Shield Society will have been a harbinger.

She fails to mention that this is precisely what happened before the war. Mishima was not a harbinger, but an anachronism. His "heroic Japan" of kamikaze, emperor-worship and pure spirit was based on nineteenth-century nationalist fantasies that had thrived in the maelstrom of industrialism and imperialism. Just as there are still neo-Nazis in Germany, there are some Japanese who still cling to the old nationalist symbols. How seriously would Yourcenar take a modern German artist if he were to resurrect Aryan supremacy, the German soul, swastikas and all the rest of the prewar mumbo jumbo to combat the flabbiness of his Americanized times? If Fassbinder, say—an artist who had much in common with Mishima—had suddenly taken to measuring people's skulls, would he have been "a harbinger"? No, it would have been taken, quite rightly, as another one of his pranks—a disquieting prank, certainly, just as Mishima's were, but a prank nonetheless.

Yourcenar, I find, has little understanding of Mishima's deliberate dandyism. She calls the theatricality of his grand gestures and his absurd uniforms the inevitable consequence of his being a man of the theater, "just as a professor brings a professorial style to his political actions." I wonder whether it was not more than that: whether theater was not the main point of the exercise.

Four months before he died, Mishima was asked by a magazine journalist whether he did not think his ideas were anachronistic. Mishima's answer was:

Anachronistic? Yes, perhaps. But, wearing one thing which is old, however modern one looks otherwise, is dandyism—as a spiritual attitude. Chivalry is dandyism. It's like wearing clothes in the latest fashion, but smoking a very old pipe. Likewise, sticking to an anachronism in one's spiritual life is dandyism.

Nobody knew Mishima as well as he knew himself.

Mishima picked his way through the Japanese past as carefully and as selectively as he did with European literature, like a connoisseur of rare curiosities. What he came up with perfectly fitted his dandyism. Take *Hagakure*, for example, an eighteenth-century text on The Way of the Samurai, stressing the constant readiness to die—its author, a samurai called Yamamoto Jocho, died of old age. Mishima wrote a book about it, and Yourcenar quotes from it with the same solemn tone that Schrader adopts in his film. *Hagakure* was already an anachronism when it was written, indeed an elaborate form of dandyism of a warrior class with no more wars to fight. Hardly anybody in Japan takes it seriously. Mishima pretended that he did.

To be sure, Mishima disliked the vulgarity of modern times. But, as Baudelaire said in *The Painter of Modern Life,* a text that Mishima probably knew by heart, that is one of the marks of the dandy. Baudelaire's definition of the dandy was pure Mishima:

It is a kind of cult of the ego. . . . It is the pleasure of causing surprise in others, and the proud satisfaction of never showing any oneself. A dandy may be blasé, he may even suffer pain, but in the latter case he will keep smiling, like the Spartan under the bite of the fox. [He refers to the Spartan who refused to cry out when a fox was gnawing at his vital parts, a Mishimanian image par excellence.] Clearly, then, dandyism in certain respects comes close to spirituality and to stoicism. . . . Dandyism is the last flicker of heroism in decadent ages. . . . Dandyism is a setting sun; like the declining star, it is magnificent, without heat and full of melancholy. But alas! the rising tide of democracy, which spreads everywhere and reduces everything to the same level, is daily carrying away these last champions of human pride.

Need one go any further? It was Mishima's misfortune that he took this kind of thing seriously. One wonders why somebody of Yourcenar's stature could not regard it with more skepticism.

If she had, she would have been less surprised by the fact that Mishima taught his protégé Morita European table manners shortly before dying the samurai death. Mishima, like many nineteenth-century dandies, was raised with the kind of snobbery that comes with feeling one's class privileges slipping. His grandmother came from an illustrious samurai family, and felt that she had married beneath her station. She greatly influenced the young Mishima—a point that both Schrader and Yourcenar make, quite rightly. The European manners that Mishima often affected were typical of the old upper class. His samurai fantasies were not necessarily in contradiction to this. He wanted to remain an aristocrat, a knight of a special brotherhood in a vulgar age. Being Japanese, the only tradition of knighthood he could fall back on was The Way of the Samurai, as expressed in such flamboyant works as *Hagakure*.

However, as Baudelaire pointed out, the select band of dandies has to keep on surprising its audience, in an unending round of costume changes. Dandies are life's practical jokers who must fool people into thinking they are something they know themselves they are not. They are like exhibitionists who feel alive only when watched. Mishima knew very well he was not fooling many Japanese after decades of his antics. As he once remarked, "I come out on the stage determined to make the audience weep, and instead they burst out laughing." To really shake people up, he had to resort to something very extreme. Posed photographs of Mishima dying by the sword, choking in mud, being run over by a truck, having his skull sliced with an ax, were no longer enough: only the real thing would do. And his countrymen, as well as people in the rest of the world, were duly shocked. One can almost hear him laughing up there, having pulled off the ultimate prank.

But let us not be conned into thinking that he stood for more than himself. It would be best to concentrate on his books as works of art, not as props for grand statements about the author's life and death. This does not mean that certain Japanese were justified in trying to prevent Schrader's film from being shown in Japan. But I do think most Japanese are right in regarding Mishima's seppuku as little more than the pathetic act of a very gifted buffoon.

1985

Oshima Nagisa

JAPANESE SEX

It is remarkable how often Japanese radicals turn to pornography. It is equally remarkable how often Japanese pornography tends toward cruelty and violence. The connection between Japanese politics and sexual violence, then, is something to explore. And the work of Oshima Nagisa, former student activist, bad boy of the Japanese New Wave cinema, director of *Ai No Corrida* (*In the Realm of the Senses*—perhaps the only intelligent hard-core porno film ever made), dandy and TV personality, would be a good starting place.

What is interesting about Oshima is not his rebelliousness but the form of his rebellion. What in particular has Oshima rebelled against? Aesthetically, the answer is easily given, especially so far as his early work is concerned. Oshima rebelled against Ozu Yasujiro, or rather the tradition that Ozu represented. In his postwar films, such as *Late Spring*, for example, or *Tokyo Story*, or *Early Summer*, Ozu refined a minimalist, classical style which Japanese think of as so quintessentially Japanese that they are always astonished at Ozu's appeal abroad. Ozu's camera almost never moved, and its gaze was usually fixed at the eye

level of people sitting on a tatami floor. Every shot was beautifully composed, with not a flower arrangement, a piece of furniture or an actor
out of place. There was no room for improvisation. In one typical instance, Ozu made an actress go through the act of picking up a teacup
dozens of times, until she got it absolutely right.

Ozu's plots tended to follow the predictable course of what the
Japanese call "home dramas" (Ozu was not much interested in plot):
girl takes care of old father; old father tells girl to get married; girl says
no, father says yes, girl gets married, both are sad, but such is life. Ozu's
world is like the seasons, hence the titles of many of his films. Harmony and tradition impose their natural order, which it is foolish to oppose. Since chaos is to be feared and freedom an illusion, any attempt
to go against the seasons, so to speak, will end in tragedy. To learn this
lesson—which Ozu's characters usually do—is to achieve maturity and
wisdom.

Oshima joined the Shochiku studios as a young assistant director
just as Ozu was making some of his late masterpieces there. Now, I am
sure Oshima would be the first to recognize Ozu's genius, for, despite
his conservatism, Ozu was a master, whose films are deeply moving.
But back then, in the late 1950s, Oshima loathed the kind of thing Ozu,
and especially the hacks who copied his style, stood for: "I absolutely
could not stand the films that were mass-produced by the studio in
which I worked: tear-jerking melodramas and flavorless domestic dramas in which imbecilic men and women monotonously repeat ex-
changes of infinitely stagnant emotions."

Oshima wanted to destroy the harmony of this artificial world,
which was so comforting to a Japanese audience, buffeted by high-
speed economic development, Americanized pop culture and the still
fresh memories of wartime catastrophe. He hated this hoary naturalism
so much that he refused, in his own future work, to use the color green,
redolent of gardens, nature, softness. Oshima wanted to express a
world of concrete and violence. What was needed was not naturalism
but "bold fiction and free structure." Cameras would be handheld, cuts
would jump, and "on a very technical level, I tried to eliminate completely all scenes with characters sitting on tatami while talking." You
can't get much further away from Ozu than that.

If all this sounds rather un-Japanese, indeed rather French, rather
nouvelle vague, this too was deliberate. In the 1960s, when Oshima

made his technically boldest films, he felt more affinity with French directors of his age than with his Japanese masters. Yet Ozu, too, had been inspired once by untraditional models. His earliest films, made in the 1920s, were so-called nonsense films, zany comedies, whose gags were so loosely strung together that the effect was often surreal. As a student, Ozu wrote fan letters to Lillian Gish. Like many Japanese, he became more "Japanese" as he grew older.

Oshima's cinematic style has changed a great deal during his career, from handheld nouvelle vague grit to the almost static aestheticism of *Ai No Corrida*. But the idea that filmmaking is a form of liberation—political, sexual, social, all three—is a constant theme in his thinking. In 1968 he called the collaborators on one of his best films "my fellow Guevaras." The picture was *Death by Hanging* (1968), about the execution of a Korean accused of murder. To make the film at all was to break a taboo of sorts: not many Japanese artists have shown a sympathetic interest in the plight of Koreans in Japan. One of his "Guevaras" on the movie was Adachi Masao, who disappeared soon after. He has been hiding somewhere in the Middle East for the last twenty years, after being involved in Red Army terrorism. Adachi was once a promising director of violent porno films.

Criminality, of one sort or another, is a theme of most of Oshima's films. His characters include rapists, murderers, sexual deviants and, in the most celebrated case of O-Sada in *Ai No Corrida,* a passionate maid who cut off her lover's penis—after strangling him, of course. Interest in underdogs and sympathy for antiheroes were common attitudes everywhere, particularly in the 1960s: Bonnie and Clyde, Butch Cassidy, Belmondo in many things, good and bad. One of Oshima's most interesting essays is about James Dean and his influence on Japanese cinema. But perhaps the idea of the artist as a semicriminal outsider himself is less common—though by no means unknown—in Europe or America than it is in Japan. Indeed, until not so long ago—about a century at most—it was more than an idea: print artists, fiction writers, actors and playwrights really were on the fringe of an underworld. The prostitute, the gangster and the playwright were part of the same scene: the licensed quarters of theaters, teahouses and brothels.

It may have been presumptuous of Oshima to claim, in 1978, two years after he made *Ai No Corrida,* that he thought "only from the viewpoint of 'suffering' women like O-Sada." But unlike the many Shochiku films about poor, virtuous people battling through life with a tear and a laugh (the so-called *shomingeki,* or small-folks dramas), Oshima was never sentimental about the downtrodden. Films such as *Tomb of the Sun* (1960), about life in an Osaka slum, or his debut, *Town of Love and Hope* (1959), are tough-minded without being politically strident. There is always an element of voyeurism in watching the sordid lives of slum-dwellers in a comfortable cinema, but, even so, *Tomb of the Sun* is voyeurism of a high order.

Oshima's interest in criminal outcasts is more than voyeurism, however. He is on their side, intellectually, because he sees crime as a political, or metapolitical, act. In the collection *Cinema, Censorship and the State: The Writings of Nagisa Oshima,* Oshima makes a point regarding Masumura Yasuzo's movie about a gangster, played by Mishima Yukio, the novelist. Normally, Oshima wrote, Masumura "depicted modern heroes and heroines. He portrays and praises characters who expose their desires straightforwardly and act upon them." Mishima's gangster, however, is a wretched figure. This, Oshima implies, is a reactionary view, not at all in keeping with Masumura's usual standards. Oshima's criminals are never wretched, even though they might come to sticky ends.★ Their crimes represent our deepest desires. Even the "hero" in *Violence at Noon* (1966), who goes around the country raping and killing women, earning himself the sobriquet Daylight Demon, is not entirely beyond the pale: "At the press conference announcing the production, I said I made the film because I am the Daylight Demon, and Sato Kei, who plays the demon, said the same thing."

This must be properly understood: Oshima is not so politically incorrect as actually to admire a rapist. His point is that every society deserves the criminals it gets, and that the society, rather than the criminal, is usually at fault. Further than that, he sees crime as the only refuge of people who have no political power to effect change and expand their freedom. Crime, in other words, is a substitute for politics.

★In real life the story of O-Sada, heroine of *Ai No Corrida,* actually had a relatively happy ending. After cutting off her lover's penis, she fled the scene carrying the object of her affections in a silk purse. She was later arrested, and spent some time in jail. But after her release she opened a bar in Tokyo, where she delighted her faithful patrons by making a grand entrance every night at eleven sharp. She would be greeted with loud cheers, and the men would briefly cup their genitals.

Crime includes sexual deviance. So is the preponderance of sex and violence in Japanese entertainment a sign of political desperation? I think in some cases it is.

The extraordinary cruelty of nineteenth-century woodblock prints by, say, Yoshitoshi, or the stylized violence of many Kabuki plays, or indeed the celebration of murderous antiheroes in the plays by Tsuruya Namboku (1755–1829), can be read in different ways. One interpretation is that in the imagination—the theater, the brothel, the novel, the print—anything goes. Japanese morals are social, not religious, and so it is all right to fantasize. Indeed, fantasy is the institutionalized escape from an oppressive society. Another interpretation is that the taste for sadism and excess in the early nineteenth century, the fin de siècle, the 1920s and the 1960s was a reflection of a society in great flux. The dates, interestingly enough, correspond pretty much to similar developments in the West.

Both interpretations are plausible. But there is another one, namely that Japanese social life was so politicized—by removing any chance of actual political discourse—that assaults on social taboos were the only way to rebel. Japan under Tokugawa rule, lasting from 1603 to 1867, was a police state, or, more precisely, a spy state. Political opposition to the shogunate was dangerous. There were government informants everywhere. As in totalitarian dictatorships, social control was maintained by circumscribing every aspect of people's lives, including their dress, the way they decorated their houses, even the manner of their death. Suicide, for example, was a samurai privilege. The many Kabuki plays about love-suicides by commoners were in effect celebrating criminal acts.

It is often said—not least by Japanese themselves—that the Japanese are not a religious people, and that sex and violence are therefore not subject to religious constraints. Sadean or Buñuelesque or indeed Rushdiean attacks on the Church, one might conclude, have no counterparts in Japan. But in fact they do. Apart from a relatively short period of extreme emperor worship, the presence of an official Church is indeed not so apparent in Japan. But religion, ethics and law were all instruments of political control. To challenge the state was to challenge religion, and vice versa.

It might seem far-fetched to project the social system of Tokugawa

Japan onto Oshima's work. After all, there are no shoguns, no sumptuary laws, no official isolation from the outside world. Japan has a democratic form of government. There is freedom of the press. And so on and so forth. Yet you can see how Oshima's preoccupation with sex and violence is very much the result of political frustration. You can even trace, in his own films and writings, how and when this came about.

In 1960 Oshima could still write about his film *Night and Fog in Japan* that it was a "weapon of the people's struggle," but he would rarely use that kind of political rhetoric again. The film itself was a New Left critique of the Communist Party in student politics. The political context was the general failure of the left to stop the revised U.S.–Japan Security Treaty in 1960, which was forced through parliament by Prime Minister Kishi, the former vice-minister of munitions during the war. It was an event of crucial importance in postwar Japanese politics, which scarred leftists of Oshima's generation for life. Never before had so many people come out in protest against government policy, and never would so many do so again. Whatever the rights and wrongs of the treaty itself, it was to be the last serious challenge to the virtual monopoly on power of an elite of bureaucrats, corporations and conservative politicians.

The story, or rather the argument, of this rather talky picture is structured around a wedding. As the ceremony unfolds, the failures of the student movement are rehearsed, over and over, in monologues, in debates, in appearances at the wedding, quite literally, of an accusing ghost from the past. It is an interesting film, with limited popular appeal, but it upset the studio bosses enough for them to pull the movie from distribution. Oshima called this "a massacre." What killed the film, he wrote in "protest against the massacre of *Night and Fog in Japan*," was "the same thing that killed Kamba Michiko and Asanuma Inejiro, and I protest with unrelenting anger." Kamba was a female student who got trampled to death during a clash between students and riot police in the 1960 antitreaty demonstrations. Asanuma was the chairman of the Japan Socialist Party, who was assassinated by a right-wing extremist in that same year.

So far as political failure was concerned, Oshima knew what he was talking about. He had been a student activist at Kyoto University, where he studied law. His organization was forced to disband in 1951, after the

"Emperor incident." The students wanted to have an open discussion with the emperor during his visit to the university. When this was refused, they demonstrated with a placard imploring the emperor not to lend himself to deification again. As a result, the Kyoto Prefecture Student Alliance was banned. It was revived in 1953, but was crushed after a violent demonstration that followed the university's refusal to let the students meet on the campus. Oshima's professor Takikawa Yukitoki published a statement saying that the authorities should have been tougher on the students after the Emperor incident. This was the same man who had been purged in 1933 for writing a liberal paper. Takikawa's example had inspired Oshima to study law. And now it had come to this.

But 1960 was really the left's last stand, even though there were to be more student demonstrations during the 1970s. Its failure, which Oshima blames on the authoritarian communists as much as on the repressiveness of the government, bred nihilism and despair. In that year Oshima made another film, apart from *Night and Fog in Japan,* entitled *Cruel Story of Youth.* It is about a handsome young man and his girlfriend, whose games of mild sex and violence escalate to the point of death. He gets killed by gangsters; she jumps from a speeding car. All hope is lost, dreams are smashed. Kicks are all that's left.

It is tempting to compare *Cruel Story of Youth* to the more famous *Ai No Corrida,* made sixteen years later. The story of Abe Sada and her lover, Kichizo, is also about a sexual game ending in death, but the spirit is different. Whereas an air of despair and nihilism drives the actions of the young couple in *Cruel Story of Youth,* O-Sada and her lover, Kichisan, are not nihilistic at all, nor frustrated. On the contrary: they have voluntarily locked themselves up in their passion. Even though freedom, in their small private utopia, proves elusive, sexual love is celebrated with almost revolutionary gusto. Passion is all. They communicate only through their bodies, in the language of sex. When they speak, it is to heighten their passion. What is subversive about the film is that it positively wallows in the power of female sexuality. O-Sada is not a passive tool for her lover's pleasure, the usual pattern in Japanese porn, where the simpering heroine spends most of her time trussed up in ropes. No, in this case his penis is her instrument of pleasure. She is on top. He gives, and she sucks the life out of him.

But it is a brittle paradise they live in. Obsessions cannot be satisfied: one always wants more. Nor can the lovers completely isolate themselves from the world. In an ominous display of displaced sexual energy, soldiers are already marching outside the sliding doors of Kichi and Sada's love nest, off toward the war in China. The story took place in the 1930s. However much we might try, we cannot change anything: order will prevail. "I think that our only route to freedom," Oshima wrote in 1965, "and our only route to pleasure can come after we have first recognized that freedom and pleasure are not possible in this world." In a way, is this not what Ozu was saying, too?

Well, yes—but only in a way. An important footnote to Oshima's essay "The Concept of Demons" mentions the work of Wakamatsu Koji. He was at least as deeply involved in the protest movements of the 1950s and 1960s as Oshima was, but, after the defeat, he turned to the production of pornographic films, or "ero-ductions."

The showing of one of these at the Berlin Film Festival in 1965 caused a rumpus in Japan. The film, entitled *The Secret Act Inside Walls,* shows people having various kinds of sex in a high-rise public-housing apartment. On the wall, as though watching over the proceedings, is a portrait of Stalin. The idea, so Oshima's editor guesses, is to show the limitations of the proletarian struggle for power. It is a plausible explanation, in keeping with the almost tragic spirit of many activists turned pornographers.

I am not aware of any of Wakamatsu's ero-ductions actually being banned in Japan. I suspect it is because they are not taken very seriously. Oshima's *Ai No Corrida,* on the other hand, drew so much international attention that the police decided to bare their censorious teeth. The film, produced by Anatole Dauman, was shot in Japan but developed and edited in Paris. It still has not been shown in Japan in an unmutilated form. The bizarre ways in which sex scenes are censored—genitals obscured by black squares, and so on—turn acts of tenderness into something prurient. One third of the film was doctored in one way or another. But at least it was not banned. Then a book came out in Tokyo, containing the script of the film, as well as still photographs. This was the chance for the police to crack down. Oshima, who was not the publisher of the book, was charged with obscenity.

It was the police, and not government censors, who charged Oshima, since obscenity is in the criminal code, as a convenient, ill-defined left-over from prewar days. Censorship is actually prohibited by the constitution. Oshima's attitude to the trial was as brave as it was succinct: "Obscenity? What's wrong with obscenity?" The outcome was a Japanese compromise: the charges were dropped, but the book was banned. This compromise was reached because Oshima put his prosecutors on the spot. He asked them to define what was obscene about the book, and they could not come up with a reasonable answer.

Why, in any case, would the sight of genitals, or of adults making love in a wholly conventional manner, offend anybody's sensibilities in a culture that had never connected such matters with sin? The answer is that it wouldn't, really. Normally the fantasy world of the brothel or the pornographic work is tolerated—even, until not so long ago, institutionalized in special licensed quarters. But once in a while the state must show its power to keep people in their places, to show who is boss. The sight of naked genitals has nothing to do with sin: it is just a convenient peg, as it were, for showing the fist of authority.

In an essay about morality, "Between Custom and Crime: Sex as Mediator," Oshima describes a meeting with a conservative politician who asks him about the provenance of manners and customs. Mores, says the politician, have more power to change society than politics. Oshima disagrees. It is true, he writes, that manners and customs are changed by "guerrillas," and that new mores begin as expressions of dissatisfaction with a political system that uses customs to support the status quo. But—and here Oshima puts his finger on the sorest point of Japanese politics—"it is not, as the LDP Dietman said, that mores have more power to change society than politics; rather the forces unable to change society through politics shift to manners and customs." That is why Oshima makes movies. And the subversiveness of his work explains his cri de cœur that "to make films is a criminal act in this world."

Laws, in a society such as Japan's, blur with customs: not in the manner of laws based on precedents, as is the case in Britain, but in a vaguer sense—something more akin to the idea of absolute harmony. Propagandists for absolute harmony, or unity, do not recognize conflicts of interest, or individual rights vis-à-vis the authority of the state. Harmony protects the natural order, the existing hierarchy. If the law is used to safeguard this hierarchy against pornographers and other potential troublemakers who upset the customs and manners that foster deference to the people in power, then the law will be corrupted. This has often been the case in Japan. And this is why Oshima's voice is so refreshing, so bracing, of such critical importance.

Oshima, the critical spirit, however, is not what most Japanese see today. His voice is not exactly muted, but it has lost much of its edge. He still looks striking. The last time I saw him he was dressed in a pea-green suit and a maroon (or was it purple?) shirt. He is a much-favored guest on Japanese television shows, grinning his way through quizzes and counseling distressed housewives in agony-aunt programs. He spends longer and longer between film projects. But when he does make a movie he still manages to break taboos. His 1986 film *Max, mon amour* features Charlotte Rampling having an affair with an ape. And the previous one, *Merry Christmas, Mr. Lawrence* (1983), with David Bowie as a British officer in a Japanese POW camp, is the only Japanese film, so far as I know, that shows Japanese brutality toward Europeans.

This last film, despite its grim subject matter, revealed a side of Oshima that was always there but has grown stronger over the years. It is a rather showbizzy side, rather flash, like his purple or pea-green suits, rather interested in pop figures and performance. From student activism to pornography to show-business dandy: not a bad summing-up of postwar Japanese culture.

1992

Tanizaki Junichiro

THE ART OF CRUELTY

Two short stories, by Tanizaki Junichiro and Akutagawa Ryunosuke, appeared within ten years of each other: Tanizaki's "The Tattooer" in 1910, and Akutagawa's "Hell Screen" in 1918. The stories are remarkably alike. "The Tattooer" concerns Seikichi, a tattoo artist in the decadent phase of the Edo period, around the 1840s let us say, whose ambition is, as the author puts it, to engrave his soul into the skin of a beautiful woman. It takes time to find the perfect human canvas for his masterpiece, but when he catches a glimpse of the exquisite feet of a young teahouse girl he knows his goal is near. "This," he feels instinctively, "is a foot to be fed by men's blood, a foot to trample on their bodies."

The girl with the enticing feet visits his studio, and Seikichi shows her a picture of a beautiful princess watching with rapture the execution of a prisoner. The girl confesses that she feels the same inclination as the cruel princess. The tattooer's eyes gleam with pleasure. Seikichi drugs her and works on her fair skin day and night. When she wakes from her stupor, the legs of a tattooed spider on her back appear to move from her shoulders down to her waist. The tattooer is exhausted, his soul caught forever in the female spider's web. The girl is transformed into a sexual demon, every man her slave. Both are ecstatic with the beauty of it all.

Akutagawa's story also concerns an artist, a painter at the court of the most powerful lord in Kyoto. The artist, Yoshihide, has a taste for cruel and violent scenes, which he insists on seeing to the last horrible detail before transforming them into art. His handsome young assistant is made to strip and is tortured by snakes and birds, or tied up in excruciating postures.

Yoshihide, a melancholy and macabre man, has only one tender spot, his daughter, whom he loves deeply. Yoshihide's lord takes a fancy to this beautiful girl, but his advances are refused.

Yoshihide is commissioned to paint a screen depicting a scene from hell. He asks his lord for a favor. In order to convey the full horror of the main image, a burning ox carriage containing an elegant court lady in the throes of a ghastly death, he needs to see the scene with his own eyes. It can be arranged, the lord promises in pleasant anticipation. A carriage is provided with a gorgeously dressed woman inside. And, just as the carriage is put to the torch, Yoshihide notices with a mixture of horror and fascination that he is watching his own daughter being burned to death. His screen is of course a masterpiece. On the day after its completion, Yoshihide hangs himself.

Both stories are romantic, beautifully (though in the young Tanizaki's case, somewhat floridly) written, and quite perverse. They are amoral—not immoral—in the sense of Oscar Wilde's dictum about there being no moral or immoral art, only good or bad art. Indeed, in both works, art for art's sake is taken as far as it can go: nothing, not even death, is too much of a sacrifice for the sake of beauty.

One might be tempted to find something peculiarly Japanese about these works, a sense of beauty unfettered by Christian morality. This has been argued by some Japanese critics, who have pointed out that Tanizaki's aesthetic was not so much an attack on morality, or humanism, as completely indifferent to such concerns. In this he differed from many Western "decadents," who were too busy rebelling against religious constraints to be completely free from them. It is also possible to speculate that artists who grow up in a highly formalistic culture become obsessed with genuine emotions, whose sincerity can be tested only by going to violent extremes—double suicide as the only proof of enduring love, and so forth.

But the aesthetics of cruelty in Tanizaki and Akutagawa are not especially Japanese. When he wrote "The Tattooer," Tanizaki was an enthusiastic reader of Oscar Wilde, and it shows. His preoccupation with femmes fatales, at least in his early works, was influenced by Flaubert, Baudelaire and Wilde as much as by Japanese literature.

The same is true of Akutagawa. He set many of his stories in Japanese history, but his literary sensibility was deeply influenced by European writers. In "Cogwheels," the melancholy record of the author's incipient madness, Akutagawa constantly refers to Western literature, which lends his hallucinations a strangely bookish quality, as if he lived with literary ghosts:

> Back in the room I thought of calling a certain mental hospital. But to go there meant death to me. After much hesitancy I started reading *Crime and Punishment* to distract myself. The page I turned to, however, was from *The Brothers Karamazov*. . . . It was a passage of Ivan's being tormented by the Devil's Inquisition. Ivan, Strindberg, de Maupassant, myself, in this room . . .

This is not to say that either man lacked originality, or that Japanese culture and society are not reflected in their writing. But there are more rewarding ways to approach these great writers—in Akutagawa's case I use the word "great" with some hesitation, in Tanizaki's with none—than to seek what might or might not be quintessentially Japanese. Why, for example, did two authors of such similar backgrounds, with, at first, such similar literary tastes, end up almost as opposites?

Both men were born in the old "Low City" of Tokyo. Both were fascinated by the West, though neither ever went there. Both escaped, if that is the right word, from politics and social issues, into aestheticism. But Akutagawa turned away from macabre fantasies to the kind of solipsistic autobiographical writing that Japanese critics like to classify as the purest literature: that is to say, literature without plot, concentrating instead on minute shifts in the author's mood and details of his often uneventful daily life.

Tanizaki, on the other hand, remained an unashamedly popular writer, whose taste for drama, heady eroticism and baroque fantasy never flagged until he died, aged seventy-nine, in 1965. (Akutagawa took his own life in 1927, when he was thirty-five.) In an essay on Tanizaki, Mishima Yukio once remarked how his beautiful aunt would look quietly joyful whenever Tanizaki's "perverse" works were mentioned. "Tanizaki's literature," wrote Mishima, "was first of all delicious, like Chinese or French cuisine."

Tanizaki's main literary theme was sex, particularly sadomasochistic sex—hence his interest in ladies' feet—while Akutagawa grew more and more absorbed by egotism, the absence of universal values, disgust with himself, and death. These diverse preoccupations are already visible in the two short stories described earlier. Tanizaki's hero, Seikichi, turns his muse into a demon, but finds erotic fulfillment. Akutagawa's artist creates his masterpiece, but has to sacrifice the only person he loved. His obsession turns to disgust, and his life becomes meaningless, not worth living.

Tanizaki's *Childhood Years: A Memoir* is invaluable as a guide to his personality. Brimming with his early erotic inclinations, it is a wonderful portrait of the artist as a child. It has been observed that in a sense he remained a child for his entire life. Certainly childhood nostalgia runs through most of his books. Thus we learn of such childlike entertainments, indulged in by Tanizaki and his friends, as the "basket game." The young schoolboys would lie down together in baskets, dubbed "courtesans' bedchambers," pretending they were clients and prostitutes in an elegant brothel. Then there were the many grotesque murders to capture the young imagination. One such case, later turned into a popular play, which delighted Tanizaki, concerned the murder of a former bar girl by her common-law husband. A salient detail was that her face had been disfigured with a knife. Photographs of the result, along with those of popular actors, were displayed at the local fair. Even more to Tanizaki's taste—the boot being, so to speak, on the other foot—was the stylish geisha O-ume, who stabbed her lover with a kitchen knife. "I suppose," observed Tanizaki's mother, "that's what they must mean when they talk about a 'real woman'!" The adult Tanizaki would doubtless have agreed.

Tanizaki's worship of women was inspired by his mother, apparently a great beauty. He was by all accounts, including his own, a mama's boy and an impossible crybaby. Long past his toddler's years, Tanizaki still found his mother's breast irresistible—though not so much for the taste of milk, he thought, as its "sweet smell and the gentle warmth." Compare this to Akutagawa's description of his mother in *Death Register* (translation by Donald Keene):

> My mother was a madwoman. I never once experienced anything resembling maternal affection from her. She would always be sitting by herself in the family house in Shiba, her hair twisted around a comb, puffing away at a long-stemmed pipe. Her face and body were both very small. Her face—I can't explain this— was always an ashen color, with no suggestion of living vitality.

Another source of Tanizaki's inspiration, we are told, was a picture of the Madonna belonging to his grandfather, who was a member of the Russian Orthodox Church. "Gazing with inexpressible reverence into the Virgin Mother's eyes, so full of tenderness and mercy, I felt I never wanted to leave her side."

Nagai Kafu, novelist, translator of Baudelaire and lifelong devotee of brothel life, praised Tanizaki's early work, specifically "The Tattooer," for its style—its urbanity and its "profound, mysterious beauty arising from carnal terror." Whenever Tanizaki's woman-worship becomes sexual, his pure goddesses are transformed into demons. They are still unutterably beautiful, made even more so, perhaps, by the terror they inspire.

One interesting aspect of Tanizaki's femmes fatales is that they are often highly Westernized women—brash, colorful and a little vulgar. This prompted one Japanese critic, Eto Jun, to remark that Tanizaki's masochistic worship was a metaphor for modern Japan. Japan worshiped the West just as Tanizaki's literary heroes sucked the feet of bitch goddesses. But then Eto, who has had a bee in his bonnet about America ever since the Occupation after the war, *would* say that. In fact Tanizaki's worship was ambivalent. The West, like his cruel mistresses, was seductive but dangerous. He once likened Western culture to a sweet and deadly drug. In his younger years he expressed the desire to be killed by the drug. Later on, after moving away from Tokyo in the

1920s, he turned more and more to the traditional Japan of his childhood, which still lingered in Kyoto.

The sluttish Western woman appears even in the account of his childhood, perhaps more as a creature of the imagination than anything else. Tanizaki describes a group of young English ladies in an establishment called the Grand Academy of European Culture, set up in the foreign quarter of Tokyo. These attractive ladies teach English on the first floor, but there is a mysterious second floor to the house, where the young Japanese pupils are not permitted to go. It is described by a friend of Tanizaki's, who took a clandestine peek, as a den of luxury. There is speculation that these foreign ladies do more than teach English when well-to-do Japanese gentlemen come to visit.

Despite worshiping his grandfather's Virgin Mary, Tanizaki was never a religious or even particularly spiritual man. And, despite his considerable scholarship in Japanese, Chinese and Western literature, he was not an especially intellectual writer. Indeed, his reputation was that of a sensualist, and therefore, in certain highbrow circles, not to be taken very seriously. There was not enough anguish and soul-searching in his books to please the advocates of "pure literature."

Akutagawa, on the other hand, pleased them much more; plenty of soul-searching in his work. He died with a Bible beside his bed. And yet he never found God. In "Cogwheels" an old man suggests that Christianity might be the answer to his angst:

> "If even *I* could become . . ."
> "There's nothing hard about it. If you just believe in God, in Christ the Son of God, and the miracles Christ did . . ."
> "Devils I believe in . . ."
> "Then why not believe in God? If you believe shadow, I don't see how you can help believing light also."
> "But there's some darkness that has no light in it."

Perhaps Akutagawa's attraction to Christianity was partly aesthetic, as was Oscar Wilde's: both enjoyed the style of religious ritual and imagery. But I think it was more than that. Akutagawa, though never a political writer, was very aware of the spiritual dislocation that accompanied Western-style modernization. Not that he had a reactionary yearning for traditional Japan—far from it. That, as far as he was concerned, was all bankrupt. What he sought was a universal spiritual ethos that could save him from the sense of alienation that led to morbid solipsism and pure egotism. Donald Keene, in his introduction to *Dawn to the West,* summed it up well: "Egoism could be transcended through divine grace, but not by a careful observance of any code of etiquette."

Akutagawa's minute description of his mental anguish, leading up to his suicide, is a moving document. You sense the life being drained from him, leaving nothing but intellect, icily, horribly lucid, when not fading in and out of hallucinations. In "A Fool's Life," written as a kind of suicide note shortly before he killed himself, he compares himself to Icarus, his mind equipped with artificial wings by Voltaire:

Unfolding these man-made wings, easily he glided up into the sky. Bathed with reason's light, human joy and sorrow sank away beneath his eyes. Over squalid towns, letting irony and mockery fall, he soared into unobstructed space, heading straight for the sun. That with just such man-made wings, scorched by the sun's radiance an ancient Greek had hurtled into the sea, dead. He'd seemed to have forgotten . . .

All this might suggest that Akutagawa was a more profound writer than the hedonistic Tanizaki, who was too busy with his sexual obsessions to have much time for Voltaire, Icarus and the sun's radiance. But I wonder if it is true. I wonder if Tanizaki, through his deep understanding of eroticism, did not get closer to human nature than Akutagawa ever did. And, what is more important, he managed to convey this in his art. Tanizaki's prose lives. Perhaps Akutagawa, burned out out at such an early age, knew that his prose was dying. Perhaps that is why he could no longer bear to live.

1988

Yoshimoto Banana

PINK DREAMS

In Tokyo in 1992 two Japanese films achieved great success with a public consisting largely of young girls and homosexuals. They had a common theme. Both were about young women forming relationships with gay couples. One was called *Okoge,* meaning fag hag; the other was *Kira Kira Hikaru,* which might be translated as "Shining Brightly." In *Okoge,* directed by Nakajima Takehiro, a spirited young woman called Sayoko offers her bedroom to a male couple she has befriended at the beach. While the men make love upstairs, she crawls into her futon in the living room and leafs through a book of Frida Kahlo paintings. She can only enjoy the passion of her two "lovers" vicariously, but at least she is spared the oppressiveness of more conventional arrangements.

Kira Kira Hikaru, directed by Matsuoka Joji, is a less anarchic and more ambivalent film. The story revolves around an arranged middle-class marriage, which would be conventional enough were it not for the fact that the husband is gay and the wife is alcoholic. She wants her husband's lover to join the ménage, but she would like to have a baby, too, to please her parents. She craves freedom, but becomes confused when she achieves it—a common enough dilemma. The fascination with male homosexuality among young women is not unique to Japan either, but it is nonetheless a remarkable phenomenon.

Japan can easily give the impression of being a country of fag hags. Comic books for young girls feature beautiful youths falling in love with aristocratic men, or androgynous rock stars. Japanese girls like David Bowie at his most camp. The film of E. M. Forster's *Maurice* played to full houses, mostly of young girls. Luchino Visconti was a teenage idol, as was his star, Helmut Berger. The most popular theater company for young girls is the all-female Takarazuka, based in a dreamlike little spa near Osaka, with pink bridges and pink houses and a large pink theater. One of the most popular Takarazuka roles—apart from Rhett Butler and Lieutenant Pinkerton—is that of a young woman at the court of Louis XVI who grows up as a boy named Oscar. As a dashing military officer, Oscar falls in love with a Swedish aristocrat, who is already in love with Marie Antoinette. But Oscar in turn is adored by her/his groom, who is unaware of his master's female identity. The play is entitled *Rose of Versailles*.

All this would be camp, if it were knowing. But it is not. Young Japanese girls appear to find the pink bridges, the gay romances, the rock stars in drag, the girls dressed as boys who fall in love with other boys, beautiful. *Akogare*—romantic longing—is the term they use for this dream world, far removed from the demands of reality. What would be the highest of camp in another context can become cute in Japan, redolent of childhood. It is rather like the chosen name of the author Yoshimoto Banana. "Banana" is the kind of sobriquet that would suit a Brazilian drag artist. But the publicity photograph of the author hugging a little puppy dog is cuteness personified. The fact that her father is the most famous philosopher of the 1960s New Left gives her name an extra air of incongruousness, as though there were a young German novelist called Banana Habermas.

Yoshimoto Banana's extraordinary success—more than 6 million books were sold in two years while she was still in her twenties—has made her so famous that the Japanese foreign ministry was handing out copies of her book to foreign visitors at the 1993 G-7 Summit in Tokyo. They may not have realized what peculiar fantasies lurk behind Yoshimoto's cute exterior.

Yoshimoto Banana's stories are clearly related to the androgynous teenage universe of Takarazuka and girls' comics. The characters in *Kitchen,* a book of two short stories, include a transsexual father and a boy who dresses up in his dead girlfriend's school uniform. Yet there is nothing overtly kinky about these transformations. In the title story, a young girl called Mikage, who is left alone in the world after her grandmother dies, goes to live with Eriko, the transsexual, and his/her son, Yuichi. She more or less lives in their kitchen, cooking delicious food, trying to soothe her lonely heart. In a way, the kitchen is to Mikage what drag is to Eriko: a refuge from loneliness after the death of a loved one. Yuichi explains how his father became his mother:

> "After my real mother died, Eriko quit her job, gathered me up, and asked herself 'What do I want to do now?' What she decided was, 'Become a woman.' She knew she'd never love anybody else. She says that before she became a woman she was very shy."

In the second story, entitled "Moonlight Shadow," Hiiragi's taste for wearing his dead girlfriend's clothes is equally matter-of-fact. And it, too, is an escape from loneliness. His girlfriend, Yumiko, died in a car crash, together with his brother Hitoshi. Hitoshi's girlfriend is called Satsuki, and the story is told in her voice. She wants to know why Hiiragi insists on going around in Yumiko's school uniform:

> When I asked him if he wore it for sentimental reasons, he said that wasn't it. "Things are just things, they can't bring back the dead. It just makes me feel better."

What cooking is to Mikage, jogging is to Satsuki. As Satsuki says,

> His sailor outfit—my jogging. They served exactly the same purpose. . . . Neither recourse was anything more than a way of trying to lend some life to a shriveled spirit. It was a way to divert our minds, to kill time.

The Italian scholar Giorgio Amitrano pointed out the connection with girls' comics in his introduction to the German edition of *Kitchen.*

He wrote that Yoshimoto's stories, with their odd sexual disguises and morbid emotions, are not only like many Japanese girls' comics, but also owe much to horror movies and the impressionistic style of Kawabata Yasunari's novels. This is more weight than the book can possibly carry, but the point is well taken, for a fascination for horror and death is as much part of girls' comics as the cuteness and androgynous fantasies.

The tone of Yoshimoto's stories is strange, for it veers from childlike naïveté to flights of bizarre fancy, which is just like most Japanese comic books for teenagers. Sometimes her prose is direct and simple, and sometimes it reads like a young girl's diary, filled with poetic sadness: "Suddenly, to see that the world was so large, the cosmos so black. The unbounded fascination of it, the unbounded loneliness . . ."

Children often dream of flying out the window of their bedrooms, following some fairy or another to a never-never land without parents, to a new family of children and freaks. Yoshimoto's characters are a bit like such dreaming children—except that they are not children; they just dream like children. Instead of fathers and mothers, there are the surrogate fathers and brothers, dressed in women's clothes.

But neither of her stories celebrates or even suggests new sexual possibilities, as one might assume. Indeed, sex, like real parents and siblings, is absent. Yuichi never becomes Mikage's lover, and neither does Hiiragi become Satsuki's. Not sex but death permeates both tales: the death of Eriko, stabbed by a mad suitor; the death of Mikage's grandmother; and the deaths of Satsuki's boyfriend and Hiiragi's girlfriend. Death, loss, the melancholy fleetingness of life, these are brooded over endlessly with the feverish sensibility of Victorian children's tales. This is where *Kitchen* is both contemporary and very traditional—hence, perhaps, the perceived shades of Kawabata, who, incidentally, wrote some of his stories for an audience of young girls. But it is a pop version of Kawabata, as though *The Izu Dancer* or *Snow Country* were written for the Takarazuka theater.

The two most common phrases in classical Japanese literature, as well as in modern pop songs and in Yoshimoto's book, are sadness (*kanashimi*) and nostalgia (*natsukashisa*). Translated into English, this can sound odd: "The sound of his voice made me want to weep with nostalgia." Or "Somewhere deep in my heart I felt I had known her long ago, and the reunion made me feel so nostalgic I wanted to weep tears of joy." Weeping tears of nostalgia is not something one comes across often in Western literature. Not that the emotion doesn't exist, but it is not usually so histrionically expressed; or, rather, what sounds histrionic in English is perfectly ordinary in Japanese. Perhaps "nostalgic" isn't even quite the right word for *natsukashii,* but I don't know of a better one.

Nostalgia is closely linked to that other key element of Japanese aesthetics: *mono no aware,* the pathos of things. Sadness about the transience of life is, in Japanese art, a thing of beauty. Again, like nostalgia, it is not easy to translate. But you find instances of it all through Yoshimoto's book:

> When I finished reading I carefully refolded the letter. The smell of Eriko's favorite perfume tugged at my heart. This, too, will disappear after the letter is opened a few more times, I thought. That was hardest of all.

Nostalgia is one reason why so much in Japanese art is about reliving the past, or fixing the flow of time, as in a haiku. The ghosts of the dead appear in Noh plays rather as Christ did to his disciples after the crucifixion. Sometimes they return to torment or exact their revenge, and sometimes to liberate the living from being haunted by death. And sometimes just to say good-bye. In "Moonlight Shadow," Satsuki sees her dead boyfriend for one last time, when he appears one night on a river bank:

> My tears fell like rain; all I could do was stare at him. Hitoshi looked sadly back at me. I wished time could stop—but with the first rays of the rising sun everything slowly began to fade away.

The beautiful pathos of things is linked to the Japanese cult of purity, of uncorrupted youth, of the cherry blossom in full bloom. It is the fleetingness of the cherry blossom's life (about a week in Japan) and the speed at which decay and corruption spoil the pure beauty of a young boy or girl that bring on the sense of exquisite sadness. Here is where classical Japanese aesthetics meets the world of Takarazuka, girls' comics and Yoshimoto's stories. For in all these instances there is a deep nostalgia for the purity of youth, before sex roles are clearly defined, before social hypocrisy corrupts, before the rot sets in. In Japanese fiction of the seventeenth and eighteenth centuries, homosexuality was often celebrated for this reason: boys' love was considered to be purer than the heterosexual kind; it was uncontaminated by the demands of reproduction and other family duties.

Since family duties are (or at any rate were) particularly onerous in Japan and sex roles so rigidly defined, it is no wonder that young girls so often long to stop time and to retreat into a fantasy world of purity, androgyny and prepubescence. Yet, of course, women have written about sexual love. Lady Murasaki wrote about little else in her *Tale of Genji.* But even she, who still enjoyed a high status in the rarefied sphere of the Heian court, was filled with sadness: she pined, she longed, she was nostalgic. Subsequently the status of Japanese women steadily declined and women's stories, whether written by women or men, became sadder and sadder. Love so often ended in tragedy because there was no room in Japanese society for love. Marriage had nothing to do with romantic love. And women who loved outside the home, in fiction and in fact, overstepped their social borders, and their passion had to end in death. Sex in the fiction of the Edo period (1603–1867) was almost entirely confined to the licensed quarters. But only men wrote about this floating world of paid love. Ihara Saikaku's *The Life of an Amorous Woman* (1686) is one of the masterpieces of this genre. Women, being confined to the brothel or the home, hardly wrote anything at all. They were the sacrificial victims of love in the male imagination, and often in reality too.

Love, wrote Tanizaki Junichiro in 1932, was liberated for the Japanese by European literature. He meant that romantic love in modern Japan had become a serious subject, not an excuse for dramatic suicide. Before there was only sex, with prostitutes, actors, boys; now sexual love would strike a blow for individual freedom. Women writers took up this theme too. But it is interesting that one of the greatest literary masterpieces of the early modern period (and indeed of modern Japanese literature *tout court*) should still be so traditional, in content and in form. It is a novella entitled *Growing Up,* written by Higuchi Ichiyo and published in 1895. The story is of a young girl growing up in a licensed quarter of Tokyo. What makes her sexual awakening, her growing up, so sad is that we know how she will end up—in the brothel with her elder sister. Freedom, as this story shows, belongs to the child. The loss of innocence means bondage, not freedom. To become a woman is to enter the prison that society has provided—in this case a whorehouse, but it could just as well have been the home.

Things have changed since 1895, to be sure. Japanese women have more freedom than ever before. One of the most remarkable statistics of modern Japan is that in recent years more women than men have initiated divorce proceedings. (In Higuchi Ichiyo's time, a woman did not even have the right to ask for a divorce.) And yet, as far as sexual love is concerned, things have not changed as much as it may seem. For the alternative to pure sex is still very often a sad nostalgia for lost innocence.

What has changed is that the description of sex, from a predatory point of view, is no longer a male preserve. A young woman writer called Yamada Emi made her reputation by writing novels about working as a dominatrix in an SM club, and her passion for black men. In *Bedtime Eyes,* she describes her lover, a black GI, as a sweating sex object. His character is as flat and featureless as the courtesans in pornographic woodblock prints of the Edo period. Foreigners, and especially black men, have taken the place of prostitutes in the Japanese erotic imagination. A recent nonfiction best-seller entitled *Yellow Cab,* by Ieda Shoko, featured examples of wild sexual adventures enjoyed by Japanese women visiting New York. This is not the love that Tanizaki talked about, but at least it is women doing all the talking.

Sex with foreigners, in fantasy or in fact, is a long way from the pink dreams of innocent gender-bending. And yet there is a connection. Just as the licensed quarters were a traditional escape for men from the duties of family life, sexual adventurism overseas has become a modern escape for many independent women. Marriage for most Japanese women is still a social trap, commonly known as "the graveyard of life." It means the end of a career, of economic independence. And, since heterosexual love in Japan usually means marriage, an increasing number of career women are stuck with celibacy, with or without trips abroad.

The alternative is of course the sexless intimacy of the fag hag and her chosen friends. The heroines of Yoshimoto's fiction are not exactly fag hags, nor are they innocent. Mikage and Satsuki are young women, but grown-up sexual relationships are still beyond their grasp. Instead, in the security of their private kitchens, they dream nostalgic dreams, and shed melancholy tears about the passing of time. This is the stuff of great Japanese poetry, and absolute kitsch. Yoshimoto Banana is not yet a mistress of poetry, but she is a past master of kitsch.

1993

Edward Seidensticker

AN AMERICAN IN TOKYO

Of all the emotions one might associate with Tokyo, that most modern of cities, nostalgia would not rank high in the minds of most people. Yet that is precisely what many lovers and literary worshipers of Tokyo feel: a poignant sense of what has been lost. The aficionado, wandering through the Tokyo streets, finds his memory jolted with reminders, like pleasant little electric shocks, of what once was and is no more. One such aficionado, Philippe Pons, the Tokyo correspondent of *Le Monde,* put it well in his book *D'Edo à Tokyo:*

> Walking through Shinjuku in the company of a friend and initiator, who picks up fragments of his memory, collected in the course of his own wanderings, is to walk in the traces from which emerges a kind of archeology of illusion.

It is of course the city's very modernity, the unhinging pace of change, that elicits nostalgia; for it is only memories that lend a sense of continuity, of meaning, to a place which, without them, would be little more than a kaleidoscopic bazaar of senseless gimmicks, spurring its denizens to buy and sell and live faster, ever faster.

Edward Seidensticker, perhaps the most distinguished living celebrator of Tokyo in the English language, is steeped in nostalgia. *Tokyo Rising: The City Since the Great Earthquake,* continuing where his *Low City, High City* left off, from the Great Kanto Earthquake of 1923, when much of the city burnt to a crisp, is suffused with the melancholy remembrance of things past. This elegiac mood is deepened by Seidensticker's wry commentary on the changes that continue to chip away at his great affection for the city. But then grouchiness about the present is inevitable in literary nostalgia, which necessarily precludes enthusiasm for the new. And, if expressed with sufficient wit, there is as much pleasure to be derived from grouchiness as from its concomitant desire to catch the shadows of the old before they fade forever.

In his Tokyo elegy Seidensticker follows, sometimes literally, in the footsteps of an author he much admires, and about whom he has written a classic book: Nagai Kafu. Kafu (he is always known by his first name) lived from 1879 to 1959, and saw his native city almost completely destroyed twice: during the earthquake in 1923 and again during the fire-bombings in 1945. He wrote novels, short stories and discursive essays of varying quality, but he was a master at evoking the changing moods of his city—change wrought by the seasons, but also by the hands of man. The prevailing mood of everything Kafu wrote is nostalgia.

Like all romantics, Kafu was an escapist. His entire life can be seen as an escape from the stern, stuffy, eminently respectable world of his father, a businessman and a bureaucrat who embodied the mixture, so typical of his time, of social conservatism and an unshakable faith in Western-style progress. He was the kind of Meiji patriarch who agreed with the famous Kabuki actor of that era that "the theatre of recent years has drunk up filth and smelled of the coarse and the mean." And, like the actor, he wished "to clean away the decay."

Kafu did not wish to clean away anything: he wallowed in decay. He disliked progress as much as conventional morality, and from a very early age he sought refuge precisely in the coarse and the mean, among the actors, comedians, musicians and prostitutes of the old city, the Shitamachi, or, as Seidensticker translates it, the Low City, to the plebeian east of Tokyo, where history cast its longest shadows. Kafu was a rebel, to be sure, but in his loathing of the modern world and his morbid love of decay (when he wasn't visiting brothels, he was prowling around cemeteries) he was a rather reactionary rebel. Or perhaps "reactionary" is not quite the right word; like Seidensticker, he liked to mourn for the past without really wishing for its revival, for he was always too curious to see what silliness people would come up with next.

As a young man, Kafu spent some years in America, partly in Kalamazoo, Michigan, which was not at all to his taste. He was happiest roaming around the brothels and opium dens of Manhattan's Chinatown, where his connoisseur's nose picked up his favorite odor of decadence. Back in bustling, brash, modern, Meiji Japan, he turned his back in disgust on the literary world, with its coteries, its academic positions, its prizes, and spent the rest of his life in the company of geisha, strippers, whores and a few scattered fellow enthusiasts of the low life, which revolved around such noted red-light districts as the Yoshiwara in the heart of the Low City. In his book on Kafu, half of which is biography and half translation of Kafu's stories, Seidensticker quotes the following passage, so typical of Kafu's mood:

> There was a sad, plaintive harmony in the life and scenes of the Yoshiwara, like that of Edo plays and ballads. It was not the creation of novelists who put their skills to the uses of their tastes. And it was not limited to the Yoshiwara. In the Tokyo of past days there was a sad harmony in the crowded lowland flats and in the quiet hilly sections, too. . . . But time passed, and the noise and glare of the frantic modern city destroyed the old harmony. The pace of life changed. I believe that the Edo mood still remained in the Tokyo of thirty years ago. Its last, lingering notes were to be caught in the Yoshiwara.

That was written in the 1930s. Here is Seidensticker describing exactly the same place more than fifty years later, long after the old houses of pleasure were transformed into gaudy massage parlors, known as "Turkish baths" (*Toruko*) until a Turk objected and they were renamed "soaplands."

One may not come upon much that looks Turkish beside a Yoshi-wara street, but the more ornate styles of Europe and the ancient Orient are most of them there, with an occasional touch of Egypt among them. It is all very interesting and amusing, but a result of anti-prostitution has been to make the Yoshiwara slip yet a bit further from the height of other ages. The more dignified houses went away, and the less dignified ones stayed and became less dignified all the time.

What strikes the reader is a similarity not just of taste—that for solitary wanderings through the old quarters of ill repute—but of tone: wry and melancholy. Life is no longer what it was. Of course it never is. Perhaps it is better now that people are more prosperous, own cars and television sets and whatnot. "So it may be argued," writes Seidensticker. "Yet variety is lost, uniformity prevails, and for some this is a development to be lamented. Certainly a stroll through the Low City of a summer evening is not the fun it once was."

Like Kafu, Seidensticker can be said to have sought a kind of refuge in the back alleys of Tokyo: a refuge, possibly, from the smug, prosperous, progressive America of the Truman and Eisenhower era—a fine time, perhaps, but not congenial, especially outside the largest cities, to those with a romantic temperament and unorthodox tastes. This might explain why Japan after the war proved so alluring to American romantics with a penchant for low life. Like Isherwood's Berlin or Henry Miller's Paris, Tokyo offered freedom from the straight and narrow social restraints that prevailed back home. To be sure, such restraints existed for the Japanese themselves, but they were rarely, if ever, applied to foreigners, for foreigners were beyond the pale anyway.

The lure of Japan has, over the ages, proved especially irresistible to homosexual men. Truman Capote, during a trip to Tokyo, declared himself to be in heaven. J. R. Ackerley found love there that was more pleasing and certainly safer than his fleeting affairs with sailors and guardsmen in London. Seidensticker describes a quarter in Shinjuku that used to be a red-light district and is now "the homosexual capital of the nation" and, with its hundreds of bars, bathhouses and short-term hotels, is "in the running for the designation homosexual capital of the world." Its cosmopolitanism has been somewhat tarnished by the arrival of AIDS, which has prompted many establishments to bar foreigners from their premises. Nevertheless, the romance of guilt-free male bonding (as common today as it was in the samurai past) and the lissome charms of Japanese boys still attract many Western men, who, even after reaching a certain age, continue to find love in Japan.

Such freedom has its price. For the sense of being beyond the pale, of living as a permanent outsider in a provincial and often xenophobic society, can get on one's nerves. This is how the so-called (so-called among fellow stragglers in Tokyo) Seidensticker syndrome is born: the love that can turn to hate and then back to love again at enormous speed. There is a way to short-circuit the syndrome, which is to do something akin to Zen meditation, to reach a point of nonthinking, a spiritual mellowness Zen adepts call *satori,* which is to say a point where nothing matters anymore: I'm OK, you're OK, everything's OK. This, to his eternal credit, Seidensticker has always refused to do. His *This Country Japan* reprints his last column for the newspaper *Yomiuri,* just before returning to America in 1962, after having spent more than a decade in Japan. He wrote:

> There we are. I have felt recently that I might be getting mellow, becoming a reasonable meadow mouse. The Japanese are just like other people. They work hard to support their—but no. They are not like other people. They are infinitely more clannish, insular, parochial, and one owes it to one's self-respect to preserve a feeling of outrage at the insularity. To have a sense of outrage go dull is to lose the will to communicate; and that, I think, is death. So I am going home.

Seidensticker has approached the city in a variety of ways, but two themes stand out: language and popular culture, particularly the culture of sex, and, since Tokyo provides or promises to provide so much sex, this is appropriate. The language of Tokyo, expressed in popular songs, in the names of bars and restaurants, in street slang and advertising slogans, is often a mixture of Japanese and English. A superficial observer might conclude from this that Tokyo and, by extension, Japan and the Japanese are hopelessly Americanized. It is hard to measure such things, but this conclusion would be only partly correct at best. As

Seidensticker observes, "Among the pleasures of modern Japanese is that its use of one's own language so often requires explanation." What, you might well ask, is a *"mobo"* or a *"maihomu papa"* or a *"nopan kissa"*? Well, *mobo* is shorthand, current in the 1920s, for modern boy, a young man of fashion; a *maihomu* (my home) *papa* is a house-proud family man; and a *nopan* (no-pants) *kissa* is a bar offering the services of nude waitresses. The English language used in this Japanized way is ornamental, expressing a mood of exoticism or modernity. It sounds cosmopolitan, but isn't.

There was a song, popular just after World War II, which perfectly expressed the quasi-cosmopolitanism of modern, urban Japan. It was entitled "Tokyo Boogie Woogie," and went something like this:

> Tokyo Boogie Woogie.
> Rhythm. Wowie Wowie.
> My heart goes pit-a-pat. Tick-a-tack.
> A song of the world. A happy song.
> Tokyo Boogie Woogie.

It might be a song of the world, but only a Japanese could make sense of it, despite the jazzy English phrases. One of the interesting things about Tokyo is that it is at once utterly fashionable, utterly up to date, utterly metropolitan, and utterly parochial. Tokyo people like foreign things—or at least things that sound and look foreign—without necessarily liking foreign people.

Tanizaki Junichiro caught this idea wonderfully well in his novel *Naomi*. The two main characters are a man called Joji and a girl called Naomi. Joji is a dull office worker, born in the provinces, and Naomi is a floozy from the Low City, a kind of bitch goddess of Tokyo lowlife. She adopts every Western fashion: high heels, lipstick, all the newest dances, and the latest hybrid slang. Joji is so besotted with her that he becomes her slave. He is the provincial Japanese in love with the image of the exotic West, as, in a way, is she. But neither, despite all Naomi's fashionable posturing, is remotely Westernized, in the sense of being a citizen of the world. They are citizens of Tokyo, and their feet remain firmly planted in Japanese soil.

Tanizaki often used sex as a metaphor for culture. The clash between

Western fashion and Japanese tradition is apparent in many of his great female characters. Seidensticker's use of sex is somewhat similar. Through his descriptions of brothels, *nopan kissa,* peep shows and pornography, one catches the spirit of the Japanese metropolis. He has clearly done his homework in this department with the thoroughness of the true enthusiast, and one could not wish for a better guide to the arcana of the wonderful world of Japanese sex.

There is much to be said for this approach: the back alleys rather than the main avenues, low rather than high life, popular rather than highbrow culture. And it is easy to empathize with his preference for the old, messy, increasingly déclassé streets of the Low City, rather than the ritzy, suburban sprawl to the west of the High City, which is where all the action is nowadays. The center of Tokyo, certainly as far as nightlife is concerned, has shifted from the east to the west, from Asakusa to Shinjuku, a suburb that was still an outpost 100 years ago. Shinjuku is now where the literati and artists seek their pleasures.

Seidensticker is almost as disdainful of these literati and what he calls "the odorless rarefaction of the High City intellectual world" as Kafu was in his day. They are usually described as "artistic types" or "intellectual and literary people" who "read difficult publications and discuss constitutionalism and such things." Again, anyone who has busied himself with the frivolous chatter of many Japanese intellectuals, or *"intellis,"* as they call themselves, cannot fail to see some merit in Seidensticker's disdain.

And yet nostalgia can sometimes cause one to miss out on what is interesting about the new. One of Seidensticker's saddest laments is that Tokyo no longer has such writers as Tanizaki, Kafu or Kawabata to celebrate the city's moods. "No novel conveys a sense of Shinjuku as a place, no novel is suffused with affection for it. Shinjuku has no regional literature. It may be said that Tokyo has had none since the war." The implication is that modern, bustling, high-rise, high-tech Tokyo lacks poetry.

I am not sure this is quite true. The great Shinjuki novel is perhaps yet to be written, but, especially in the 1960s, the quarter was celebrated in drama and the movies. It was the center of experimental theater, much of it, as always with experiments, dross, but some of it as good as anything of its kind in the world. Seidensticker does not do justice to the excitement generated in Shinjuku by such playwrights as Terayama Shuji or Kara Juro. The performances by the latter's troupe are mentioned in one sentence, as being "conspicuous for their lurid colors." This is a bit like saying that Fellini's films are notable chiefly for their odd costumes.

Whether or not they were to one's taste, the films of Oshima (among them *Diary of a Shinjuku Thief*) and the plays of Terayama, Kara, Suzuki Tadashi and others were as important to the cultural life of Shinjuku as the *nopan kissa* or the massage parlors. And the underground theater of the 1960s and 1970s was as nostalgic in its luridly colorful way as Seidensticker's books. Playwrights, poster designers and novelists showed a particular interest in the 1920s, a relatively liberal period associated with the catchphrase *"ero, guro, nansensu"* (erotic, grotesque, nonsense), and the immediate postwar years when most of the artists prominent in the 1960s grew up. They evoked the atmosphere of the postwar ruins and the liberal 1920s in the same way Seidensticker does: through popular music, slogans, slang, movies and so forth. They, too, had a horror of the homogenized, anonymous, conformist prosperity of the economic miracle. Far better, they seemed to say, to live passionately in the midst of ruins than boringly in the riches of concrete and glass.

"Perhaps," writes Seidensticker, "what has happened to the High City, now so close to being the whole city, is among the things encompassed by the voguish expression 'postmodern.' A city that is urban in the abstract may be what the future holds." It is an interesting notion: life experienced entirely vicariously through television, advertising and other mass gimmicks; life without odor, barely human, homogenous and cold as the modern architecture Seidensticker deplores.

Perhaps, indeed. But one of the most remarkable things about Tokyo is the way the Japanese, unlike the inhabitants of many Western cities, have managed to make the machine age more human. Television, instead of being a sinister flickering presence behind closed curtains on deserted city streets, has been dragged out into the open. It is everywhere—not only in shop windows, but on giant screens looming over the crowds, in taxis, on trains, in coffee shops and in restaurants. The same is true of music, blaring forth constantly from every corner, Mozart mixed with "Tokyo Boogie Woogie." It is as though Japanese can only enjoy themselves in crowds, with everything going on full blast. The effect is not restful, to be sure. It is cacophonous, relentless, often irritating, but it is not inhuman, and it contains a peculiar kind of poetry, for which at some future date, when the city has been transformed yet again, some writer will feel the deepest nostalgia. One may only hope that he or she will express it with the wit and style of a Kafu, or a Seidensticker.

1990

Wilfred Thesiger

WILFRED OF ARABIA

When people or their ideas become the object of cults, it is time to watch out. For cults by their very nature are beyond criticism. The beauty of cult worship lies in its irrationality. Cultists substitute exultation for thought.

Wilfred Thesiger, adventurer, writer and photographer, has become a British cult figure. His autobiography, *The Life of My Choice,* received the highest praise in Britain and was a best-seller to boot. I once expressed some doubts about Thesiger to a British admirer of his and got slapped on the wrist: Thesiger is a Great Man, a *real* traveler, unlike those smart-alecky young writers today who parachute in and out of places; Thesiger really *knew* the people he wrote about; he lived with them; he loved them. Not for him the effete banter of literary London. He prefers the company of *real* people, noble people, pure people, like Marsh Arabs, tribal warriors in Kenya or stern nomads of the Arabian desert.

To be sure, there is much to admire about Wilfred Thesiger. His book on the Marsh Arabs in southern Iraq, with whom he lived for about five years during the 1950s, is a unique document of a vanished way of life. What was left before the slaughter of the Iran–Iraq war surely now is lost forever. Thesiger's prose survives, however, as well as his excellent black-and-white photographs, which have been beautifully reproduced in *Visions of a Nomad,* an album that spans much of Thesiger's traveling life. It is divided into three parts: Africa, meaning Ethiopia, Sudan and Kenya; the Arab world, consisting of Arabia, Yemen, Morocco, Lebanon and Iraq; and Asia, mainly Iran, Afghanistan, Pakistan and India.

In between the pictures of noble graybeards in Persia, armed Arab youths in Oman and naked warriors in northern Kenya, we are offered snippets of Thesiger's likes and dislikes. He hates tourists, cars, airplanes: "Airports represent to me the ultimate abomination, everything that I most detest in our civilization." He does not care much for Europe, "either its people, its towns or its landscape, and I certainly have no wish to visit America, Australia or New Zealand."

On the other hand, Thesiger loves "relaxed and graceful tribesmen," with whom he can share "comradeship"; he has had a "life-long craving for barbaric splendour, for savagery and colour and the throb of drums . . . for long-established custom and ritual, from which I would derive later a deep-seated resentment of Western innovations in other lands"; and he loves shooting large numbers of animals.

Apart from the shooting, which he admits is no longer fashionable now that wildlife has been largely depleted, there seems to be nothing especially objectionable about Thesiger's views. Most of us can sympathize with his distaste for, as he puts it in *The Marsh Arabs,* "that drab modernity which, in the uniform of second-hand European clothes, was spreading like a blight across the rest of Iraq." For "Iraq" read "the entire developing world."

Indeed, Thesiger deserves praise for his sympathy for remote peoples, his deep understanding of their ways, and the healthy skepticism toward the White Man's aims in those places where the sun never used to set. His tolerance and curiosity must have been rare among colonials of his generation (Thesiger was a colonial by profession, if not necessarily by inclination). And if Thesiger appears, at times, a bit condescending in his passion for barbaric splendor, well, as Osbert Sitwell once said, "A certain love of the exotic was, perhaps, innate in those of English blood, counterpart indeed, of our proud insularity."

One can understand why the British have taken Thesiger to their hearts. He is the quintessential English eccentric, forever embarking on impossible adventures in impossible countries, among impossible people; the well-bred aristocrat—his uncle, Lord Chelmsford, was viceroy of India—reveling in excruciating discomfort and horrid food. He is like a character in a John Buchan story. He is what English romantics like best: the last of a kind.

There is, as I said, nothing ostensibly wrong with all this. And yet . . . I wonder about the nature of Thesiger's romanticism. His empathy with tribal people is fine and good, but his admiration for the noble warrior tends to border on cultishness. His sympathy for browns and blacks is wholly admirable, but his preoccupation with racial purity strikes me as suspect. His tolerance for native customs is to be commended, but his delight in violence, killing and other more exotic forms of nastiness comes rather close to ghoulishness. About his taste for blood he is at least entirely honest. It was developed early in life. As Thesiger's father wrote to his mother:

> Billy goes out shooting every day but does not get much as his only weapons are a tennis bat and empty cartridge case which he hits at the birds. He says he can't get them flying but if they would only sit for him he is sure he could kill one. His sporting instincts are very strongly developed.

Indeed they were. Billy (Wilfred) was three at the time.

In *The Life of My Choice,* Thesiger offers his hunter's philosophy in asides, in between descriptions of how he bagged ever more hippos, lions, boars and whatnot. "I believe that most men have an inborn desire to hunt and kill and that even today this primitive urge has only been eradicated in a small minority of the human race." Maybe so, but those are not the members of the human race that interest Thesiger. He was happiest when in the company of such "savage, and good-looking people" as the Danakil of Abyssinia, for whom a man's social standing depended on the number of men he had killed and castrated. He describes in *The Marsh Arabs* how he charmed even the dourest of tribal friends by offering them his gun. "You can usually get on terms with people by helping them to kill something" is his typical throwaway remark.

Now it may be that I misunderstand him: that this is an example of the last Great White Hunter's cynical wit. But I don't think so. For one thing, Thesiger is not an especially witty writer. For another, he clearly approves of the desire to kill. This is not just confined to animals either: he kills men with equal zeal. Some of his wartime exploits as a guerrilla in Libya, paving the way for Montgomery's victory, make for a chilling read. He would drive up to German canteens: "Inside men were talking, laughing and singing. I fired a long burst into the tent. . . . During these operations we must have killed and wounded many people, but as I never saw the casualties we inflicted my feelings remained impersonal."

Well, that was war. Thesiger might be a cold fish, but that is no reason to condemn him. It is when the killing becomes highly personal and is justified by a kind of warrior code that I begin to feel queasy. The Bedu, nomads of the Arabian desert, represent the kind of life and manners Thesiger most admires. He decided to live with them, to share their hardships and, above all, their comradeship. "I knew I could not match them in physical endurance, but, with my family background, Eton, Oxford, the Sudan Political Service, I did perhaps think I would match them in civilized behaviour." He admits, though, that even he could not live up to their impossibly high standards.

On the next page we are informed that

inevitably these Bedu had little veneration for human life. In their frequent raids and counter-raids they killed and were killed, and each killing involved the tribe or family in another blood-feud to be settled without mercy—though in no circumstances would they have tortured anyone. I soon acquired the same attitude, and if anyone had killed one of my companions I would unquestionably have sought to avenge him: I have no belief in the "sanctity" of life.

This is where Thesiger's romanticism, to me, becomes objectionable. To hell with materialist civilization, where men are protected by law and fight out their differences in parliaments; to hell with those "fat little gourmets," those weak townsmen who choose "that easier life of lesser men"; hurray for the "warrior race," the "handsome race," the "savage crew," the always "happy and cheerful" comrades and their "wild and lawless lives." What Thesiger admires in his tribal comrades is not simply their colorful customs and friendly disposition, but their worship of physical power. Thesiger is in love with racial macho.

When racial macho dovetails with ideals of racial purity, as it inevitably does in a certain strain of nineteenth-century romanticism, things become truly sinister. Here is Thesiger on the sixteenth-century Muslim invasion of Abyssinia, the country of his birth:

> For the first time for more than two thousand years Abyssinia had been invaded, though not conquered, by an alien race. The inhabitants of the country had been decimated, their land ravaged, much of their unique ecclesiastical heritage destroyed; but as a race they had not been mongrelized.

Thesiger's admiration for this great race knows no bounds. Their former emperor, Haile Selassie, whose reign was not without blemish, is described in the worshipful tones of a true believer (the memoirs are dedicated to his memory). Haile Selassie thought he was the Elect of God. His power, in other words, was based on magic. This is not especially unusual. Nor, alas, is it particularly unusual for Western pilgrims to worship such power. But it is the kind of naïveté (let us assume that that is what it is) that lends support to ghastly abuses, famines and massacres.

His emperor-worship aside, Thesiger is not a very emotional writer. Nor is he especially interested in politics—given his love for ancient tribal ways, he probably detests politics, for it smacks of that lesser life of the cities. He does get excited about some major issues, however, and his sympathies are entirely predictable. The treatment meted out by Mussolini's forces to the Abyssinians, quite rightly, enraged him. He is equally emphatic in his condemnation of the "intolerable rule" of Jews in Israel. "Seldom," he tells us, "can a greater wrong have been inflicted on an innocent people." That Palestinians were not the only innocent people who had been wronged is not worth mentioning. There is one passing reference to a lot of "hysterical Tunisian Jews with the Star of David sewn on their clothes." Why they were hysterical is left to our imagination. But then the Jews are a mongrelized race, and Israel has built the kind of society Thesiger loathes—all those airplanes, schools and so on.

Thesiger rather disapproves of schools, at least where his tribal comrades are concerned. Eton, of course, was a very fine thing, for him. But Marsh Arabs, we are told, only learn to be discontented with tribal life. Education spoils them forever, for they are no longer people who "know no world other than their own"—one of Thesiger's conditions for true comradeship.

What, one wonders, was the real nature of this comradeship? Was it sex? After all, the Middle East was favored as a playground by upper-class homosexuals who felt that the price, in guilt or social disgrace, for sex at home was too high. Thesiger disclaims any interest in sex. It is true that, especially in *The Marsh Arabs,* he shows great enthusiasm for dancing boys and concern for the private parts of young men; he was a master of circumcision, a service much sought after in the Marshes, which he performed with relish. Still, it is entirely possible that sex per se is indeed of little interest to him. Comradeship comes in many forms. British warriors, particularly of the Victorian and Edwardian age, often liked the company of young lads (think of Gordon of Khartoum and his school for runaway boys), without actually, as it were, having them.

One thing is clear: Thesiger has little interest in women. They hardly figure in his writing, or pictures, at all. And when they do, it is often in a derogatory way. Mostly they are passing figures in the background. He describes, in a throwaway line, how women were treated by some of his favorite people, the Amhara in Abyssinia: "The slave woman who brought us food was rewarded with a handful stuffed into her mouth by her master."

The odd thing about Thesiger's native comrades is how little his prose brings them alive as individuals. This is especially true of his memoirs. He tells us that he felt deeply about these people—more deeply than about any white men—but he confines his descriptions to the splendidness of their racial stock, their capacity to take hardship and pain (a clue, perhaps?), their always cheerful disposition and so forth. We hear very little about what they were actually like. Maybe the author is being discreet, but a similar discretion, happily, is not applied to fellow English eccentrics.

The extraordinary Lieutenant Colonel Orde Wingate, who helped defeat the Italians in Africa and the Japanese in Burma, is described with a vividness lacking in Thesiger's sketches of his native friends. Wingate, we learn, would issue orders while brushing his body hair with a toothbrush. Even in the intense African heat, Wingate never washed, but he would sometimes "lower his trousers and cool his bottom in the occasional waterholes, from which, incidentally, others would have to drink."

Thesiger doesn't mention the nineteenth-century German novelist Karl May among his favorite authors. Being English, he may not have heard of him, but Thesiger bears an uncanny resemblance to a Karl May hero revered by millions on the European continent: Old Shatterhand. As a child, I used to read about Old Shatterhand's Wild West adventures in Dutch translation. He seemed a splendid fellow, were it not for the annoying detail that he was German (annoying, that is, for a reader born in the shadow of World War II). Like Thesiger, Old Shatterhand was an eccentric loner; he felt comfortable only in the company of his trusted Indian comrade Winnetou. Like Thesiger, he was happy to help his native friend in killing things. And, like Thesiger, he saw most white men as corrupters of the noble native soul. Old Shatterhand, also, took a voluptuous pleasure in hardship. And, just as Thesiger evokes Eton, Oxford and his proud family lineage as his tribal colors, Karl May's readers are left in no doubt that Old Shatterhand's qualities are good German qualities.

May's romanticism falls well into what the French called the *malaise allemand*. (His personal malaise took a mystical turn: he invented an imaginary paradise called Dschinnistan, a spiritual Eden without a trace of industry or materialism.) Gordon Craig, in his study *The Germans,* quotes Nietzsche's description of this German malaise: "a barbaric and enchanting discharge of ardent and gay colored things from an unrestrained and chaotic soul . . . an art of exaggeration, of excitement, of antipathy to anything regulated, monotonous, simple and logical." In other words, something rather like Thesiger's barbaric splendor, savagery, color and throbbing drums. An even more Thesigerian note is struck by the writer Ludwig Tieck: "Human beings must learn to kill each other. That is nobler than falling through destiny. . . . Honor, fame, etc. are the warrior's pleasure and life. . . . The desire for death is the warrior-spirit. Romantic life of the warrior . . ."

Craig explains the German disease as an essentially bourgeois phenomenon. Romanticism served as an escape from the feeling of political impotence. Hence its decline in the heady run-up to the 1848 bourgeois revolution, and its reemergence after the failure thereof. Ultimately, these German dreams culminated in the nightmare of the Third Reich.

Thesiger's dreams, though related to the German movement, differ in one important respect. The origins of his romanticism, I believe, are not bourgeois but aristocratic. His remark about family, Eton and Oxford infusing him with the standards of behavior that might match those of the Bedu people is revealing. As is his observation that Eton taught him a lasting respect for tradition and a veneration for the past. There is also his interesting comment that he could never convert to Islam, not because he believed in Christianity but because of his family tradition. Most revealing of all is his relationship with the Druze in Lebanon during World War II. Thesiger was "conscious of their pride as a warrior race . . . I saw myself as their leader rather than their commanding officer." The Romantic *Wandervögel* becomes a tribal chieftain.

Thesiger is indeed one of the last of his kind, an aristocrat who has seen his kultur disappear in a world of grubby politicians, vulgar tradesmen, and narrow engineers—in short, the world of those lesser men he so despises. Thesiger has lost his Herrenvolk. The airplane, the tourist and education for all (those ghastly lesser schools) are symbols of the drab uniformity of the modern world, no doubt, but also of the loss of feudal power, of tribal magic and aristocratic droit du seigneur. Happily for Thesiger, he can still find remnants of that old world among the Herrenvolk of Africa and Arabia. The distance from the playing fields of Eton to the hunting fields of the Samburu or the Danakil is not so great after all.

So by all means let us admire Wilfred Thesiger, his adventurism, his crisp prose and his photographs. He is a gifted and courageous explorer and a more than competent writer. But we can still stop short of admiring what he stands for.

1988

Baden-Powell

BOYS WILL BE BOYS

In the famous eighteenth-century Japanese document entitled *Hagakure,* there is one passage I find particularly arresting. The author, an elderly samurai named Yamamoto Jocho, advises his readers, presumably young followers of Bushido, or The Way of the Samurai, always to "carry rouge and powder with one," for "after rising in the morning, or after sobering up, we sometimes find that we do not look very good. In such a case we should take out the rouge and put it on." This, he went on, is especially important when going out to do battle, for one must be beautiful even in death.

Yamamoto wrote this tract setting out the rules of warriorhood at a time when Japanese warriors had little else to do but worry about rules, appearances, style, for the major battles had been fought and the time was set for almost three centuries of uninterrupted peace. The old samurai was evidently worried that peace would sap the manly virtues of the warrior caste, and wished to make sure the young retained their vigor through constant training of body and mind. The inevitable happened: warriorhood without wars was soon reduced to a set of stylish postures, adding another form of theatrical behavior to a period already so rich in dandyism. No wonder Mishima Yukio admired it so.

Lord Baden-Powell, affectionately known as B-P, hero of Mafeking and the World Chief Scout, approved of Japan and of the samurai spirit in particular. There was nothing unusual about this, for many Edwardians found much to admire in a Spartan code that extolled such virtues as self-sacrifice, obedience, bravery and comradeship. The Russo–Japanese war of 1905, when the great Russian bear, so it was thought, was defeated through sheer Japanese pluck, elicited considerable enthusiasm in Britain, and B-P was especially impressed by the way Japanese soldiers were prepared to blow themselves to bits for their emperor and country.

In this, as in so many enthusiasms (building empire, disciplining boys, shooting animals, etc.), Baden-Powell was a man of his time. Less common, perhaps, though by no means completely eccentric, was his love of acting in drag, which he called skirt-dancing. Possibly related to this, and if not then certainly in Yamamoto Jocho's philosophy, was a curious personal habit noted in Tim Jeal's superb and exhaustive biography *The Boy-Man: The Life of Lord Baden-Powell:* even during the partly self-inflicted rigors of roughing it in the African veldt, B-P insisted on using scented soap in his collapsible bathtub.

It is a small detail, but it seems so at odds with B-P's cultish adherence to what he called "the flannel-shirt life," that peculiar predilection of hearty English gentlemen to revel in discomfort, and at such complete variance with his often stated fears of effeminacy, that it makes one wonder. Is there a point at which machismo turns into its opposite? And, if so, did B-P, like Yamamoto's samurai (not to mention Mishima), cross that line?

Jeal's notes on the Chief Scout's acting career suggest that he did—rather often, in fact. Baden-Powell was essentially a man of the theater. His was a life of poses, fancy uniforms, strange oaths, flowery speeches, medallions, mottoes and jamborees. The most famous Boy Scout maxim, "Be Prepared," reflected the Chief's narcissism. Great military men are often great poseurs, which doesn't necessarily make them closet sissies, but there does seem to be a lot of muscle-flexing for the benefit of mama. (As in B-P's own case, there is usually a great mother hovering closely behind our great heroes.) Certainly, skirt-dancing is a venerable masculine tradition in Britain, still carried on in some very rough pubs. And yet, to one not raised in that tradition, some of B-P's theatrical roles suggest a strong feminine streak in the old scout which, combined with an equally strong fear of females, could help one to explain, without wishing to be too Freudian, his general attitudes to life and politics.

B-P's theatrical talents were already in evidence as a schoolboy at Charterhouse. His role as the termagant Mrs. Bundle in Charles Dibdin's ballad opera *The Waterman* was so much admired that the butler in his house saved part of his dress. In the army one of his more romantic roles, in a production of William Brough's *The Area Belle,* was as a guardsman named Tosser who falls in love with Penelope, played by a young officer by the name of Kenneth McLaren, whom B-P judged a "wonderfully good lady." Tim Jeal's description of the play is one of the more amusing passages in his book. "I'd choose to be a daisy if I might be a flower," sang Penelope, as she entered the stage. "Where can Penelope be?" exclaimed the love-struck Tosser. "I am longing to embrace her." One can be sure that much hearty fun was had by all.

B-P took McLaren under his wing, and would henceforth refer to him affectionately as "the Boy." This relationship might well have been the closest he ever enjoyed with anyone apart from his mother. When the Boy was captured by the Boers, while B-P was holding the fort at Mafeking, B-P wrote to him daily (such still were wars in those days) and consoled himself by looking at photos of the Boy on his desk. It is hardly surprising, then, that when the Boy finally decided to get married, his wife found little favor in B-P's eyes. And when B-P himself, after years of procrastination, got married at the age of fifty-five, his bride, Olave, declined to invite the Boy to their wedding. The arrows of jealousy will find their target, even if those of Eros are denied.

Which begs the inevitable question: Was B-P a closet queen? The question has been raised so often, about so many imperial old boys (Kipling, Lawrence, etc.), that this angle has become a bit of a cliché. Still, in B-P's case the pointers are hard to ignore.

Henrietta Grace, B-P's mother, was by all accounts rather a monster, who commanded, and duly received, her sons' absolute devotion, as well as a considerable chunk of their incomes to keep her in the style to which she had accustomed herself. Her main aim in life was what she called "getting on." Jeal begins his chapter on Henrietta Grace, aptly entitled "That Wonderful Woman," with a quotation from her most famous son: "The whole secret of my getting on lay with my mother."

Getting on in British society, then as now, meant doing battle in the class war: in the case of the Baden-Powells, battling to move from middle to upper class. This in itself involved a large amount of theater. The family name, for example: Powell was changed by H.G. to the more distinguished-sounding Baden-Powell (that all-important hyphen) by attaching her husband's first name, Baden, to his surname. Baden had the added advantage of sounding vaguely Germanic—an advantage because of the German connection of the royals and the then fashionable association with Teutonic vigor. When this association lost its shine later in the century because of Germany's increasing rivalry with Britain, more stress was laid on the Powell side. H.G. even laid claim to a bloodline that went back to Athelystan Glodrydd, prince of Fferlys, whoever he may have been.

Getting on meant living beyond the family means, but since Mrs. Baden-Powell was absolutely "determined not to make any new friends unless very choice people indeed," this sacrifice had to be bravely borne. The house in London—indispensable for wining and dining the choicest available—was maintained at vast expense, severely cramping the styles of H.G.'s sons for most of their lives. But it must be said in H.G.'s defense that her strategy paid off: the family, particularly through the efforts of B-P, got on—at the price, of course, of a permanent social neurosis, but that is a common British condition to this day. B-P's fondness for camping out in Asian deserts and African veldts was a welcome and, in his time, customary respite from the class war back home.

The presence of formidable mothers is generally not a help in the battle of the sexes, to be sure, but it does not automatically drive sons into the arms of boys, either. Jeal does not say that it did. He finds stronger evidence for B-P's desire for his own sex (in the mind, if not actually in the camp bed) elsewhere. But even there, where the indications seem most obvious, one must bear in mind that what may strike a modern reader as homosexual behavior often was not regarded as such by a man of B-P's class and time.

Take, for instance, the case of the photographs. B-P had an old friend (rifle corps and football first XI) called A. H. Tod, who taught at Charterhouse after retiring from the army. One of Tod's amusements was to take the boys out and photograph them in the nude. His work can no longer be seen, alas, for the pictures were destroyed in the late 1960s—supposedly to protect Tod's reputation. But Jeal quotes one source describing them as "contrived and artificial as regards poses"—Charterhouse boys as Greek athletes, perhaps, throwing javelins, or dancing between the trees like fauns. In any event, they were much admired by B-P, and visits to his alma mater were preceded by pleasant anticipation of another peek at his friend's art.

It is possible, of course, that B-P's interest was purely artistic, and it is true that fondness of the male nude was as conventional among the late Victorians as, well, skirt-dancing. B-P's enthusiasm for naked men went further than art, however. During the Great War he took great pleasure in watching soldiers "trooping in to be washed in nature's garb, with their strong well-built naked wonderfully made bodies." This, too, would not be necessarily significant if it were not for his equally pronounced distaste for the female body ("pinkish, whitish, dollish women"), or indeed anything to do with female sexuality. Interest in girls, which, despite his warnings, he could not fail to note among many young men in his charge, he regarded as a temporary disease ("girlitis"). It would soon pass, he was convinced, with a sufficient regimen of the flannel-shirt life. Masturbation was of course the very devil's work, and sex to him, though unfortunately indispensable for procreation, was so much "beastliness." No wonder he suffered constant migraines—not to mention torrid dreams of soldiers putting their hands in his pocket—during the time he dutifully cooperated in the production of three children. No wonder his headaches ceased the moment he forsook the marital bed for the more rugged quarters of his balcony.

Added up, these various horrors and fancies do indeed lead somewhere near the conclusion drawn by Jeal, that B-P was a repressed homosexual who sublimated his desires on a grand scale. There is a school of thought, gaining currency among some conservatives, that the Victorian repression of sex was not such a bad thing, since, as in the Chief Scout's case, it resulted in prodigious creative energy. Jeal lends support to this argument:

> When a gifted man's deep anxieties about his sexual nature and his personal manliness coincide with a nation's fear of impending decline through lack of virile qualities, the basic ingredients exist for a remarkably potent creative brew.

Indeed so. But a potentially dangerous one, too, for it is the brew from which great dictators emerge.

Which leads us to the next question about B-P, and others like him: Was he a proto-fascist? Were the Boy Scouts part of the same brew as Hitler Youth? Leftist debunkers of the Chief Scout's mythology have argued that he was, though admittedly not a murderer, certainly a racist, authoritarian, reactionary breeder (if that is the right word) of cannon fodder for a belligerent empire. The best-known book to make this case is *The Character Factory,* by Michael Rosenthal. One of the aims of Jeal's book is to debunk the debunkers, specifically Mr. Rosenthal.

He largely succeeds. B-P was no more racist than most Englishmen of his time—indeed, in many ways, less. Jeal has little trouble attacking Rosenthal's rather conventional "progressive" view that B-P was a conservative elitist, for the Chief Scout's ideals were far from conservative; in fact, they were rather radical, having much in common, as Jeal says, with Fabian socialism and the aesthetic politics of John Ruskin. And if the sight of uniformed boys swearing oaths around campfires strikes one as particularly right-wing, one might ponder the fact that these spectacles are most common in the few people's republics still remaining. But Jeal's main line of attack against the progressive debunkers is to argue that B-P did not intend to breed "militarists" so much as "good citizens."

This may be missing the point, for what are good citizens? Good citizens of Sparta were not like those of Athens. B-P himself had some strong ideas on the subject. A pamphlet written by the hero of Mafeking in 1907 to promote the idea of "Peace Scouts" states, "The main cause of the downfall of Rome was the decline of good citizenship among its subjects, due to want of energetic patriotism, to the growth of luxury and idleness, and to the exaggerated importance of local party politics." This is not a recipe for militarism, to be sure, but, like many radicals of various persuasions, Baden-Powell associated party politics, materialism, commerce, intellectualism—in short, urban life—with decadence. He sought to stop the rot by, so to speak, throwing away the books and making for the bush. Typically, he believed that the virtuous pioneering spirit of America had been destroyed by "over-civilization."

Like Ruskin and, it must be said, many romantic fathers of political extremism, B-P had a profound contempt for the bourgeoisie—possibly because they stood for a society that forced him to suppress his most hidden desires. And so he dreamed of a premodern order of purity, self-reliance, comradeship and discipline. B-P's Boy Scout movement didn't have military aims: what the Chief Scout aimed at was to revive the warrior spirit in peacetime, rather like the old samurai and his Bushido. Indeed, he went further: he hoped to achieve world peace and brotherhood through the warrior spirit. Despite his old-fashioned notions of patriotism, he was as much of an internationalist as the most ardent Marxist.

In the class war, though getting on all right himself, he wanted his movement to transcend class, just as he wished it to transcend race and nation. As for Empire, his ideals led to an interesting dilemma felt by many a British adventurer in the bush. For B-P was in Africa ostensibly to civilize the natives, but in many respects he admired their customs more than the flabby ways of the white man. He deplored the destruction of "the tribal system of training and discipline" to make way for the "widespread provision of cash wages, bad temptations, and such teachings of civilization as they can gain from low class American cinema."

Those bad temptations just won't go away! To help his scouts resist them, he found some use for the tribal folklore he had picked up among the natives: blowing the kudu horn at morning call, handing out African amulets for special merit, that sort of thing. Perhaps The Way of the Tribal Warrior was better than that of the wage-earning, moviegoing, party-voting suburbanites back home, but surely members of the latter were closer to our definition of good citizens in a modern democracy.

It is true that much of B-P's tribalism was boyish, not to say infantile, more than it was sinister. Pictures of the old Chief Scout in shorts, surrounded by his loyal scoutmasters (his "Boy-Men," as he called them), roaring with good clean hearty laughter, suggest not so much fascists as outsize boys who refuse to grow up. Such refusal was a common Victorian and Edwardian affliction. B-P was apparently so moved by James Barrie's *Peter Pan* that he went to see the play on consecutive nights. The kudu horn, the amulets, the campfire yards, the lusty community singing: Jeal is surely right that "for many men, Baden-Powell among them, the Boy Scouts provided a blessed illusion of reclaiming their stolen childhoods."

But was B-P's movement really as innocuous as Jeal says? Was it really all boyish romance "in a different moral world" from the National Socialist and Communist youth movements of the 1930s? And, if it was, was this a matter of circumstances or because "the fundamental, moral ideals of the two organizations could hardly have been more distinct"? I am not quite as sanguine about this as Jeal appears to be, for I am more inclined to think that B-P's brand of back-to-naturism, tribal nostalgia and youth worship always contained a kernel of noxious idealism which, if it had developed under different conditions, might well have ended up in the same moral world as the Hitler Youth or the Red Pioneers.

To be sure, despite B-P's brief flirtation with the ideas of Hitler and Mussolini (not as unusual in the 1930s as some people like to believe), his Boy Scouts never became tools of an authoritarian state. B-P's movement was more akin to the German *Wandervögel,* city boys mooning about with rucksacks, trekking through forest and dale, letting mountains echo with their soulful folk-songs. Like B-P, they rejected "over-civilization," politics, city life: they, too, made a cult of the flannel-shirt life, of nature, of youth. They were consciously antipolitical. As one enthusiast (quoted by Joachim C. Fest in *The Face of the Third Reich*) observed:

> Does not political activity all belong to that urban civilization of yesterday, from which we fled when we set up our community of friends out in the forests? Is there anything more unpolitical than the *Wandervögel*? Were not the Meissner festival and its formula a repudiation of the party men who were so anxious to harness

youth to their political activities? Is not the sole task of the free German communities to educate free, noble and kind people?

Instead of politics there was a cult of beauty—male beauty. This was splendidly recorded in Herbert List's photographs of blond nature boys sitting on rocks or bathing in lakes—rather similar, one imagines, to the pictures taken by B-P's Charterhouse friend. The pure idealism and antipolitical nature of the *Wandervögel* movement were what made it so attractive and so vulnerable to political manipulation, for in time the celebration of youth, of nature, of male comradeship, of antiurban, antibourgeois sentiment was harnessed to a most sinister cause, which also insisted on being above party politics—though not nation or race—in the name of a beautiful new order. One figure to emerge from the *Wandervögel* was Baldur von Schirach, leader of the Hitler Youth. Descriptions of him quoted by Fest sound a familiar note:

[He was] a big, pampered boy of good family who laboriously imitated the rough, forceful style of the boys' gang. His unemphatic, rather soft features held a hint of femininity, and all the time he was in office there were rumours about his allegedly white bedroom furnished like a girl's.

There is no evidence that Schirach was homosexual, or that male femininity, any more than the presence of great mothers, is a clear sign of homosexuality, or that homosexuals are any more attracted to extreme ideals or antipolitical romanticism than heteros. But there is a connection between authoritarianism and communities based on male bonding, particularly when they seek to replace or at least put themselves above politics, family life, in short, the boring suburbanites. This is sometimes forgotten in our own enlightened times by those who see the bourgeois family as uniquely oppressive and homosexuality as a liberating force. It can be thus, but it can also be the other way around: family loyalty, as all totalitarian regimes well know, is a great obstacle to state control, whereas the collective loyalty of bonded males is often a help. It is also true that some of the more notorious leaders of boys' bands (Gabriele D'Annunzio, Oswald Mosley) were not homosexuals but, on the contrary, compulsive womanizers; but this is really no more ironic than B-P's neurotic homophobia or the vicious persecution of homosexuals in Hitler's Reich.

The best examples of overt homosexual authoritarianism are the samurai and the Dorians. In their book, *The Love of the Samurai,* Watanabe Tsuneo and Iwata Jun'ichi lament the passing of the aesthetic cult of boy-love (*shudo*) upon which, they say, The Way of the Samurai was based. The Way of Boy-Love specifically promoted the loving submission of beautiful boys to more experienced men. What destroyed this unique system of beauty, loyalty and male nobility were those old enemies of the romantic mind, capitalism and industrialization. As they put it rather charmingly, "Modernization resulted in beauty being taken over by women!" Why? "Because in traditional societies one regarded oneself as being, while in the modern, one sees oneself as having." Previously one was born an aristocrat or a peasant, and an aristocrat had to be more beautiful than the common man, whereas the modern bourgeois have "no need of being beautiful themselves. They relate themselves to beauty by 'having' a beautiful woman."

So much, then, for the modern view of seventeenth-century Japan. What about this poem composed in Greece by Theognis, in the sixth century B.C.:

> You want to buy an ass? a horse?
> You'll pick a thoroughbred, of course
> For quality is in the blood.
> But when a *man* goes out to stud—
> He won't refuse a commoner
> If lots of money goes with her.

Theognis was deeply worried about modern decadence, and advocated boy-love, discipline and hierarchy to preserve the noble traditions of the past. As his translator, Dorothea Wender, put it, "He presents to us the distress and confusion of those who live in an age of transition from one set of values (based on agrarian, hereditary nobility) to another (based on money and the city)."

The distress and confusion of Victorian gentlemen, particularly those on the fringes of nobility with aspirations of getting on, were just as acute. Likewise with Japanese dandies pining for the samurai past, or even perhaps aesthetes falling in love with one another and Stalinism in Cambridge. In *Plato and the Platonists,* Walter Pater, one of Oscar Wilde's mentors, drew the comparison between the Dorians and Victorian England. Dorian youth, he wrote, left early the mushy comforts of the suburban home to be educated in public schools:

> It involved however for the most part, as with ourselves, the government of youth by itself; an implicit subordination of the younger to the older, in many degrees. . . . [They ate] not reclined, like Ionians or Asiatics, but like heroes, the princely males, in Homer, sitting upright on their wooden benches. . . . [They] "became adepts in presence of mind," in mental readiness and vigour, in the brief mode of speech Plato commends . . . with no warm baths allowed; a daily plunge in their river required. . . . Youthful beauty and strength in perfect service—a manifestation of the true and genuine Hellenism, though it may make one think of the novices at school in some Gothic cloister, of our own English schools.

This, much more than the Teutoniuc earnestness and racism of the Hitler Youth, would have appealed to B-P and his Boy-Men. "Youthful friendship 'passing even the love of women' . . . became an elementary part of their education. A part of their duty and discipline." Indeed, indeed. And if such a system weighs heavily on individual freedom and, in times of peace, "may be thought to have survived the original purpose," well, says Pater, "An intelligent young Spartan may have replied: 'To the end that I myself may be a perfect work of art, issuing thus into the eyes of all Greece.' "

B-P was himself a work of art, in the eyes of his mother, in the eyes of all the world. And in being so he gave many boys much innocent pleasure. He never was a fascist, but his ideals lent themselves to fascism elsewhere. Britain was too bourgeois to turn into a Sparta, and the aggressive energies of youth had a ready outlet in the empire. As B-P observed:

> This nation does not need more clerks in the overcrowded cities of this little island. . . . No! The nation wants men and wants them badly, men of British blood who can go out and tackle the golden

opportunities, not merely for benefiting themselves, but for building up and developing those great overseas states of our Commonwealth.

Those days are over now. We live in meaner times. One shudders to think what might happen if the energy of British youth—jobless, ill-educated, ready for any action—were to be turned to some great cause, against clerks whom B-P so despised. One can already hear the words of salvation in the mind of some future Spartan: discipline, sacrifice, comradeship—Be Prepared!

1990

Louis Couperus

THE EURASIANS OF
THE DUTCH EAST INDIES

In 1900 Holland seemed to be at the height of its colonial power in the Dutch East Indies, today's Indonesia. In 1899 the sultans of Acheh had been defeated and the whole island of Sumatra had been brought under Dutch rule. The smaller islands, such as Lombok, the Moluccas and the Lesser Sunda Islands, were subjugated in the 1880s and 1890s. And Java had already been colonized for some time before that.

As it turned out, complete Dutch control over its Asian colony was only to last for about fifty years. But of course nobody could have known that in 1900. To the Dutch governors, planters, businessmen, administrators, police officers, scholars, geographers, soldiers, bankers, travelers, railway engineers, schoolteachers and their wives, 1900 must have felt like the best of times.

It was also just then, at the very peak of Dutch control, that an idea of nationhood began to emerge among native intellectuals. Radeng Adjeng Kartini advocated—in Dutch writings—education for women. And in 1908 young Javanese intellectuals founded the Budi Utomo, the first nationalist association. National independence was not their immediate aim: they wanted a bigger say in the way they were governed. And there was growing sympathy for this view in Holland. The "liberal" policy, which meant the liberty of Dutch planters to exploit the colonies as they saw fit, was replaced by the "ethical" policy, which took a fuller account of native interests. But full independence would come only after a world war, during which the Japanese shook the foundations of European rule, by showing the white imperialists, sometimes literally, without clothes.

In fact the Europeans always were vulnerable. Colonial rule, in Indonesia as well as, say, India, had to be based to some extent on bluff. The idea of European supremacy had to seem natural and, for it to appear that way, the Europeans themselves, as much as the native populations under their control, had to believe it to be so. As soon as the colonialists lost faith in their natural right to rule—a loss that Nirad C. Chaudhuri, speaking of the British in India in *Thy Hand, Great Anarch!* memorably characterized as "funk"—the colonial edifice, built over time, often haphazardly, would begin to rot: slowly, at first imperceptibly, but relentlessly, until the whole thing came toppling down. Perhaps it is so with all authoritarian systems. Loss of nerve was certainly a factor in the collapse of the Soviet empire. So perhaps Mountbatten and Gorbachev had something in common.

But in the Dutch East Indies in 1900 I suspect that only a sensitive novelist, passing through, would have been able to pick up the smell of decay, or at any rate to put the smell into words. Louis Couperus was such a novelist. And his *The Hidden Force,* written during a year-long stay in the East Indies, is one of the masterpieces to come from the colonial experience. It is still regarded as a great book in the Netherlands. Couperus was famous in Britain and the United States as well during his lifetime: fifteen books were translated; Katherine Mansfield and Oscar Wilde were among his admirers. But he has been largely forgotten outside Holland.

The Hidden Force is a story of decay, fear and disillusion. The writer's vision of Dutch colonialism is that of a solid Dutch house, slowly crumbling in hostile, alien soil. The Dutch characters, even van Oudijck, the chief local administrator, or resident, initially so "practical, cool-headed, decisive (due to the long habit of authority)," are defeated by the hidden forces of the land they rule. The nature of these hidden, or silent, forces is indistinct. It is not quite black magic, associated with Javanese mysticism, although that plays a part. Couperus, a romantic of his time, certainly believed in the supernatural: "I believe that benevolent and hostile forces float around us, right through our ordinary, everyday existence; I believe that the Oriental, no matter where he comes from, can command more power over these forces than the Westerner who is absorbed by his sobriety, business and making money."

One character in the novel who commands such power (but power over little else) is van Oudijck's native opponent, the regent Sunario. He is the heir to a long line of local sultans. The Dutch administration kept these nobles on as vassal rulers with colorful ceremonial trappings and some administrative duties, such as tax-collecting. Van Oudijck, an "ethical" administrator, respected Sunario's father, a Javanese aristocrat of the old school, but sees Sunario as "a degenerate Javanese, an unhinged Javanese fop," an "enigmatic *Wayang* puppet," gambling and indulging in native hocus-pocus. Sunario, for his part, views the Dutchman as a crude, base, foreign infidel, who has no business upsetting the sacred bonds and privileges of ancient aristocratic rule.

Couperus, in this book at least, is not an apologist for colonial rule. Quite the contrary. His descriptions of van Oudijck's priggish love of order, hard facts and hard work, and the same man's patronizing view of natives and contempt for half-castes, so typical of Dutch colonial administrators, are full of mocking irony. Van Oudijck's disdain for the Eurasians is not always personal. His first wife had Javanese blood, and he loves his two children, even though his daughter, Doddy, looks and speaks like a typical Indo-European. It is the *idea* of the "Indo" that van Oudijck cannot abide—the idea of something less than pure. Van Helderen, a Creole born in the Indies, warns the Dutch wife of a civil servant that the native population, "oppressed by the disdain of its overlord," is likely to revolt at some stage. He sounds oddly prophetic. She, Eva Eldersma, a bored, artistic Dutch woman, trapped in the colonial life, had sensed something ominous in the air. She thinks it is the strangeness of the landscape, the climate, the people, whom she doesn't understand. And van Helderen says to her, "You, as an artist, feel the danger approaching, vaguely, like a cloud in the sky, in the tropical night; I see the danger as something very real, something arising—for

Holland—if not from America and Japan, then from the soil of this country itself."

There is no doubt that Coupcrus felt the danger on his travels through Java. And, remember, this was written when Dutch power appeared unassailable. But Couperus was not a prophet, so a vague sense of unease, of something being out of kilter, must have been palpable. There must have been a feeling, among at least some of the Dutch, of walking on treacherous ground, which could suck you in, however sturdy your big Dutch boots might be. To describe this feeling as guilt would be wrong and anachronistic. It might have been closer to a sense that the Europeans had bitten off more than they could chew, or a nagging awareness of the hollowness of their bluff.

Van Oudijck resists such feelings until near the end of the book, when he too is defeated by the silent forces of the East, forces manipulated, perhaps, by his opponent, the puppetlike Sunario. The struggle between the two men is a struggle between two types of power: one is supposedly rational, open, bureaucratic; the other is magic, shadowy, mysterious. The hidden force of Sunario is associated with the night, with moonlight, while the power of the resident is exercised mainly in daylight. The resident's ceremonial sunshade, or *pajong,* is often described as a "furled sun."

One is reminded of the descriptions of Trinidad in V. S. Naipaul's *The Overcrowded Barracoon.* In "Power?" Naipaul tells how black plantation slaves would turn the world upside down at night. Then, in the dark, half-forgotten remnants of African magic would transform their abject existence as slaves into a glorious parallel world of kings and queens. Naipaul describes this as a pathetic fantasy, and Couperus writes about the hidden force as something quite real. But both writers, like Conrad, are sensitive to the horror, that lies behind such concepts.

The conflict between van Oudijck and Sunario comes to a head when the behavior of Sunario's brother becomes impossible. He gambles and drinks and, instead of efficiently carrying on his tax-collecting and other duties, steals money from the treasury to pay his debts. The resident decides to take the unprecedented step of dismissing him, which will mean a frightful loss of face for an ancient noble family. The regent's mother, a princess, is so outraged that she throws herself at the resident's feet and offers to be his slave if he can only forgive her son.

But van Oudijck stands firm. He cannot afford to compromise. Principle is principle. A decision, once taken, must not be revoked. For he "was a man with a clear, logically deduced, simple, masculine sense of duty, a man of a plain and simple life. He would never know that under the simple life, there are all those forces which together make the omnipotent hidden force. He would have laughed at the idea that there are nations that have a greater control over that force than the Western nations have."

Then horrible things start to happen. The resident's young wife, Leonie, as promiscuous as she is narcissistic, finds herself being spat on with blood-red *sirih* juice, apparently from nowhere, as she stands naked in her bath. (Couperus's description of slimy splatters dribbling down her breasts, her "lower belly" and her buttocks shocked his Dutch readers profoundly; in the original English translation such passages were bowdlerized.) Malevolent spirits stalk the resident's mansion. Stones sail through the rooms. Sinister figures in white turbans appear and disappear, like ghosts. Glasses shatter; whiskey turns yellow. The resident's family leaves the haunted mansion in terror. Even his servants flee from the house. But the resident stays put, working on his papers, ignoring the noises, the broken glass, the soiled beds, the hammering overhead. He has these phenomena investigated, "punctiliously, as if he were investigating a criminal case, and nothing came to light."

The resident and the regent come to a kind of agreement in the end—what agreement, the reader never knows—and the torments stop. But, like Dutch supremacy itself, the resident's authority begins to disintegrate at the moment of its peak. And, again as was the case with the Dutch colonialists, the subversion, the fatal loss of nerve, occurs inside the ruler's own heart.

Van Oudijck had ignored his wife's sexual adventures, even though everyone else knew. He had been blind to her affairs with his half-caste son—her stepson—and with a handsome Eurasian boy called Addy, even though regular hate mail pointed these things out to him. He had not been aware of the jealousies that soured the air in his residency. But now, suddenly, after he had resisted the hidden forces through sheer force of will, the tropical poison begins to sap his spirit too. For the first time in his life the resident feels the pangs of hatred and jealousy, and he becomes superstitious too, "believing in a hidden force that lurked he knew not where, in the Indies, in the soil of the Indies, in a profound mystery, somewhere, a force that wished him ill because he was a European, a ruler, a foreigner on the mysterious, sacred soil." The moonlit Javanese night had exacted her revenge.

The Hidden Force opens an interesting and fresh angle on the idea of Orientalism. For Couperus employed all the symbols that became the clichés of East and West, which Edward Said, in *Orientalism,* has identified with colonial apologetics: the East representing the passive female principle (the moon), and the West the vitality of the sun; the West being modern, rational, logical, industrious, creative, idealistic, and the East mysterious, mystical, torpid, sensual, irrational. And so on. But, far from using these images of Occident and Orient to justify colonialism, Couperus shows the futility of European rule. For the hidden force of the East will vanquish the West, with all its rational pretensions.

More than that, it is desirable that it should do so. Van Oudijck's spiritual defeat is also a kind of parable of enlightenment. To be sure, he loses the attributes that made him into the perfect Dutch administrator. Where he had been stern and decisive before, he "now had the inclination to hush things up, to gloss things over . . . to muffle with half-measures anything that was too sharp." His vitality has gone. His skin turns sallow. He shows all the danger signs of giving in to the torpor of the East, of "going native." This happens, quite literally, at the end of the book, when Eva Eldersma, the artistic Dutch lady, goes to say good-bye to him before leaving for Europe—she, too, has been defeated; she will never come back. She finds van Oudijck living in a native village, or *kampong,* in "a typical Indies mess." He has found a kind of happiness there, living with a native woman and her extended family. He has lost his principles, but he has gained an insight, for his principles no longer blind him to reality. He has accepted the Indies for what they are.

The European dread of going native, which Couperus describes so beautifully, was a fear on two fronts: political and sexual. Both are of course linked. We laugh now at the image of Englishmen or Dutchmen in the jungle or the bush, dressing up for formal dinners in the tropical heat. But there was a real purpose to this, for the stiff suit was one of the necessary caste marks to impress their subjects, as well as themselves, of the Europeans' natural right to rule. Letting go of European proprieties, or "principles," was a step toward letting go of power. In colonial households (Eva Eldersma's, for instance), "It was always a struggle not to surrender to lassitude, to let the grounds go wild . . ." When Eva's husband is too hot and tired to dress for dinner in a black jacket and stiff collar, she "thought that terrible, unspeakably dreadful."

No wonder the Europeans felt horribly humiliated when they were forced to bow, dressed in rags, to Japanese guards in the World War II concentration camps. The Japanese knew perfectly well what they were doing. Like the black slaves in Trinidad, they turned everything upside down, except that this was for real. As the Dutch writer Rudy Kousbroek, himself a former prisoner of the Japanese, has pointed out, the most common expression among the Dutch survivors was "We were treated like coolies"—that is to say, much like the way the Dutch treated many of their colonial subjects.

Then there was the sex. People forget what a sexual, even sexy, enterprise colonialism was—and I don't mean just metaphorically, in the sense of the virile West penetrating the passive, feminine East. No, colonial life was quite literally drenched in sex. White men would enter the *kampongs* and take their pleasure with native girls for a few coins, or even for nothing if the men were cheap and caddish enough. Europeans enjoyed the droit de seigneur in the *kampong,* and anyway, native women and half-castes were supposed to be unusually highly sexed. They still had this reputation when Eurasians, called "Indos," moved to Holland in the 1940s and '50s, usually to settle in The Hague, where I grew up. Girls of Indo or Indonesian extraction at my school were all supposed to be "hot."

Casual tropical sex is personified in *The Hidden Force* by Leonie, the resident's wife, and her Indo lover, Addy de Luce. Both live for seduction. Neither of them has anything but sex on his or her indolent mind. They are born voluptuaries. Leonie loves Addy. Every woman and girl loves him, with "his comely, slender sensuality and the glow of his tempter's eyes in the shadowy brown of his young Moorish face, the curve of his lips meant only for kissing, with the young down of his moustache, the feline strength and litheness of his Don Juan limbs."

The European fear of letting go, of being "corrupted," of going native, was to a large extent, I suspect, the northern puritan's fear of his (or her) own sexuality. If Couperus had shared this fear, his book would have been another Victorian morality tale. But he is not a puritan. He doesn't judge his characters, even the voracious harebrain Leonie, harshly. Indeed, one feels that he himself would have fancied Addy.

A dandy, a homosexual and a romantic, Couperus understood the sensuality of colonial life perfectly. He was attracted to the sun—in the Mediterranean, as well as in the East—for just that reason. He cultivated the image of torrid indolence. His rooms in Europe would be heated to a tropical temperature, as though he were an orchid, and he pretended to spend most of his time dreaming. In truth, of course, like Noël Coward, who affected a similar pose, he worked very hard. But with his carefully tended, overrefined sensibility, he should have been more in sympathy with Sunario, the "degenerative Javanese," than with van Oudijck.

Couperus's readings were legendary. He would complain if the flowers onstage weren't exactly right. He did not read his prose so much as declaim it, in his high-pitched theatrical voice, like a male Sarah Bernhardt. My grandmother once attended one of these performances in a small Dutch town. Sixty years later she could still remember how Couperus not only had the flower arrangement changed after the intermission, but also changed his socks and tie to ones of a slightly different shade of gray.

And yet Couperus, however rarefied in his tastes, did not try to identify himself with the Javanese. He grew up in the Dutch East Indies, where his father was a colonial official, but remained completely European. He describes Sunario from the same ironic distance as he does van Oudijck. If Couperus felt close to any group in particular, it was with those who were neither one thing nor the other: the Creoles and Indos. Both van Oudijck and Sunario are pure in their ways—the principled, full-blooded Dutchman, or Totok, and the refined, pure-blooded Javanese—and that, in Couperus's eyes, was precisely what was wrong with them. For Couperus celebrated the ambiguity he himself personified: a Dutchman grown up in the Indies; a homosexual married to a devoted mother/wife; a master of the Dutch language, but an exotic outsider in Holland—"an orchid amongst onions," as one of his obituarists called him.

The only characters in *The Hidden Force* who are entirely at ease with themselves, despite their European pretensions, are the Indos: Addy and his extended family, and van Oudijck's half-caste daughter Doddy. They appear to have the best of both worlds. But I suspect this is a reflection more of Couperus's sympathies than of real life. For in fact the Eurasians probably had the worst of both worlds. Indos who were acknowledged by their Western fathers were legally Europeans, but they were subject to subtle forms of discrimination in a society obsessed by race and color. Many Creoles hardly spoke Dutch; others, like van Helderen, who prophesied the native rebellion, spoke it almost too precisely. Like van Oudijck, most Totoks respected the Javanese as a civilized race—perhaps more civilized in their way than the Europeans—but despised the Indos. The Indos were commonly regarded by the Dutch as lazy and stupid, as well as oversexed. People made fun of their efforts to speak proper Dutch. Even Couperus has some sport with this—something that is lost in translation. The Indos overcompensated by disdaining the natives, as though this would make the Dutch accept them as equals. In fact, of course, it just made them seem more despicable.

In *Het Oostindisch Kampsyndroom,* Rudy Kousbroek, who has written brilliantly about this extraordinary social geography, described his native Dutch East Indies thus: "Our tropical paradise was a madhouse, whose people looked down on one another in ways that no outsider could ever fathom. It was a factory of inferiority complexes, which produced all manner of contorted behaviour that still has not entirely disappeared."

The fusion between Dutch and East Indian never took, culturally or politically, except in some individual instances of people highly educated in both cultures. Yet it is that blend, that ambiguity, if you like, that state of having the best of both worlds, that many Dutch writers born in the East, including Couperus and Kousbroek, have yearned for. This can result in mawkish regret. But the best of these writers came to see that their dream was bound to fail, as long as one side had its boot on the neck of the other. It would not work, no matter how well-meaning or idealistic the ruler might be. Of course, many rulers were neither. Van Oudijck was both, which is why he couldn't understand why his native subjects hated him: "There was no logic in it. Logically, he should be loved, not hated, however strict and authoritarian he might be considered. Indeed, did he not temper his strictness with the jovial laugh under his thick moustache, with a friendly, genial warning and exhortation?"

His insight into the tragedy of European colonialism made Couperus a great writer. And his sympathy for the hybrid, the impure, the ambiguous, gave him a peculiarly modern voice. It is an extraordinary thing that the art of this Dutch dandy, writing in the flowery language of fin-de-siècle decadence, should still sound so fresh. We should be grateful. For, now that the dreams of ethnic purity are making a comeback, his voice is more urgent than ever.

1994

PART II

Satyajit Ray

THE LAST BENGALI

RENAISSANCE MAN

On a visit to Calcutta I was told a story about Louis Malle. The French film director had spent some time in the city to film part of his famous—in India notorious—1969 documentary *Calcutta*. One day Malle was shooting a riot, a not uncommon scene in Calcutta. This infuriated a Bengali policeman, who ran up to Malle threatening to smash his camera. Malle objected. "Who do you think you are?" shouted the policeman. "Louis Malle," replied the director. "Ah," said the Bengali with a sweet smile, *"Zazie dans le métro."*

It is no doubt an apocryphal tale, but one hears many such stories in Calcutta. It tells you something about the atmosphere of the place—an extraordinary combination of squalor and high culture, violence and civility.

I was told this anecdote by a successful newspaper editor called Aveek Sarkar. We met in his office, housed in an old building in the center of a commercial district where beggars and ricksha-wallahs dodged in and out of the hopeless traffic jams, while families, the children naked, the adults in flimsy clothes, washed themselves by burst waterpipes. Aveek was dressed in a dhoti, and smoked Montecristo cigars. He offered me a fine Scotch whiskey, and talked about Bengali poetry. Every Bengali is a poet, he said. There are at least 500 poetry magazines in the state of West Bengal, and when Calcutta celebrates the birthday of its greatest poet, Rabindranath Tagore, poetry bulletins are published by the day, sometimes even by the hour. "We don't look to the rest of India, which is intellectually inferior," he said. "Our literature is related to French literature, not Hindi. I don't even read Hindi. Calcutta is like Paris."

Aveek introduced me to Satyajit Ray, the film director, graphic designer, composer of music and author of children's stories. He lives in a grand old apartment building in an elegantly crumbling area known as South Calcutta. His workroom is stacked with books—anything from Bengali literature to fifteenth-century Italian art to modern British theater design. There are inkstands, pens and paintbrushes, and an old-fashioned gramophone. And in the midst of this sits Ray, a tall, handsome man, dressed in a dhoti, drinking tea. He speaks English with a refined baritone drawl, rather like an aesthetic Oxford don. Without having seen Calcutta—or, indeed, his films—one might mistake him for a brown sahib, a genteel colonial relic. He is actually something far more complex than that; he represents a style historically and socially rooted where many of his films take place, in the decaying grandeur of his native city.

Ray had been very ill. He still appeared weary. "It's a frightful bore making films in India these days," he said. He complained about the state of the Bengali film industry. Cut off from a large potential audience in Bangladesh by a government ban there on Indian films, there are not enough Bengalis to sustain the industry anymore. Compared to the average movie produced in Calcutta today, Ray said he would rather see a splashy Bombay musical: "At least there's plenty of action and pretty girls."

His latest film, *The Home and the World* (1984), had been completed from his hospital bed, by issuing instructions to his son. It is possible that some of Ray's genius will be carried on to the next generation, but not likely. Genius cannot be taught. Besides that, India has changed too much. It is almost impossible now to make the kind of understated, humanist movies that Ray did. The style is not fashionable—but then it never really was. One of the most remarkable things about Ray's films is that they ever got made at all.

In an essay about the Japanese cinema, in his book *Our Films, Their Films,* Ray commented on Kurosawa's masterpiece, *Rashomon:* "It was a kind of film that immediately suggests a culmination, a fruition, rather than a beginning. You could not—as a film-making nation, have a *Rashomon* and nothing to show before it." It is hard to disagree, but this makes Ray's achievements all the more baffling. For what, in the Indian cinema, laid a foundation for *Pather Panchali,* Ray's first film, made in 1955? It had the maturity of a culmination of something, while in fact it was only the beginning. As early influences Ray cites the humanism of Jean Renoir, the technical economy and realism of Rossellini and De Sica, but he had no Indian masters to follow or to challenge. Yet unlike so many "arty" Asian films, Ray's work was never a reflection of half-understood Western styles. From the very beginning, his films were unmistakably his own. How did he do it? What, if not Indian cinema, was his artistic source?

"The raw material of the cinema is life itself. It is incredible that a country which has inspired so much painting and music and poetry should fail to move the film-maker. He has only to keep his eyes open, and his ears. Let him do so." Ray wrote this in 1948, seven years before his first film was shown. It offers at least a vague and general answer to the question above. There is more to Ray, though, than a sensitive pair of eyes and ears. To find clues to his particular vision one must, I think, go back much further than Renoir or Rossellini, back to the Bengali renaissance of the 1820s and 1830s.

The Bengali renaissance was the product of a small number of families, often divided among themselves in cliques. These families—the Tagores, the Debs, the Rays, the Ghoses, the Mallicks—were mostly high-caste Hindus, and were collectively known as the *bhadralok,* literally, gentlemen of substance. The British called them the "educated natives." While the Bengali elite had been large landowners, the *bhadralok* attained social prominence in the late eighteenth and early nineteenth centuries by acting as middlemen for the East India Company and private British traders. Some were clerks, fixers, contractors, translators, minor civil servants or tax collectors who made fortunes by fleecing the old landlords, who often ended up in penury (the theme of one of

Ray's best films, *The Music Room,* 1958). Their main enthusiasm was modern education, for which they had an almost unquenchable thirst: science, English literature, European philosophy, and politics. They organized reading societies, established English-language schools, stocked libraries, started printing presses, and published newspapers. The *bhadralok,* in other words, were the first Indian urban middle class: modern men who tried to fuse European liberalism and enlightened Hinduism. Anxious to be cosmopolitan, they were still steeped in their own past.

Their position was often ambivalent. Since they were colonial middlemen, their interests lay with the British Empire, which their political ideals would ultimately lead them to oppose. Their sons and grandsons, frustrated by the lack of political power on the one hand and the inertia of Indian traditions on the other, often turned to Marxist radicalism. The reformist zeal of the *bhadralok* left a legacy in Bengal of Marxist government and occasional terrorism. The cultural sophistication, the fruit of the Bengali renaissance, produced thousands of garrulous coffee-shop philosophers, millions of poets and the occasional genius, such as Rabindranath Tagore and Satyajit Ray.

Tagore's grandfather, Dwarkanath, was a typical example of the pioneering *bhadralok.* He started off as the chief native officer of the East India Company's opium and salt department, but in true *bhadralok* style later owned several English-language newspapers. A British friend described him as "a Hindoo with an enlarged mind and a truly British spirit." He might have said the same about Satyajit Ray's grandfather, Upendrakisore Ray, an accomplished musician of Western classical music, a graphic artist, a composer of songs and a writer of children's stories. Upendrakisore launched the children's monthly magazine called *Gandesh,* which Satyajit revived in 1961 and in which most of the short stories in *The Unicorn Expedition and Other Fantastic Tales of India* first appeared. Few renaissance men maintain the same level of excellence in everything they put their hands to. Although Ray's stories, written for teenagers, never quite scale the heights of his films, they are filled with the same spirit.

His characters reflect the gentle patrician humanism so typically *bhadralok,* and so typical of Ray's work. There is Shonku, the scientist-inventor, whom Ray himself calls "a mild-mannered version of Professor Challenger," one of Arthur Conan Doyle's creations. Professor Shonku travels around the world showing off his strange inventions— a computer the size of a football that knows the answers to a million questions, or Corvus, the crow genius. Like Ray himself, Shonku is cosmopolitan, at home in most capital cities, thirsty for new knowledge, but at the same time he remains very Indian in his fascination with the metaphysical. His adventures take him to Zen gardens in Kyoto and to Tibetan monasteries where he learns how to fly off to an imaginary land filled with imaginary unicorns. The Shonku stories, in the manner of Verne and Wells, humanize science. The author's attitude, his humanism and his faith in science, remind one of a more self-confident age in the West, an age in which we still believed in progress, an age before Auschwitz and the invention of the atom bomb. Indians (and most Asians, for that matter) often like to make the neat distinction between scientific Western civilization and spiritual Eastern civilization. Professor Shonku, again a bit like his creator, quite successfully manages to straddle both.

The sad appeal of *bhadralok* culture is that it flowered so briefly. Ever since the British shifted the capital of the raj to New Delhi in 1912, Calcutta has been a city in decline. Its European elegance had always been somewhat anomalous in the steamy climate of Bengal. But Calcutta somehow managed to wear its decadence with a certain amount of grace; the anomaly of high culture in the midst of squalor is a kind of dandyism. It is a common theme in Ray's work, and a common trait in many of his characters. One of his stories tells of a middle-aged man who used to be a successful amateur actor and earned a decent living. Now reduced to genteel poverty, he is suddenly asked to fill in as an extra in some tawdry local film. His only line is "Oh!" as he is knocked down in the street by the star of the production. He rehearses the scene endlessly on his own, trying to recapture his old élan. He does the scene perfectly.

> But all the labour and imagination he had to put into this one shot—were these people able to appreciate that? He doubted it. They just got hold of some people, got them to go through certain motions, paid them for their labours and forgot all about it. Paid them, yes, but how much? Ten, fifteen, twenty rupees? But what

was twenty rupees when measured against the intense satisfaction of a small job done with perfection and dedication?

He walks away without waiting for his pay. He is too good for such a sordid business.

Apu's father in *Pather Panchali* is also too cultured for his surroundings. He is a poor literary Brahmin dreaming of writing a masterpiece, while his family almost starves in a village of illiterate peasants. And the landlord in *The Music Room* ignores his debts and pawns his possessions so he can still pretend to live in aristocratic style. Ray is never sentimental about these dreamers. "It is true," he has said about *The Music Room*, "I am interested in all dying traditions. This man who believes in his future is for me a pathetic figure. But I sympathize with him. He might be absurd, but he is fascinating."

The sad nobility of being out of step with one's surroundings or time can go much deeper than the simple contrast between poverty and dreams. In a way, the entire *bhadralok* culture, its refinement, its liberalism, its sophisticated attempt to bridge East and West, was out of step—just as Calcutta, the old colonial capital, has been out of step for a long time with the development of India. Although Ray himself, like Tagore, at whose school he studied art, believes in the enlightened values of the liberal *bhadralok,* he gently mocks the proponents. Not only are some of the Bengali intellectuals in his films a little absurd, but they wreak havoc upon the emotions of innocent people by being carried away by their ideas to the exclusion of all else. This is particularly true of films based on Tagore's stories. Bhupati, the pipe-smoking journalist husband in *Charulata* (1964), is typical. His head, usually buried in books, is so full of new ideas that he loses sight of the people around him. His young and beautiful wife, Charu, is bored and frustrated, endlessly peering through her binoculars at life outside the claustrophobic women's quarters. Bhupati, the modernist, is still a traditional Indian husband who takes his wife for granted. He encourages his young cousin, Amal, a literary youth, to keep her company. The inevitable happens. Charu falls in love. Amal runs away to escape his guilt. Bhupati learns his lesson.

In the first scene of Ray's *The Home and the World* we see Nikhil reading Milton in English to his young bride, Bimal, who doesn't understand a word. The story takes place in the first decade of this century, when Bengal was partitioned by Lord Curzon, effectively dividing Hindus and Muslims. Nikhil is a large landowner. His grand mansion reflects his culture: part of the house, particularly the women's quarters, is in the Indian style, while the drawing room, with its crystal chandeliers, grand piano and cut-glass ornaments, is Victorian English. Nikhil sees it as his mission to get his wife out of the women's quarters ("Purdah never was a Hindu custom") and into the Victorian drawing room. To please her husband, she takes singing lessons from an English lady and learns to recite English poetry. He finally gets her to break the taboo of purdah: she opens the door of the women's room and walks through the hall to the drawing room, where she is introduced for the first time to a man who is not a relative. The home, as it were, is suddenly opened to the world.

Sandip, the revolutionary demagogue, seduces women the way he seduces the masses: he dazzles them with his ruthless charm. This supreme egotist, justifying his actions by a kind of Nietzschean nihilism, writes in his diary that "whatever I grab is mine. . . . Every man has a natural right to possess, and therefore greed is natural. What my mind covets my surroundings must supply." He covets Bimal, and she falls for him, stealing her husband's money for Sandip's cause (to Sandip, sex and his cause come down to much the same thing). Sandip's present cause is boycotting British goods. He forces the poor Muslim traders, who cannot survive by selling expensive and inferior Indian goods, to burn their British products. Those who won't are robbed and sometimes killed. For the cause, Sandip exploits communal tensions between Hindus and Muslims, leaving them to slaughter each other in riots.

Nikhil, the gentle humanist who believes in the freedom of choice, does not dare to intervene for fear of losing his wife. He allows his friend to stay in his house, for otherwise "Bimal would regret it. She would not stay with me out of her own choice. That would be unbearable." When Bimal finally sees through her lover's deception, Sandip escapes the chaos he has caused. Nikhil tries to stop the killing and is shot dead. Barbarism has proved to be a stronger force than Nikhil's enlightened ideals.

Nikhil and Sandip, the radical and the humanist, the two faces of modern Bengali culture. "We both decided to have nothing to do with irrational conventions," says Nikhil at one point in the film. "He was just more radical than I." It is telling that, besides Ray, the Bengali filmmakers of greatest importance, Ritwik Ghatak and Mrinal Sen, are both Marxists. Ghatak, who was four years younger than Ray, was a communist sympathizer until his death in 1976. People who champion Mrinal Sen's films often accuse Ray of being sentimental, lacking in class analysis, or even of being "feudal." It is certainly true that Ray is less interested in analyzing the human predicament politically than in showing how people behave, how they react to love and death. With Sen—though, oddly enough, less with the more radical Ghatak—one sometimes feels that he is more interested in ideas than in people.

Unfortunately, the weakness of *The Home and the World,* compared, say, to *The Music Room, Charulata* or the Apu trilogy, is precisely that the characters represent ideas, preventing them from wholly coming to life. This accounts, perhaps, for the unusual—for Ray's films, that is— wordiness of the movie. Ray's best scenes are often silent: the death of Durga, Apu's sister, in *Pather Panchali,* or the look on the face of the starving husband at the end of *Distant Thunder* (1973), set during the great famine in 1943, when his wife tells him she is pregnant. Words could never express the emotional intensity of those silent moments. Words, at least to one who cannot understand Bengali, appear to detract from the realism in *The Home and the World;* they express literary and political ideas rather than feelings.

Ray suffered a heart attack while making *The Home and the World,* but I think the relative weakness of the film (it is still a masterpiece compared to most movies) cannot be explained by Ray's ill health alone. The flaws are also in Tagore's original story. Tagore's biographer Krishna Kripalani wrote that Nikhil, "who is compounded of the Maharishi's [Rabindranath's father] religious insight, of Gandhi's political idealism and of Tagore's own tolerance and humanism, is too shadowy to be real." Sandip, however, "the Machiavellian patriot, the unscrupulous politician, the splendid wind-bag and shameless seducer is, on the other hand, very real." In Ray's film it seems more the other way around. Nikhil, played by Victor Bannerjee, reveals a brooding complexity, while Sandip, played by Soumitra Chatterjee, appears as more of a caricature.

The most convincing character is the woman in the middle, superbly acted by Swatilekha Chatterjee. As is the case with many Japanese heroines, Bimal's shy and submissive exterior hides a character that is stronger and more passionate than that of either of the men who appear to dominate her. One is reminded of the women in Mizoguchi's films. Both Ray and Mizoguchi managed to get great performances out of their leading men, but the most powerful roles are usually for women. (Strangely, however, women hardly figure at all in Ray's short stories.)

Japanese critics like to call Mizoguchi a "feminist" (they use the English word). And many of Ray's films, such as his latest one, deal with the emancipation of women. But neither director—least of all Mizoguchi, a traditionalist to the core—is a radical feminist in the political sense of the word. Ray once said in an interview, "A woman's beauty, I think, also lies in her patience and endurance in a world where men are generally more vulnerable and in need of guidance." This is precisely what Mizoguchi would have said. It is what the Japanese mean by feminism. The transition from Asian tradition to Western-influenced modernity, a constant theme in both Ray's and Mizoguchi's work, often focuses on women. Still the bedrock of tradition, they offer solace. But it is also those same traditional women whose emotions are most affected by modernization.

There may be a religious element in this brand of feminism. Japan and India, particularly Bengal, share strong matriarchal traditions of worshiping mother goddesses. This, by the way, is a thread running through Ritwak Ghatak's films, where women sacrifice everything for their men. Ghatak, a keen student of Jung as well as Marx, tends to mix religious and political metaphors: his suffering heroines stand for the downtrodden peasants, for sacrificing goddesses, and even for his motherland, raped by the British imperialists and their Indian capitalist lackeys.

We speak of Western civilization because of shared religious, philosophical and political traditions. Do such widely different countries as India and Japan have enough in common (Buddhism, perhaps?) to allow us to talk of a distinct Eastern civilization? Tagore, as his statements in China and Japan made clear, believed so. In his fascinating essay about Japanese cinema in *Our Films, Their Films,* Ray, though a little more tentatively than Tagore, reaches the same conclusion. He quotes his old professor at Tagore's academy as saying: "Consider the Fujiyama. . . . Fire within and calm without. There is the symbol of the true Oriental artist." Mizoguchi and Ozu, Ray says, "both suggest enormous reserves of power and feeling which never spill over into emotional displays." Well, this depends on what one means by emotional displays. But I think I know what Ray means. The emotions under the surface, the long spells of apparent calm, suddenly interrupted by an emotional climax—a look of terrible grief, a stifled scream, a burst of silent tears—the image of the woman betrayed by weaker men, biting her sari or kimono in anguish: these mark the style of Ray's films, as they do that of Mizoguchi's. Perhaps this offers a hint of what makes Ray's films seem, for lack of a better word, Asian.

Ray's films, like those of Mizoguchi, indeed of most Asian masters, are often accused of being slow. To those for whom only perpetual action can stave off boredom this may be true. But the lingering over everyday details, the moments of complete calm—compared by Ray to the slow movements in music—are necessary to express the intensity of the emotional highlights. The slow realism of the classic Asian cinema is a bit like the Japanese Noh theater or the English game of cricket: the slowness—which, to me, is never boring—draws you into the world expressed on the screen, the stage or the playing field. This process is more than entertainment—it is not always entertaining. And it is not a matter of slowing down life to the pace of real life—that really would be boring. Rather, it slows down moments in life sufficiently to, as it were, catch reality.

It is a form of realism that has almost died out in the Japanese and Indian cinema. Commercial pressures, especially acute in a place like Bengal, with only a very small educated audience, are partly to blame. With the advent of television, videos and other new entertainments, the film industries have opted for safe formulas: song and dance in India, soapy melodrama in Japan. But I do not believe this is the only reason for the cinematic regression.

Ray made the following point about the great Japanese directors:

I am not saying that these masters did not learn from the West. All artists imbibe, consciously or unconsciously, the lessons of past masters. But when a film-maker's roots are strong, and when tradition is a living reality, outside influences are bound to dwindle and disappear and a true indigenous style evolve.

This was certainly true of Ray, Mizoguchi, Ozu, even Kurosawa. They all imbibed the work of such different directors as John Ford, Frank Capra and Jean Renoir. But they also were steeped in their own aesthetic traditions, which was the very condition that made their art universal. This is what has changed. Few young Japanese filmmakers are at home in Japanese painting, as Mizoguchi was; few Indian filmmakers could compose a score of Indian music, as Ray does. What is left, in this world of instant communications, is a constant exposure to Western fashions, which, without a strong traditional culture to absorb them, become meaningless ornaments. These ornaments are merged with the showy conventions of local pop culture. The result is often profitable, sometimes entertaining, but never a masterpiece. There are still serious films being made in India, but they tend to be melodramas containing political messages. Both in style and in content they are parochial in a way that Ray's films never are. One fears it will be a long time before another Satyajit Ray appears in India. He is one of the last true cosmopolitans, and perhaps the very last Bengali renaissance man.

1987

Nirad C. Chaudhuri

CITIZEN OF

THE BRITISH EMPIRE

Nirad C. Chaudhuri is in many ways a most unusual Indian. Fellow Indians sometimes dismiss him with a casual flick of the wrist. "Oh, him," said a journalist from Bombay, whose opinion I sought— "just a cantankerous old fellow." A more charitable Bengali scholar called him "a kind of museum piece, a nineteenth-century relic." But many Indians continue to read him.

Chaudhuri, born in 1897, has spent a lifetime kicking against the myths and shibboleths held by the majority of his countrymen: he has ridiculed the pacifism of Mahatma Ghandi; he has exposed Hinduism as a form of xenophobic power worship; he has castigated Indian nationalism for being corrupt, self-seeking and destructive; he has mocked the pretensions of Anglicized Indians and vented his spleen at the stupidity and philistinism of the British in India, while at the same time beginning his first and most famous book, *The Autobiography of an Unknown Indian,* with the following dedication:

To the memory of the British Empire in India, which conferred subjecthood on us but withheld citizenship, to which yet every one of us threw out the challenge *Civis Britannicus sum,* because all that was good and living within us was made, shaped, and quickened by the same British rule.

It was this sentiment, perhaps more than anything else, that most irritated Indians, not to mention British liberals: the former because of nationalist pride, the latter for reasons of colonial guilt, or, as Chaudhuri himself would put it, degeneracy of national character.

"Just a cantankerous old fellow." "Totally irrelevant." "A reactionary relic." No matter how often these mantras of dismissal were recited, Chaudhuri refused to go away or shut up. His voice is as strong, idiosyncratic, erudite, garrulous and at times cantankerous as ever. *Thy Hand, Great Anarch! India 1921–1952,* his chronicle of the intellectual life and times of a no longer unknown Indian, is almost a thousand pages long. Indians, as Chaudhuri himself tells us, and as anybody who has ever sat next to an unknown Indian on a plane or train will know, love to talk. It testifies to Chaudhuri's eloquence, wit and intellectual brilliance that he can go on at such length without once becoming a bore.

Chaudhuri's theme is decadence. It permeates everything he writes. "It is a fatality with me," he writes in the introduction, "that wherever I go the spectre of decadence treads at my heels like the Foul Fiend." The title itself, a quotation from Alexander Pope, refers to this foul fiend: "Thy hand, great Anarch! lets the curtain fall; / And Universal Darkness buries All!" In his first book he described the decadence of Bengal, specifically the decline of high culture in Calcutta, which flowered briefly in the nineteenth century, inspired by Western learning that came with British rule. This decline, in Chaudhuri's account, is but part of a larger decadence, that of the British empire itself, which, like all decadent empires, "ceased to create or defend values associated with [it]."

In *Thy Hand, Great Anarch!* the empire dies, in Chaudhuri's view, squalidly and ignobly, leaving at least a million slaughtered Hindus and Muslims in its wake. The death of Empire spelled the death of the British people. They died, as Chaudhuri put it to me in his Oxford house, savoring his words, "not as the noble Roman perishing in his marble bath, but as cheap hussies in a whorehouse." But even that is only part of a much greater death, for the Universal Darkness is descending upon us all—upon America, where he thinks the gulf between technological mastery and social and cultural depravity is widest, but also upon "the least civilized of the non-European human groups, e.g. those in Africa," who are "socially and culturally as decadent as the Europeans."

Personally, Chaudhuri tells us, it has been his aim in life to navigate through the currents of history—never to be carried away by them. His prescription to remain untainted by the decay around him is to cultivate the "capacity to shake off the fetters of the present. No one who is in bondage to it can have any true view of life. . . . Fashion, the tyrant of humanity taken in the mass, had no hold on me." This has lent an aristocratic detachment to his views, and the ability to see through the received opinions that give comfort to lesser minds than his. While he picks his way through the debris of modern civilization, he sounds a warning to his fellow men.

But Chaudhuri's writing is so much more than a mere warning; his vision of doom is integral to his art, an expression of foreboding, but also of fascination. There are loud echos of Burke in his elitist conservatism, to be sure, but also of the refined urbanites of Cavafy's poem "Waiting for the Barbarians," obsessed by the menace without. He wants to warn us about the impending disaster, but cannot avert his fascinated gaze, not wanting to miss a minute of the action. As he put it in his first autobiography,

> In my student days I used to be specially drawn towards these periods of history in which some great empire or nation, or at all events the power and glory of a great state, was passing away. I was induced to agonized fascination by these periods, and the earliest experience I had of this feeling was when I read about the final defeat of Athens at the hands of Sparta. I seemed to hear within me the clang of the pickaxes with which the long walls to the Peiraeus were being demolished, and was overwhelmed by a sense of desolation which men have when they see familiar landmarks suddenly disappear or witness the unexpected *bouleversement* of the purpose they had assumed to be inherent in the unfolding of their existence.

The curious thing about highly civilized men drawn to the spectacle of barbaric violence done to high civilization is that it is never entirely clear which holds the greater attraction; the dying civilization or the Sturm und Drang that topples it. Chaudhuri is a connoisseur of everything that is fine and lofty. He is at home in the literature of Europe; he is an amateur of classical European music, testing his wife on her knowledge of Beethoven on their wedding night; he is a student of Mogul miniatures and architecture, and a proud champion of the great Bengali writers and poets. He is also a student of war, with a deep knowledge of military history. In his house in Oxford hang several portraits of Napoleon. When I commented on this, he remarked, "We are great Napoleon worshipers, you know." For a moment I was taken aback. Admirations for great power and the love of high culture do not always exist in harmony. But one can imagine why a Bengali born at the zenith of the British raj would associate the one with the other. And one can also see why the decline of power can be relished and deeply regretted at the same time.

Bengal, especially Calcutta, was and still is a perfect place to observe cultural, social, political decay. "Life in Calcutta," wrote Chaudhuri in his first book, "was the symbol and epitome of our national history, a true reflection of the creative effort in our modern existence as well as of its self-destructive duality." It was there, in the grandiose capital of the raj, that high-caste Hindus imbodied European civilization during the nineteenth century, partly through mimicry of their British masters, but mostly through literature. Great libraries were founded, grand houses built, stocked with books, fine European furniture, and paintings. There they still stand, for the inspection of tourists ("that abomination, the white tourist," says Chaudhuri), who pose for pictures before the busts of Queen Victoria covered in bird droppings, and gaze at the cobwebbed chandeliers and the gilt-framed prints of the Battle of Waterloo. Calcutta for the Hindu gentry, the *bhadralok,* was a city of poetry readings, religious reform movements and musical evenings. This modern Indian culture was known as the Bengali renaissance. Chaudhuri came of age in its twilight.

In many ways he is a typical *bhadralok,* an aristocrat of the mind, who taught himself to read and, where possible, quote from the European classics—in English, of course, but also in French, Italian, Latin and Greek. Steeped in this remarkable high culture of Calcutta, Chaudhuri saw it gradually deteriorate into the sad caricature it has become today.

Bengalis still chatter away in their crumbling coffee shops about structuralism, deconstructionism and postmodernism, and there are Satyajit Ray's films to admire, but the great days of the renaissance ended around the turn of this century. And, writes Chaudhuri, "from 1921 onwards the influence of Bengal in Indian politics began to decline." India's fate was to be determined more by Gandhi's mass movement than by Calcutta's cultivated *bhadralok.* "In the cultural field the same decline became perceptible to me, and I myself took some part in what might be called the Bengali *Kulturkampf.* With independence, the eclipse of Bengal was completed."

Again and again Chaudhuri points out the confluence of power, or decline in power, and cultural decay. Later in *Thy Hand, Great Anarch!,* referring to the postcolonial British, and specifically to Sir Richard Attenborough's naive and sentimental liberalism ("The worship of Gandhi is, in the British above all, unqualified imbecility and a sure proof of the degeneration of the British character"), he turns a famous saying upside down: "Loss of power corrupts, and absolute loss of power corrupts absolutely." Maybe so. But was loss of power really the reason for cultural decadence in Bengal? What is the connection between culture and power? Are they truly Siamese twins who live and die together?

At first sight Bengal would seem to prove Chaudhuri's case. Having created more or less in their own image a vigorous Bengali elite, the British, like a suddenly panicked Dr. Frankenstein, did their best to snuff it out, or at least rob it of power. First there was the attempt to divide Bengal in 1905 between Muslims and Hindus, causing riots, communal bitterness and a permanent British distrust of unruly Bengal. Then there was the transfer of the Indian government from Calcutta to New Delhi in 1912. There were practical reasons for this, to be sure, but behind it was a cultural prejudice. The British who ruled India during the jingoistic age of New Imperialism were no longer the hearty adventurers and high-minded gentlemen who arrived in the eighteenth and early nineteenth centuries.

In *An Area of Darkness,* a book that irritates Indians almost as much as Chaudhuri's works do, V. S. Naipaul described how in the latter half of the nineteenth century the raj had become a swaggering fantasy, expressed in bombastic monuments and racial arrogance: "To be English in India was to be larger than life."

An imperial ideal well on the way to a necessarily delayed realization was foundering on the imperialist myth, equally delayed, of the empire-builder, on the English fantasy of Englishness, "the cherished conviction," as one English official wrote in 1883, "which was shared by every Englishman in India, from the highest to the lowest, by the planter's assistant in his lowly bungalow . . . to the Viceroy on his throne . . . that he belongs to a race whom God has destined to govern and subdue."

So there was Chaudhuri, lover of Mozart, Pascal, Burke, Wordsworth and Dante, ruled by Englishmen whose intellectual tastes were adequately served by Kipling's *Barrack-Room Ballads.* Their fantasy of Englishness did not include the literary Bengali babus, for whom they felt contempt and distrust. More congenial to the British New Imperialists were the brave and philistine warriors of the northern frontiers, Muslims whose tribal pride mirrored the "muscular Christianity" of the British. The British *mission civilisatrice* had run into the sand, and Chaudhuri felt betrayed: "Any exhibition of knowledge of European life, civilization or history drove the British community in India to make the gesture which peasant boys in India make at a passing train. They expose themselves and wave their hips."

The fantasy of Englishness had the unfortunate effect that Indians, especially Bengalis, retreated into fantasies of their own: the fantasy of ancient India, a civilization whose magnificence put even its modern, humiliated descendants on an unassailable plane, or the fantasy of superior spirituality, beyond the reach of the materialist West. Bengali intellectuals, made defensive by English contempt, often became show-offs, ridiculed by Kipling in *The Jungle Book.* (It is a weakness that Chaudhuri points out and, it must be said, often exemplifies.) Kipling likened Bengali intellectuals to monkeys, the Bandar Log. When Rabindranath Tagore was awarded the Nobel Prize for literature for a book in English in 1913, Kipling remarked in a letter to Rider Haggard, "Well, whose fault is it that the babu is what he is? *We* did it. We began in Macaulay's time. We have worked without intermission to make this Caliban." Caliban would have his revenge by gloating over every British setback during the two world wars—a show of petty hatred that disgusted Chaudhuri as much as did British arrogance.

Chaudhuri felt the British contempt particularly keenly because he believed in the *mission civilisatrice*. He took Queen Victoria at her word when she said the imperial mission was "to protect the poor natives and advance civilization." He can still say without a hint of self-consciousness that "I remain a Bengali, an Indian, an Englishman, while being a citizen of the world." He is the embodiment of the highest imperial ideal, a man Queen Victoria would have been deeply proud of, and precisely for that reason a man utterly out of sync with modern India. *"L'Inde c'est moi,"* he wrote in his first autobiography. Perhaps *"Bengal c'est moi"* would have been more accurate, but even that may have been too wide a net in which to catch this lifelong maverick. He thought of giving *Thy Hand, Great Anarch!* the title "One Man Against His People." He gave that up, though, because, as he put it, he is not against any people, but against historical trends.

Chaudhuri's defense of imperialism is interesting and not easily dismissed. Empires are by definition hierarchical, but also cosmopolitan (one of the greatest promoters of the British empire, Benjamin Disraeli, was a Levantine Jew): "There is no empire without a conglomeration of linguistically, racially, and culturally different nationalities and the hegemony of one of them over the rest. The heterogeneity and the domination are of the very essence of imperial relations." But this domination, in Chaudhuri's view, is perfectly justified if power is exercised morally, indeed to protect the poor natives and advance civilization. Chaudhuri distinguishes imperialism from mere colonialism. The conquest of the Americas, and the consequent slaughter of the native population, was colonialism. The Roman empire and the British raj worked to the benefit of all.

History, says Chaudhuri, "had shown empires as protectors and reclaimers of civilization, and empires had taken over the keepership of civilizations when its creators had become incapable of maintaining them." It is true that empires impose order and often preserve native elites, whose assistance they require. The Manchus did that in China and so did the Dutch and the British. The Soviets, of course, did not—they murdered the old guard. The British raj, despite its skill at dividing to rule, kept the peace in India better than its successors have done. But the trouble with empires is that they tend to freeze the existing social order artificially: social conflicts are not solved but frozen into place. Old elites are kept in power, symbolically, without retaining real authority; their high culture survives but becomes lifeless. New hybrid elites, the compradors and middlemen, are created in the imperialists' own image. But, as soon as the imperial rulers leave, the tensions break out again, the high culture turns to dust, the new elites find themselves isolated and betrayed and, in the unlucky event of a revolution, up against the execution wall.

This does not excuse the way in which Britain left India. Chaudhuri is quite right to feel bitter about Attlee and Lord Mountbatten, the Richard Attenborough of the empire's dying days, more interested in his own liberal image than in the consequences of his actions. India was left wholly unprepared for the mass migrations and massacres that came with partition. But I am not convinced that prolonging British rule would have done all that much for the things that Chaudhuri holds dear.

Chaudhuri is an unashamed elitist, as were the great writers of the Bengali renaissance. Tagore, he says, "never had any friendliness for anybody who did not belong to an elite." Bankim Chandra Chatterji, Bengal's first novelist and a Hindu nationalist, wrote, to Chaudhuri's approval, "It is indeed a matter of hope for the Bengali people that they are imitating the English." But, writes Chaudhuri, also with approval, what Chatterji "wholly condemned and regarded as despicable was imitation by those who are devoid of talent." And, still on a high cultural note, when Chaudhuri himself learned to appreciate European classical music, he observed that "if I had heard pop music then, my chance encounter with European music would not have had any sequel. A man moored to the highest in one's own culture does not go over to barbarism, nor is he beaten by it, even if it were as strong as King Kong."

Chaudhuri's favorite word of condemnation is "crude." Bengali revolutionaries were crude. Middle-class Indians are crude. The British in India were crude. The British in their own country today are crude. Crude people cannot be good rulers. They cannot advance civilization. And so Congress rule in India is turning the country into "a Caribbean island on a continental scale."

There is a seeming contradiction between Chaudhuri's elitism and his assertion that the greatest betrayal by the British was their leaving India without having achieved a social transformation of Indian society. But there is no real contradiction there. Chaudhuri's elitism has little to do with class. He did not think his own class, the upper middle-class Hindus, were fit to rule, for they only looked after their own interests. But neither did he have any trust in the Indian masses—or any masses for that matter—for they did not understand politics; all they knew was communal hatred, which should be kept in check at all times, if necessary by force. Gandhi's greatest crime, in Chaudhuri's eyes, is that by mobilizing the masses he effectively unleashed the primitive emotions that the British had kept under control for so long. Chaudhuri's elite, the only one fit to rule, is a cultural and moral aristocracy. Only this enlightened elite could have effected a social transformation, from the top on down, with the help and might of the British; but this, as we know, was denied it.

Gandhi tried to do the exact opposite: he had no time for high culture. Indeed he tried by example to return India to the level of folk religion and the spinning wheel. His transformation had to come from the bottom up. Chaudhuri does not deny that Gandhi was a moral man, but "even after the best had been said about it, it still remained the morality of the *servus,* very pure and lofty certainly, none the less bearing in all its manifestations the unmistakable stamp of its lowly origin." But that was of course Gandhi's whole point: only through the morality of the *servus* could he make the Indian masses feel proud of themselves.

Chaudhuri's defense of high culture is deeply antidemocratic:

Neither biological evolution nor human history reveals anything like equal status for all. They do not bear witness to the achievement of anything good, great, wise, abiding, or new, by the exercise of the equal vote. The cosmic process is revealed as a living and evergrowing pyramid, whose apex is rising higher and higher, leaving more and more strata underneath.

Chaudhuri believes that democracy advances cultural decadence. Yet nowhere are the fruits of high culture so abundantly available as in the democracies of the decadent West; and many of those fruits were sown in democracies, beginning with ancient Greece. Still, when the Attlee government decided to relinquish British power in India, the preservation of high culture was not high on its list of goals: the very idea of a

mission civilisatrice had become an embarrassment. Britain was not prepared to rule by force, because it no longer seemed moral to do so. Instead it was hoped that the instruments and institutions of law and
democracy would last beyond the raj. And, to an astonishing degree,
despite corruption, economic mismanagement, political demagoguery
and communal violence, it has turned out that way. India is still a func-
tioning democracy. This might have resulted in a loss of aristocratic values, but that is a price worth paying.

It would be hard to convince Chaudhuri of that, however. His sense
of betrayal goes too deep. It is a sign of his decency and common sense
that, unlike some European participants of the Kulturkampf against
democratic vulgarity, Chaudhuri never fell for fascist poseurs in fancy
uniforms. There were plenty of them in Bengal; Gandhi's greatest political rival was the Bengali politician Subhas Chandra Bose, known to
his followers as Netaji, meaning Leader.

Chaudhuri's revenge against his betrayers was more subtle than that.
In 1970 he moved to Britain, where he is not just a cantankerous old
fellow, let alone totally irrelevant, but a literary celebrity. His newly
found role is to castigate his former masters for their crudeness, ignorance and illiterate philistinism. The Bengali babu has finally come into
his own as an arbiter elegantiarum in the pages of the Tory press. WHY I
MOURN FOR ENGLAND was the headline to a 1988 piece in *The Daily
Telegraph* in which Chaudhuri analyzed the decay of the English mind
by pointing out the sloppy, ungrammatical, imprecise use of the English language as it is spoken by the British today. He has great sport by
inserting literary allusions which he refuses to identify and which he
can be quite sure few of his readers will recognize.

As a young man in Bengal, Chaudhuri was hurt by the contemptuous laughter of arrogant Englishmen who mocked him for knowing
more about their culture than they did. Now he has the last laugh. But
irony still finds a way of catching up with its most elusive targets. Now
that every politician feels compelled to talk about "values" again, Nirad
C. Chaudhuri is fast becoming the very thing he had avoided with such
success for ninety years: fashionable.

1988

Mircea Eliade

BENGAL NIGHTS

In 1928 Mircea Eliade left Bucharest for India. He was a twenty-one-year-old student of philosophy, and an aspiring novelist. His purpose was to study in Calcutta under Surendranath Dasgupta, a famous historian of Indian philosophy. Dasgupta was so taken with his Romanian student that he invited him to live in his house.

Eliade fell in love with India. As he wrote much later in his *Autobiography,* after he had become a famous historian of comparative religion, "In India I discovered what I later came to refer to as cosmic religious feeling." He took to wearing a dhoti—"the apparel of the people with whom I wished to become one"—and eating with his hands. He had no interest in other Europeans. He despised the Eurasians, or "Anglo-Indians," whom he described as "idiots" and "fanatics." He did not feel he was a visitor in India: "I felt completely at home." And he fell in love with Professor Dasgupta's teenage daughter, Maitreyi, a talented poet already at sixteen, whose first volume was introduced by Rabindranath Tagore. The two talked secretly about marriage. Eliade thought his teacher would be delighted.

But, when Dasgupta found out about the affair, Eliade was told to leave the house at once. He had abused his teacher's hospitality. He was forbidden to see Maitreyi again. Eliade was devastated. He had tried to live like an Indian, even to become one, and now he had been rejected, like a foreign body in a healthy organism. As he put it in his *Autobiography,* "I knew that, along with the friendship of the Dasgupta family, I had lost India itself." His romance had come to an end, even if his cosmic feelings had not: he escaped to a Himalayan monastery to "find himself."

Eliade wrote up the affair as a roman à clef, which had considerable success, especially in France. It was also made into a film, which was less successful. Eliade appears to have stuck closely to the facts, as he saw them. Indeed, you hardly need a key to identify the characters. Eliade himself became a Frenchman called Alain, and Surendranath Dasgupta became an engineer named Narendra Sen, but most of the other people, including Maitreyi, kept their own names.

Bengal Nights belongs to a popular subgenre of confessional literature. The backdrop can be India or China or Japan; the story remains essentially the same: young, romantic Westerner falls in love with mysterious Oriental girl and, through her, with the mysterious Orient, only to bang his head on the prison wall of exclusive Oriental customs. It is a genre subject to spiritual melodrama; only a rich sense of humor can save the author from self-pity. But humor, so far as I can make out from his novel, was not one of Eliade's most notable qualities.

Yet the book is of interest, partly because the author was a great scholar, but also because of the existence of a kind of counterbook, written years later in response to it. The counterbook, first published in English in 1976, is Maitreyi Devi's *It Does Not Die*—an account of the same events, which gives a *Rashomon*-like spin to the story. She had become a well-known poet in India, and wrote books on Tagore, philosophy and social reform. She read *Bengal Nights* more than forty years after the event, and was so furious at the depiction of her as the willing partner in a sexual affair that she decided to respond: "In the innocent heart of a little girl there was no dirt. The filth has been created by that man in his imagination."

Whether or not they actually "did it," only she and Eliade would have known (she maintains that they did not), but I can see why she objected to his overheated prose:

> As though mad, driven, she offered her breasts to me, doubtless awaiting the thunderbolt that would annihilate us both. . . . Maitreyi was desire incarnate, her face immobile, her eyes fixed on me as though I were the embodiment of some god.

Her angry response is naive and rather Indian:

> Why did you not write the truth, Mircea? Was not truth enough? Did you write for financial gain? Yes, you did—that is the way of the West—books sell if they deal with lust, not love.

Maitreyi is so distressed that "I feel hot in the face and go and splash water on myself under the tap." She cannot sleep, for the "fire of anger is burning and along with it are burning many other things, my honour, my good name." The writing in English has the stilted feel of a period piece, and Maitreyi Devi's sense of humor is not much more in evidence than Eliade's. But, read together, the two books are a source of rich and entertaining ironies.

The India into which the young Eliade plunged was a good deal more complex than his description suggests. The Dasguptas were hardly paragons of Indian tradition: they were upper-class Bengali intellectuals who prided themselves on their liberalism, rationalism and cosmopolitanism. Although they were looked down on by the British and the Eurasians, who called the Indians "negroes" or "blacks," the *bhadralok* were in fact far more sophisticated than most Europeans in India—or in Europe, for that matter. The women in educated Bengali households were not in purdah, but mixed freely with male guests. Maitreyi even visited boys' colleges to recite her poetry. She worshipped Tagore, and read "forbidden" books by progressive Bengali writers. So far as mysticism is concerned, Maitreyi writes that "especially in the late twenties and early thirties, the higher middle class hesitated to show credulity. They were 'rational' not 'superstitious.' "

She tells an interesting story about a visit to Calcutta by a Russian couple, who performed telepathic feats in the theater. Professor Dasgupta called them "jugglers," but was sufficiently intrigued by their act to wish to test them further. He asked them to perform for the great poetic guru himself, Tagore, who believed "it was more scientific to enquire into unusual matters than to reject them outright." Perhaps inevitably, the "magic" failed to work in Tagore's skeptical presence.

These, then, were hardly the sort of people among whom one would expect cosmic experiences to occur. And, judging from her book, Maitreyi was far from being the "primitive and irrational creature" depicted by Eliade; nor was she the "pure" Indian goddess he described at other times. She was something far more interesting: an intelligent young woman who knew every detail of the customs and traditions that ensnared her, yet was unable to free herself from them. Eliade, in her view, understood too little of Indian life:

> He does not know how much even our family is bound by these irrational rules. And father, who is learned, who knows so much, does not know that happiness never depends on a person's caste or clan name. And me? I don't care about these things. Never, never will I enter into the prison house of prejudice. Even if I am not married to him I will prove with my life that I don't care for these silly customs. I don't care for anything in Hindu society.

But of course it was not to be as simple as that. After her relationship with Eliade is severed, she enters into a perfectly orthodox arranged marriage with a man who is, by her own account, decent, humorous, tolerant and loving, but for whom she can never muster the same passion she felt for Eliade. The coolness with which she accepts her fate is impressive. When her mother asks her whether she wants to meet her prospective husband before marrying him, she answers that there is no need for that. When her mother expresses surprise at this refusal of a modern, progressive innovation (brides never used to meet their husbands before the ceremony), Maitreyi answers:

> "Why should I see him? Suppose I say I won't marry him, I don't like him, I would rather marry Mr K., he is of another caste, never mind, I like him, will you then listen to me? You will begin to argue, won't you?"
>
> "Well, why won't you like him? Looks are not everything in a man, there are many handsome nitwits."
>
> "Stop talking nonsense, ma. You are all the same. You have no

courage to face the truth and specially you, you are to be blamed more than anybody else. You keep your eyes shut."

This is the same woman who seemed at first to Eliade like "a child, a primitive. Her words drew me, her incoherent thinking and her *naïveté* enchanted me. For a long time, I was to flatter myself by thinking of our relationship as that of civilized man and barbarian." By making this admission, Eliade does not flatter himself at all.

The truth—and the irony—of the Dasgupta home is that the learned professor cannot match his liberal ideas with deeds. He is as bound by the rules of caste and creed as the next man, no matter how much he has traveled abroad or conversed with other learned men, in English and in French. It is an old and common story, to be sure: what is good for others doesn't apply to one's own. Besides, knowledge can deepen prejudice as well as diminish it. Maitreyi's mother had read Maupassant, so she knows all about the immoral behavior of Europeans. How could she condone a marriage with a Frenchman after reading "Necklace"? Maitreyi sees through her parents and feels betrayed by Eliade when he fails to put up a fight. But then she doesn't put up much of a struggle either. Perhaps she counted the odds and realized the game wasn't worth the candle. Even so, the Eliade affair had shown her possibilities she could never forget.

Eliade's version of the thwarted love affair is so self-obsessed that he misses the irony of Dasgupta's contradictory attitudes. He confesses to a rather lame mea culpa. Asked whether he hates the Dasguptas for what they did, he says, "Why should I hate them? It is I who have done them wrong. What have they done? The only wrong they did was in bringing me to the house . . ." You begin to see why Maitreyi felt betrayed by him as much as by her father. But, in the context of his story, Eliade's response is plausible, even logical, for he turns everything into myth, in which all the characters behave according to type. There is little room for ambiguity. The Eurasians, living in their seedy boardinghouses, are all oversexed, vulgar and racist, as well as being idiots and fanatics. And Dasgupta behaves like a traditional Indian paterfamilias.

Eliade is a mythomaniac who presents himself as a European rationalist. In some wonderful vignettes, Maitreyi takes her former lover to task for his pedantry. In a childish caprice, she writes a poem on a favorite tree, addressing it as a friend. Eliade called this "pantheism." Maitreyi's retort: "He could not believe that this was no 'ism' but just a soaring poetic fancy."

A simple walk with Maitreyi in the country elicits this reverie from Eliade:

> Relentlessly, I forced myself to keep awake, to resist the enchantment of the fable that surrounded us. The rational being inside me was floundering in the unreality and the sanctity of our presence at the edge of that silent lake.

A prolonged fit of passion, in which he kisses her hands and they both shiver with desire, prompts the following flight of exultation:

> We had lived, confirmed, that miracle of human ascent into the supernatural through touch and sight. The experience lasted two hours and exhausted us.

And when the deed is finally done:

> While I retained my lucidity, handling my experience of love with rationality, she gave herself up to it as though it had a divine origin, as though the first contact of her virgin body with that of a man were some supernatural event.

This is not the language of a rationalist at all, but of a romantic to the core. Yet Eliade professes to be annoyed by his lover's irrationality and mythomania. After he had left the Dasgupta house, he receives a letter from Maitreyi in which she tells him that she felt his presence when she kissed a bunch of flowers. She writes that she worships him. He is to her "like a god made of gold and precious stones"; he is her sun, her life! Eliade:

> That escape into mythology pained me; it was extremely strange to see myself increasingly idealized, transformed from man into god, from lover into sun. . . . I did not want her to disappear into unreality, to become an idea, a myth; I did not want to console myself with an eternal, celestial paradise.

So both pride themselves on being rationalists. Eliade's claim rests on his status as a European intellectual, and Maitreyi's on her status as a *bhadralok*. Both accuse the other of mythomania, and both are deeply attracted to the irrational. On the one hand, Maitreyi, the Bengali intellectual, says it "was my habit to analyse everything." On the other, she turns to spiritual melodrama when the memories of her early passion haunt her. She cannot understand why this "completely alien person" still exerts such a pull on her. Why does she have this irrepressible urge to see him again?

> Can he be the reason for it all, or is it some other power, from some other place who is moving me towards an unknown destiny? Can there be someone who is the source of all knowledge and all love, and the message is coming from that direction? My agnostic mind does not like to admit it, but the doubt is never eased.

In a mood of acute anxiety about her future, Maitreyi even resorts to an astrologer. But, ever the rationalist, she is horrified at her own "degradation" in doing so.

This tension between rationalism and a fascination for the irrational, evident in both Maitreyi and Eliade, is related to another preoccupation shared by the two former lovers: purity. When Eliade leaves the Anglo-Indian boardinghouse in Calcutta to start his Bengali life with the Dasguptas, he distances himself from Harold, his Eurasian roommate: "My new life seemed so pure, so sacred, that I dared not describe it to him." When he first falls in love with Maitreyi, he asks her to recite a mantra given to her by Tagore "as a talisman against impurity." Despite being upper-caste Hindus, the life of the *bhadraloks* was neither particularly "pure," nor especially "sacred," but Eliade typically contrasts Indian purity with Eurasian impurity.

Maitreyi applies a similar conceit to the simple peasants she meets when she and her husband move to the countryside. She admires the rustic "music in their throats and poetry in their mind." She contrasts their purity with the crude British planters. "Being a globetrotter," she writes, "I have seen many nations and races, but in innocence and faithfulness that hill-tribe surpasses many."

India being India, the idea of purity is never far removed from the colour of people's skins. This is sometimes transcended by attitudes molded by class and education. Maitreyi admires the dark-skinned hill-tribes and despises the white, or more accurately red, British planters. But at the same time she worships the beauty of Eliade's skin, "white as alabaster." She also wants to be white, she says: "Is it possible, do you think?" Eliade answers, "I don't know, but I suspect not. Perhaps with powder . . ."

One of the fine ironies in the two accounts of the Eliade/Maitreyi affair is that "blackness," in a negative sense, is represented by the man who acts all the time as a faithful messenger between the lovers. Khokha is a poor relative living in the Dasgupta house. Eliade discovers him playing footsie under the table with Maitreyi: "I could not bear it. I saw that black, dirty hoof, darkened by the sun and from walking on tar, coming into contact with Maitreyi's soft flesh . . ." And when Maitreyi, years later, finds out that Khokha had been a less than honest go-between, she writes, "I watched him intently. Perspiration was glistening on his crude face. In the dim light of the candle he appeared to me like some primitive animal in a cave." So much for the noble savage.

I suspect that Eliade's interest in purity had something to do with his defence of "Romanianism," which, in the Romania of the 1930s (and, indeed, still today), had sinister political overtones. Jews, for example, were not true "Romanians." Eliade's journalistic support of Romanian fascism in the 1930s has been exposed brilliantly by the Romanian writer Norman Manea. To be sure, India served as a great and enduring inspiration for Eliade's intellectual life, but its rigid notions of social and ethnic hierarchy might also have appealed to his antiliberal tendencies.

Eliade's account of his love for Maitreyi was first published in 1933, so we have to turn to Maitreyi's book for the extraordinary coda of the affair. Eliade's novel ends with the sentence "I would like to look Maitreyi in the eyes . . ." But when they meet again, after forty-two years, in the library of the Divinity School in Chicago, he cannot bear to see her: he turns his back to Maitreyi. She asks him why he never answered her letters. He replies that their experience was "so—so sacred that I never thought I could touch it again. So I put you out of time and space." True to form, he escapes into fantasy and myth. And she, as usual, is a mixture of cool reason and romance. Her trip is meant to put a full stop behind an unresolved episode in her life. At the same time, she still has hope of rekindling the old passion. She tries to be concrete, to face the truth, to look Eliade in the face, but she also wants to restore "the light of love" in his eyes.

MAITREYI: Turn around, Mircea, I want to see you.
ELIADE: How can I see you? Did Dante ever think he would see his Beatrice with eyes of flesh?

She is angry. She resents being treated as a ghost. She stretches her arms towards him one more time: "My mind is lucid and steady. I will free him from his world of fantasy. We will see each other in this real world. 'Awake, dearest, awake.' "

At last he turns around, but still without raising his eyes to her. He quotes a phrase in Sanskrit about the immortality of the soul. She asks him to look at her, telling him she will take him back forty years. He lifts his face and stares at her blankly. It is too late. The light has gone from his eyes, and she lacks the power to restore it.

1994

V. S. NAIPAUL'S INDIA

Near the end of V. S. Naipaul's first book about India, *An Area of Darkness,* there is an unforgettable piece of writing. It is a description of his visit to the village of the Dubes. It was from there that Naipaul's grandfather left for Trinidad around the turn of the century, as an indentured laborer. Naipaul, "content to be a colonial, without a past, without ancestors," visits his ancestral village with a feeling of dread.

In fact the village is not as bad as he had expected. An old woman who had known Naipaul's grandfather is produced. She tells him a family story. Naipaul gives her some money. Then the wife of a man named Ramachandra wishes to see him. She bows before him, seizes his feet, "in all their Veldtschoen" (a wonderful Naipaulian detail, this), and weeps. She refuses to relax her grip on his *Veldtschoen.* Naipaul, horrified, asks his guide what he should do.

The next day, in a nearby town where Naipaul is staying, Ramachandra himself turns up. Ramachandra is the present head of Naipaul's grandfather's branch of the Dubes. He is a physical and mental wreck: "His effort at a smile did not make his expression warmer. Spittle, white and viscous, gathered at the corners of his mouth." He, too, clings to Naipaul, wanting to talk, to invite him to his hut, offer him food. Again, Naipaul is horrified, asks for help, tells him to go away, draws the curtains in his hotel room. He can hear Ramachandra scratching at the window.

When they meet again, in the village, Ramachandra still refuses to let go. He speaks of his plan to start some litigation over a piece of land. Naipaul was sent by God. Naipaul must help him. Another man slips Naipaul a letter. Naipaul is followed around by a crowd of men and boys. It is all too much. Naipaul wants to escape. He gets in his jeep. A young boy, freshly bathed, asks for a lift to town. "No," says Naipaul, "let the idler walk." And "So it ended, in futility and impatience, a gratuitous act of cruelty, self-reproach and flight."

I wish to recall this passage at some length because it says a great deal about the writer: above all about his pride, and his horror at the lack of it in others. The clutch of the *Veldtschoen,* the inertia of poverty, the abjectness of Ramachandra: these are what make Naipaul take flight. He is an expert on humiliation, sensitive to every nuance of indignity—see his novel *Guerrillas;* see his analysis of Argentine machismo in *The Return of Eva Perón;* see everything he has written on India.

But when Naipaul behaves badly, as he undoubtedly does in the village of the Dubes, it is without the blinkered contempt that Blimpish colonials display. Nor is he like Kipling, whose fear of the tar brush was perhaps one reason for his desire to keep the people at the club amused with cutting descriptions of the natives. This is, however, precisely the way many so-called Third World intellectuals see Naipaul: as a dark man mimicking the prejudices of the white imperialists. This view is not only superficial, it is wrong. Naipaul's rage is not the result of being unable to feel the native's plight; on the contrary, he is angry because he feels it so keenly.

Pride and rage: they go together, and they are at the heart of Naipaul's work, of *India: A Million Mutinies Now* no less than of his earlier, younger, more ill-tempered books. Pride is what enables him to empathize with people whose policies or religious views, or social customs, may be alien to him—even abhorrent. Naipaul, the fastidious aesthete and connoisseur of good wines and Elizabethan sonnets, is far removed from the rednecks he described in *A Turn in the South,* yet he senses in them a pride, an aesthetic, a feeling of independence. Rednecks may also be racists, but that, in this instance, is beside the point.

Nor is there reason to believe that Naipaul has any sympathy with militant Sikhs, Hindu nationalists, or Bengali Maoists; yet he describes them with a kind of tenderness, and a rare understanding, which is neither patronizing nor sentimental. This is because, as he wrote in the introduction to his masterly little book *Finding the Centre,* "The people I found, the people I was attracted to, were not unlike myself. They too were trying to find order in their world, looking for the centre; and my discovery of these people is as much part of the story as the unfolding of the West African background." In this case he was writing about people on the Ivory Coast.

This empathy with people struggling with their fate, trying to find their center—people who, as Naipaul has put it, reject rejection, who try to escape, however naively, clumsily or even violently, from the darkness and poverty of their past—the empathy with such people is what explains Naipaul's relative optimism about India.

Optimism might strike people who read about India in the newspapers as perverse. Around the time of publication of *India: A Million Mutinies Now,* in 1990, I read a description in a London paper of Hindu holy men storming a mosque at a time of day deemed auspicious by astrologers for destroying the Muslim shrine. They believed that the Hindu god Rama was born on the site, and were prepared to die for the sake of reinstating their idol there. The ensuing riots caused hundreds of deaths. The holy men were supported by the party, the Bharatiya Janata Party, that might one day form the government of India. One of its leaders had been touring through northern India in a Rama chariot, fanning Hindu hatred. One of his colleagues threatened to destroy 3,000 other mosques occupying Hindu sites.

This is all a far cry from the civilized secularism and Old Harrovian rectitude of Jawaharlal Nehru. And yet Naipaul's optimism is not ill-considered. For it is based on a deep truth about India: even thuggish opportunists, however much they might end up undermining it, are still part of a remarkably resilient political process, which is Indian democracy. In describing a Sikh militant whose head is in some ways still buried in the darkness of myths and holy wars, Naipaul is struck by how much he takes for granted—the constitution, the civil service, elections. Naipaul is right to say that in India "power came from the people. The people were poor; but the power they gave was intoxicating. As high as a man could be taken up, so low, when he lost power, he could be cast down." The rascals, in India, can still be voted out, which is more than you can say of many other countries in Asia.

Naipaul likes to say that he has no views. As he put it to Andrew Robinson in the *Literary Review*, "My ideas are just responses to human situations." Here, I think, he is being a little coy. Of course he has views. They are liberal views in the classical sense of the word. Naipaul's view of what he calls universal civilization is one where people have escaped from the world of myths and ritual and instinct and worship of ancestors and gods. Universal civilization "implies a certain kind of society, a certain kind of awakened spirit. I don't imagine my father's parents would have been able to understand the idea. So much is contained in it: the idea of the individual, responsibility, choice, the life of the intellect, the idea of vocation and perfectibility and achievement."

Many of the people Naipaul describes in his books are awakening to this idea—which does not prevent their responses from often being muddled. Again and again Naipaul applies his view to India:

> To awaken to history was to cease to live instinctively. It was to begin to see oneself and one's group the way the outside world saw one; and it was to know a kind of rage. India was now full of this rage. There had been a general awakening. But everyone awakened first to his own group or community; every group thought itself unique in its awakening; and every group sought to separate its rage from the rage of other groups.

The million mutinies of Naipaul's title are to be seen as signs of life, of India kicking itself out of its old inertia, the inertia of poverty, which was perpetuated in a vicious circle of karma, gods and holiness. Here, then, is the pride of the low-caste Dravidian politician dedicating his life to the struggle against Brahmin supremacy:

> In this small dark man were locked up generations of grief and rage. He was the first in his line to have felt the affront; and, from

what he had said, he was still the only one in his family to have taken up the cause. His passion was very great; it had to be respected.

And here, in one of the best passages in the book, is Gurtej Singh, the young Sikh militant, mentioned above, who resigned from the Indian civil service to fight for the cause of "my people." Gurtej was highly educated, had awakened, as Naipaul would say, and yet he had turned back to the gods, the myths and the holy men. Just as pride comes with rage, confusion comes with awakening:

> Like Papu the Jain stockbroker in Bombay, who lived on the edge of the great slum of Dharavi and was tormented by the idea of social upheaval, Gurtej had a vision of chaos about to come. Papu had turned to good works, in the penitential Jain fashion. Gurtej had turned to millenarian politics. It had happened with other religions when they turned fundamentalist; it threatened to bring the chaos Gurtej feared.

Democracy is always a messy process. In India it is bound to be messier than anywhere else. And as politicians, pushed up by the poor and the no longer quite so poor, do their best to remove the Old Harrovian legacy of Nehru, many people in India fear this mess. Naipaul fears it too. He is an orderly man. But he does not make a fetish of order. Disorder is an inescapable consequence of India's awakening. It is why he can respect the passion of men whom most Western liberals would regard with, shall I say, Blimpish disdain: the religious radicals, the Indian rednecks, so to speak. This may be another reason why so many "progressive" Third World intellectuals see Naipaul as a reactionary figure; for it is they, the admirers of Mao and Kim Il Sung, who make a fetish of order, and it is Naipaul who has the deeper understanding of the social forces that progressives claim to despise—perhaps because they are themselves still in the grip of those forces.

The fetish of order is something many progressives, in East and West (or, if you prefer, North and South), have in common with many conservatives. Mao was much admired by European leaders such as Edward Heath and Georges Pompidou. Like so many intellectual

Sinophiles—Henry Kissinger is another—they were impressed by the discipline Mao imposed, and were ready to defend the order reimposed on Tiananmen Square (even if they didn't like the methods). Many saw a unified society of busy bees, all expressing great confidence in their leaders, all working in serried ranks toward a glorious collective future. Some even saw the regimentation of China as a mark of superior civilization, so unlike our own disorderly world. Left-wing Indian intellectuals admired China so much that they developed an inferiority complex about messy, chaotic India. Nehru himself was deeply exercised about the question of why the Chinese achieved such remarkable unity, whereas India was forever on the brink of collapse and disunity. It was always India that had to take a leaf from China's book.

What all these admirers chose (and, alas, often still choose) to overlook was that China's order was the order of a slave state. It is said that Mao, however much blood still sticks to his waxy hands, restored pride to the Chinese people. If so, it was only to the People, and not to people that he gave this pride. The price for Mao's proud banners was the virtually complete destruction of Naipaul's universal civilization, which did exist in China: the individual, responsibility, choice, the life of the intellect and so on. In this respect, despite all the subcontinent's problems, China should take a leaf from India's book.

What makes Naipaul one of the world's most civilized writers is his refusal to be engaged by the People, and his insistence on listening to people, individuals, with their own language and their own stories. To this extent he is right when he claims to have no view; he is impatient with all abstractions. He is interested in how individual people see themselves and the world in which they live. He has recorded their histories, their dreams, their stories, their words.

As we know, the first thing that leaders or worshipers of the People do is to rob people of their words, by enforcing a language of wood. Naipaul's characters, most of whom talk at considerable length, never speak a language of wood. In his interviews, Naipaul insists on details: he wants to know how things smelled, felt, sounded, looked—especially looked. And where it concerns ideas, he wants to be told how they were arrived at: not just what people think, but how they think. This is also the method of his own writing. Naipaul, in *Finding the Centre:*

Narrative was my aim. Within that, my travelling method was intended to be transparent. The reader will see how the material was gathered; he will also see how the material could have served fiction or political journalism or a travelogue. But the material here served itself alone. . . . All that was added later was understanding. Out of that understanding the narrative came. However creatively one travels, however deep an experience in childhood or middle age, it takes thought (a sifting of impulses, ideas, and references that become more multifarious as one grows older) to understand what one has lived through or where one has been.

The extraordinary achievement of *India: A Million Mutinies Now* is that we can see his characters. More than that, we can see how they see, and how they, in turn, are seen by the author: Amir, the melancholy son of a raja in Lucknow, Cambridge-educated, a Marxist, a devout Muslim; Namdeo, the outcast poet, whose "ideas of untouchability and brothel-area sex, childbirth and rags, all coming together, were like an assault"; and many, many more. This is what makes the book a work of art. At this level it ceases to matter whether the writer is engaged in fiction or nonfiction, or whether you call a book such as *The Enigma of Arrival* a novel. Whatever his literary form, Naipaul is a master. The people in *India: A Million Mutinies Now* are so alive they could have sprung from a great writer's imagination.

There is, however, one thing that sets such a book apart from fiction, and that is the language itself. Whereas the writer controls every word in a work of invention, this cannot be the case in a factual account. Here there is a problem: compared to the author's own literary prose, the language of Naipaul's characters inevitably tends to sound flat. This is particularly true when Naipaul has to go through an interpreter to hear the person's story. I must admit that here and there I felt relief when a long quotation ended and Naipaul's words began.

And what words! The few paragraphs describing the decrepitude of Calcutta allow you to see that sad, wonderful, dying place. Naipaul writes like a painter. Small, visual details tell you all: the buzzards hovering over the grubby little street market behind the Grand Hotel, where people go about their minute tasks, one man walking by "carrying a single, limber, dancing sheet of plywood on his head." Or the "pink-walled room" of the Hindu activist in Bombay who worships at the shrine of Ganpati in Pali: "On the wall at the back of the Sony television there was a colour photograph or picture of this image at Pali: the broad, spreading belly of the deity a violent, arresting red, not altogether benign."

Referring to himself, Nirad Chaudhuri once wrote, "To be *déraciné*, is to be on the road forever." This could serve nicely as V. S. Naipaul's motto, too: Naipaul, the grandson of uprooted Indians, uprooted himself to come to England. He is a man continually fretting about roots—his own and those of the people he meets. One sometimes has the impression of a man traveling through the dark and rainy night, stopping at houses on the way, pressing his nose against the windows. Peering at the people inside, sitting around the family hearth, he is reminded of his own rootlessness. The assumption is that those others, seen through the window, are at home, rooted and whatever the opposite is of *déraciné*.

This must account for Naipaul's nostalgia for what he has called "whole and single societies." He has often used such words as "damaged" or "wounded" for societies that are fragmented and apparently rootless. Gandhi, the Mahatma, he told Andrew Robinson, "is a man, whose life, when I contemplate it, makes me cry. I am moved to tears . . ." This is, as always, largely a matter of pride, of dignity: Gandhi's own sense of dignity, which he imparted to the Indian masses. But it is also a question of Naipaul's admiration for Gandhi's vision of one single India, a vision of wholeness. Nehru had the same vision, albeit in a more secular way. So did Naipaul on his first visit to India. It was an idea of India which, as Naipaul writes, incorporated the independence movement, the great civilization, the great names, the classical past. "It was," Naipaul writes,

> an aspect of our identity, the community identity we had developed, which in multi-racial Trinidad, had become more like a racial identity.
>
> This was the identity I took to India on my first visit in 1962. And when I got there I found it had no meaning in India. The idea of an Indian community—in effect, a continental idea of our Indian identity—made sense only when the community was very small, a minority, and isolated.

And now Naipaul believes he has found the makings of this all-Indian community. He calls it "a central will, a central intellect, a national idea." The Indian Union, he writes, "was greater than the sum of its parts; and many of these movements of excess strengthened the Indian state, defining it as the source of law and civility and reasonableness." This may be right, even though Hindu chauvinism poses a threat to the secular state of India. But this focus on the whole, the single, the central, also reflects Naipaul's own state of mind, his nostalgia for an orderly identity. He has remarked elsewhere, quite convincingly, that Gandhi's all-Indian vision was shaped in South Africa, just as Nehru's was formed at Harrow. It is the old dream of the deracinated, a regret about things past.

But a dream is all it is. One senses the same nostalgia in most of the people Naipaul met on his Indian trip. As Naipaul himself has pointed out so many times, a common desire of those who have escaped the dark embrace of the tribe is to find the way back; nostalgia is the concomitant of change: for the educated Sikh who dreams of restoring Ranjit Singh's nineteenth-century kingdom; the urban intellectual in Calcutta dreaming of pastoral purity; for Dravidian politicians in Madras dreaming of medieval emperors who preceded the rule of the Brahmins. Whether or not they know it, the millions of mutineers, wrestling with their fates, are all on the road forever.

1991

BHUTTO'S PAKISTAN

Political autobiography, as a genre, tends to produce tiresome, self-serving, ghostwritten works. But once in a while a book stands out; not necessarily because it is better written than the usual stuff, but because it is the closest thing we have to classic mythology. The message is moral; the characters stand for Good and Evil; the story is a variation of the quest for a holy grail, involving not just hardship—"tests"—but exile of one kind or another. The authorship is often anonymous—ghostwriters seldom reveal their names.

When the heroes and villains come from countries where pure myths still cast their spells, where, as a Pakistani politician once put it to me, "words have magic," these political fairy tales follow the traditional patterns more closely than in the modern West, where the drama tends to get lost in media buzzwords, earnest political analysis, academic jargon or a ghastly combination of all three. Besides, the complexity of modern life leaves little room for mythical feats of heroism. Good and evil are not so clear-cut. Our politics, as puritans of all persuasions keep telling us, has lost its moral dimension.

We can be just as much enchanted by myths, of course, and sometimes something approaching classic myth will occur: Winston Churchill emerging from his "years in the wilderness" (exile) to save the world from evil dragons in the name of freedom and democracy (the Grail). But this could only happen in a war, and Churchill was rather exceptional in that he was the greatest narrator of his own myth—no ghostwriters for him. Great leaders since Churchill—the Iron Lady, the Gipper, even Gorby—may have aspired to mythical status, but have not been able really to pull it off convincingly.

No, for the truly inspiring tales we must turn to that mythical land called the Third World. That is where we can escape from not so much the decadence as the banality of Western life, and be enchanted once again, like children, our disbelief suspended. More than that, in the Third World we can retrieve the pure moral order that we feel is lost to us in the West. The story of Cory Aquino—made into an Australian TV miniseries—was perfect: she, a religious paragon of modesty and virtue; her opponents, symbols of villainy and greed. How enchanting it must have been in 1986 for American senators and congressmen to take a break from their daily affairs and don yellow ribbons for St. Cory of Manila.

The South Korean opposition leader Kim Dae Jung tried his hardest to be a mythical hero, and many Western reporters did their best to help him, but he never quite made the grade. His story had all the makings of the real thing: evil generals, exile, heroic hardship, the quest for freedom . . . But then something went wrong: Kim suddenly appeared less heroic, more like his opponents—aggressive, intransigent, hungry for power. Perhaps South Korea is too prosperous now, not Third World enough for fairy tales.

Pakistan, on the other hand, is about as Third World as you can get, and the story of Benazir Bhutto's quest to avenge her father's death at the hand of the wicked General Zia ul-Haq fits all the requirements of the classic myth. Her book *Daughter of the East,* clearly written to enchant Western readers, does not disappoint. The heroes are saintly; the villains drip with poison. There is excruciating hardship; there are years of exile; there is the wonderful combination of Western high life and ancient Oriental culture (at one point in the story, our heroine is "enthused with a sense of Asian identity"); and, finally, there is victory, made all the sweeter for the difficulties of the quest.

Miss Bhutto's prose, though satisfyingly breathless and emotional in parts, shows the dead hand of the ghost in others. Those interested in the true language of myths should turn to a collection of Benazir's speeches, interviews and assorted public utterances, aimed at her domestic supporters, entitled *The Way Out.* There we find the "clarion calls," the "night of the tyrant," the "streets painted in blood." To quote one typical clarion call:

> We must face the oppressor, the Tyrant, the Usurper, the unjust in whatever fashion or manner he manifests himself. The martyr is the life of history and history is woven of the threads of revolution . . .
>
> But how fragile it is. How easily it is crushed. How easily the crystal that dazzled the rainbow color in the morning light vanishes.

The martyr is of course Benazir's father, Zulfikar Ali Bhutto, who was hanged for murder in 1979, on orders from General Zia, who had ousted Bhutto two years before in a military coup. But that is getting ahead of the story. Let us begin at the beginning.

Benazir Bhutto was born in 1953 in Karachi, "my skin evidently so rosy that I was immediately nicknamed 'Pinkie.' " Very soon Pinkie began to lead what can only be called a bicultural life. There was Miss Bhutto, educated in English, first at Lady Jennings's nursery school and later by Irish nuns at the Convent of Jesus and Mary. The older students were divided into houses with such inspirational names as "Discipline," "Courtesy," "Endeavor," and "Service." This was the same Miss Bhutto who later went to Radcliffe, where she savored the delights of peppermint ice cream, apple cider, Joan Baez and peace marches. It was also the Miss Bhutto who moved on to Oxford, her father's alma mater, where she drove a sports car, sharpened her wit at the Oxford Union, and was squired around town by dashing young men in velvet jackets. Let us, for the sake of simplicity, call this stylish young woman the Radcliffe Benazir.

There is another Miss Bhutto, however—one who expresses herself better in the mythical language of *The Way Out.* This is the Benazir sitting adoringly at her father's feet at the family estate in Larkana, listening to his tales of heroic ancestors, "directly traceable to the Muslim invasion of India in 712 AD." One of these heroes, her great-grandfather, defied the British by taking an English lover. Rather than hand her back to the outraged officers of the raj, his retinue killed the woman. This, said the hero, was a matter of honor.

We might call this romantic lady the Larkana Benazir. She was the one who, as she writes in her autobiography, "loved hearing these family stories, as did my brothers Mir Murtaza and Shah Nawaz, who naturally identified with their namesakes. The adversities faced by our ancestors formed our own moral code, just as my father had intended. Loyalty. Honour. Principle."

Here, clearly, is a family born to rule. The Bhuttos are land-owning grandees in the desertland of Sindh, a backward part of the subcontinent, a kind of sandy Sicily, where politics consists of murky family feuds. Benazir's grandfather, Sir Shah Nawaz, founded the first political party in Sindh, in the days of the British raj. He was, as his title suggests, a very grand personage indeed. Benazir tells us nothing much about her paternal grandmother, Sir Shah Nawaz's second wife, for she, a humble Hindu from Bombay who converted to Islam just before her marriage, does not fit so neatly into the illustrious family annals—something, by the way, which Z. A. Bhutto's political opponents exploited in their campaigns against him: he was, they said, not a "real" Pakistani, but the son of an Indian, and a Hindu Indian to boot.

Just as there are two Benazirs (who sometimes get mixed up: only the Radcliffe Benazir could be "enthused" by her Asian identity), there are two Bhutto families: one is compared to the Kennedys, the blessed clan destined to deliver the people from poverty and oppression, but punished by political martyrdom. Like Kathleen Kennedy, "who had worn her father's parka at Radcliffe long after the Senator had been killed," Benazir "tried to keep my father near me by sleeping with his shirt under my pillow." And then there is the family inspired by Muslim martyrdom. Benazir calls her father *shaheed,* a martyr for Islam. In *The Way Out* she finds the appropriate words:

> The same dedicated workers whose courage is higher than the mountains and whose dedication is deeper than the oceans are even now ready to come forward and to sacrifice inspired by Sha-

heed Bhutto and in the manner of sacrifice known only to the political descendents of Muslim Martyrs.

It is sometimes tempting to sneer at the Radcliffe Benazir, shocked at army thugs "lolling on one of Mummy's delicate blue and white brocade Louis XV chairs," trying to act as the daughter of a Muslim martyr. So much about the Larkana Benazir smacks of kitsch; so much of the Radcliffe Benazir strikes one as half-baked. But to reconcile the two roles, or indeed, to forgo the sports cars and May Balls and risk torture or death, took extraordinary courage. After her father's execution in 1979, Miss Bhutto spent much of the next five years under appalling conditions in Zia's jails. And, after she had braved the worst at the hands of a military dictator, her political success has given hope to millions. It all makes one feel a little churlish to challenge some of her more cherished myths. But, as Benazir herself remarks when describing some fraud perpetrated by General Zia's government, "what matters is the truth." And the truth, however enchanting and moving Benazir's own tale may be, is an elusive thing.

But let us return to the story. When Benazir was still with the Irish nuns, her father was foreign minister in the government of General Ayub Khan. In 1966 the general and Z. A. Bhutto parted ways one year after India and Pakistan had fought over Kashmir. Bhutto thought Ayub Khan had been soft on the Indians. Benazir appeared to agree: "During the peace negotiations held in the southern Russian city of Tashkent, President Ayub Khan lost everything we had gained on the battlefield." But, according to Benazir, her father's resignation was a matter of democratic principles: "After my father broke with Ayub Khan in 1966, the words 'civil liberties' and 'democracy' were the ones that came up most, words that were mythical to most Pakistanis."

The general's rule, in Benazir's account, was marked with lawlessness, violence, corruption and economic failure. Only Ayub's "family and a handful of others had become rich." But now, with Z. A. Bhutto on the loose, the first crusade for democracy was about to begin. The first clarion call, so to speak, had sounded.

This is not entirely the way less partisan observers saw things. Shahid Javed Burki, for example, has some interesting things to say about the Ayub years in his *Pakistan Under Bhutto*. First of all, he argues,

Ayub's rule made far more people rich than his family and friends. Tax incentives and land reforms created a new middle class of small businessmen, entrepreneurs and middle-sized farmers. The ones who suffered were big industrialists, unskilled urban workers and the landed aristocracy. The aristocracy was Bhutto's traditional constituency. The new middle class would turn against him, as did the industrialists when Bhutto nationalized their assets. This left him with the support of landowners and the urban poor, whose interests were by no means always identical.

Burki also mentions the fact that in 1962 Bhutto wrote a long memorandum to Ayub outlining his idea for a one-party state in which the roles of the judiciary and the legislative branches of government were to be completely subservient to the all-powerful central authority. China and the Soviet Union were to be the models. When Ayub demurred, Bhutto called him timid and soft.

Z. A. Bhutto talked a lot about democracy, to be sure, but his instincts were those of the man of iron. The only hint of this in Benazir's account is a reading list he thoughtfully prepared for his daughter when he was detained by Ayub in 1968 for inciting riots. His recommended reading included anything about Napoleon Bonaparte, "the most complete man in history." This is not surprising, since Napoleon has long been a subcontinental hero. But the rest of the list included Bismarck, Lenin, Ataturk, Mao Zedong and, looking a little lost in this group of iron men, Abraham Lincoln. What they all had in common was their fatherhood of nations. That was how Bhutto saw himself.

Benazir was at Radcliffe, reading Kate Millett's *Sexual Politics*, protesting against the Vietnam War, and imbibing Western concepts of law and politics from Professor John Womack, when her father ran his highly successful campaign in 1970 as a populist man of the left. The urban workers, many of them dislocated, bewildered and left behind by Ayub's high-speed economic development, loved Bhutto's message of deliverance from bourgeois greed. Bhutto won the election in West Pakistan, while Sheik Mujib ur-Rahman, banking on the Bengali middle class disaffected with Punjabi domination, won in East Pakistan, not yet Bangladesh. Differences between the two were never resolved— something Benazir blames entirely on Mujib, who "showed an obstinacy the logic of which to this day defies me." The Pakistani army quelled Bengali unrest with extraordinary cruelty. India intervened. Pakistan split in half. Bhutto, Benazir informs us, did his utmost to stop the tragedy and avert the generals from their slaughter. (Benazir compares the massacre of tens of thousands of Bengalis to My Lai—this is the Radcliffe Benazir speaking—and to General Zia's suppression of his opponents in the province of Sindh—this the Larkana Benazir. Both comparisons are absurd.)

Again, this is not the way other people saw the same events. In *Can Pakistan Survive?* Tariq Ali, who helped Benazir with her speeches for the Oxford Union, clearly no friend of the generals, blames Bhutto for unleashing "a hysterical campaign" denouncing Mujib's position, for whipping up "an atmosphere of frenzied chauvinism in the Punjab," and for "colluding with the generals" in crushing the Bengalis. "Thank God! Pakistan has been saved," he quotes Bhutto as saying after the butchery was done.

And so the stage was set for the Bhutto years, that mythical golden age which our heroine set out to revive through trials and tribulations. Yahya Khan, the general in power during the crisis in East Pakistan, lost so much face that he had to appoint Bhutto as chief martial-law administrator and president. A new constitution was promulgated in 1973: "The people of Pakistan enjoyed the first constitution in Pakistan's history to introduce fundamental human rights and ensure their protection. . . . The first representative government of Pakistan finally had the legal framework within which to govern: the sanctioned authority that Professor Womack had brought home to me so clearly in his seminar."

So speaks the Radcliffe Benazir. The Larkana Benazir finds more inspirational words to describe the heady excitement of hearing masses of people shout, "Jeay Bhutto! Long live Bhutto!" Here is a sample from *The Way Out:*

> Jeay Bhutto. It's a lovely word. It's warm and wonderful. It lifts the heart. It elevates the spirit. . . . It means so much to us it drives us on. It makes us reach for the stars and the moon.

And another:

> In 1972, we climbed the highest mountains and built the biggest bridges because of our leadership. We had a brilliant leader, a pop-

ular leader, a strong leader, a man who for his principles and his motherland would fight and fight and fight.

Bhutto did not read Napoleon for nothing. Like Sukarno in Indonesia, a man he resembled in many ways, he had a personalized view of nation-building: the strong leader, the great man, who would fight and fight and fight, the erector of stadiums and phallic monuments, the chief cock of the country—only this kind of steely superhero could father a great nation. Those who opposed him were obstacles to progress: greedy merchants, selfish tribal chieftains, evil generals, reactionary politicos, uppity bureaucrats, obstinate judges and so forth. And so, to build a great nation and foster progress, the power of such selfish reactionaries had to be curbed. Burki quotes from one of Bhutto's speeches made a year before his downfall:

> In 1970, I promised you democracy. In 1973, I gave you democracy. . . . You and I have trusted each other, worked together. We understand each other. But there are people in this country that don't approve of our association. These people have attempted to put obstacles in our way; to stop us from building a new Pakistan. They can do this because we have allowed them to do so. Should we continue to permit them this freedom? Mustn't we change the rules of the game so that our progress towards a new and dynamic Pakistan is not continuously thwarted?

In fact, according to Burki, as well as many others, the rules had already been changed long before Bhutto made that speech in 1976. The tragedy of Bhutto is that he set in motion the very forces that brought him down. He curbed the bureaucracy by withdrawing constitutional guarantees from civil servants and concentrating more power in his own hands. Civil servants he considered hostile were jailed or dismissed. More serious, as far as his own ultimate fate was concerned, was his tampering with the constitution to limit the power of the law courts. They were denied jurisdiction over government decisions taken under the Defense of Pakistan Rule, an emergency measure enforced during the crisis over Bangladesh and retained by Bhutto for political purposes. The government appropriated the power to dissolve political parties by adopting the so-called Suppression of Terrorist Activities

(Special Courts) Ordinance. The main opposition party in Baluchistan, the National Awami Party, was banned under this rule and many of its members were jailed. (Soon after her own election as prime minister, Benazir ran into trouble in Baluchistan herself; her followers allowed the Baluchistan provincial assembly to be dissolved.)

Four months after Bhutto promised freedom of the press, three periodicals were banned and their editors and publishers were arrested. According to Tariq Ali, "The bulk of the media at all events was kept firmly under government control, serving the Bhutto régime as loyally as it had done its predecessors."

Most damaging of all were his maladroit dealings with the army. The first thing he did upon attaining power was to put the commanders-in-chief of the army and air force under house arrest. Protective custody, he called it. (General Zia used the same term when he had Bhutto arrested in 1977.) Then he appointed General Tikka Khan, known as the "Butcher of Dacca" for his zeal in crushing the Bengalis, as his chief of staff. Bhutto chose him for his loyalty, and turned out to be correct in this. (Tikka Khan is still close to Benazir.) In the case of General Zia, whom he appointed as chief of staff some years later, he was wrong.

Benazir describes Zia variously as a stage villain and an ignorant, unscrupulous, unintelligent, tin-pot dictator. This is as it should be in a myth. In fact, however, he was a rather intelligent and effective dictator and, though he looked like a villain, he had a soft-spoken charm. Like General Suharto, who has ruled Indonesia since the demise of Sukarno, Zia was a "smiling general," with all the steel but none of the flamboyance of the Napoleonic populist he replaced. He was certainly not a democrat. He set himself up to be a Muslim leader who would turn Pakistan into a real Muslim state, based on Muslim law—adultery, consumption of alcohol, gambling would result in cut limbs, whippings or death by stoning. Some of these punishments took place, but in fact he never went as far as the mullahs wanted. Aside from Pakistan's crippling national debt, perhaps Zia's worst legacy sprang from the source of his greatest political strength: the guns, drugs and general corruption of Pakistan society wrought by the Afghan war.

In hindsight one must conclude that Bhutto asked for trouble. He should never have called out the army to control the turbulent opposition after he was accused of rigging the 1977 elections. Once out of the barracks, and faced with a country running out of control, the generals did what came naturally to them: they took over.

Bhutto was arrested, and in confinement he read one of his books about Napoleon. Certainly he and his family were cruelly treated by Zia. He was sentenced to hang for murder in a farcical trial, and spent his last years in filthy jails, his only comforts his favorite cologne and the odd Havana cigar. At that point Benazir strode to the center stage. Bhutto, in his fetid cell, grabbed his daughter's hand and said, "My daughter, should anything happen to me, promise me you will continue my mission."

I have dwelled at some length on the rule of the father, because the daughter took his mission seriously: it is as Bhutto's daughter that she challenged her political opponents; in every campaign poster showing her face it was the image of the father that loomed behind her, like a guardian god. What she felt as she walked away from the prison is summed up in *The Way Out:* "If the people of Pakistan ever saw their leader kept in such a disgusting and disrespectful manner their blood would boil and from Khyber to Karachi a fierce fire would rage which no guns could wipe out."

Benazir slipped into her new role with great aplomb. The way it is described suggests the mystical transfusion of a spirit, or sacred flame. Such is often the nature of dynastic politics in Asia. The same process was described by Cory Aquino, who, kneeling in prayer, felt the flutter of her husband's spirit entering her soul, enabling her to carry on the struggle. It is impossible to pinpoint the precise moment when the visitation took place in Benazir's case. Was it in the jail scene evoked above? Or did it happen earlier, perhaps the first time Zia's thugs entered the family house in Karachi (the famous 70 Clifton) and lolled about on the begum's Louis XV chairs? This is how she tells it in *Daughters of the East:*

Once again I watch my father being driven away, not knowing where he is being taken, not knowing if I will ever seem him again. I waver for a moment, half of my heart breaking, the other half turning to ice. "Pinkie," I hear a voice call. I turn to see my brother Shah Nawaz lined up with the staff in the courtyard.

"*Usko choro!* Leave him!" I shout at the soldiers holding him. I am frightened myself at the new tone of my voice. But the soldiers step away.

The new tone of voice: perhaps that was it. It seems, from her own telling of the story, as though her entire life was a kind of dress rehearsal for the main act: the crusade to avenge her father, to return the Bhutto family to power. This is as true for the Larkana Benazir as for the Radcliffe one. The day she left for America, her father spoke of her debt to the people of Pakistan, "a debt you can repay with God's blessing by using your education to better their lives."

There is nothing wrong with this sentiment; in fact, it is a noble one. But it is important to know just how Benazir sees the nature of her political power, or, indeed, not just her own power, but political power in general. The Radcliffe Benazir realizes that politics must be divested of mythology to be lawful and subject to critical reason. Does the Larkana Benazir know this? Or, to make things even more complicated, are the Radcliffe Benazir's political ideals perhaps part of the Larkana Benazir's myth? This particular confusion is encouraged by the Western taste for exotic morality tales casting her as the fairy queen. Are her politics, and by extension the politics of Pakistan, to be a matter of compromise, regular elections and the same rules applying to all? Or will they remain a contest between Good and Evil, between great leaders and reactionary, obscurantist, wicked, uneducated hoodlums? Will the same rules apply to those who are born to lead as to those deemed beyond the pale? Her political opponents have given her little cause to feel conciliatory. Even as she toned down her fiery rhetoric during the elections, her rivals, a combination of big businessmen, Muslim fundamentalists, and former protégés of General Zia, mostly from Punjab, often used highly provocative language about her, hinting at Western decadence and communist connections. Although her Pakistan People's Party (PPP) did well all over Pakistan in the national elections, it did less well in the provincial elections. One of her rivals for the prime-ministership, Mian Nawaz Sharif, a former Zia man, still controls Punjab, the richest and largest province in Pakistan. Another strong opponent, Ghulam Mustafa Jatoi, once a close associate of Miss Bhutto's father, was elected to the National Assembly. An opposition party, the Muttaheda Quami

Movement, controls Karachi and Hyderabad, the two biggest cities in Sindh.

It will be interesting to see how she deals with her opposition. Will she be accountable as a leader, or will she carry out her mission with the arrogance of a dynastic ruler or the messianic zeal of those who think they represent that mythical concept, the will of the people? So far, she has done well: she has compromised, played by the rules, kept her cool. But these are still important questions, because it was precisely that zeal, that Napoleonic hubris, which destroyed her father.

Her book, admittedly written with a campaign in mind against the man she rightly holds responsible for her family's grief, is not entirely reassuring, because it is so full of myth, and because the heroes are above the rules which are applied to the villains. The treatment of her two brothers, for example. While Benazir and her mother were taken from jail to jail to stop them from agitating against the Zia regime, her brothers, Mir Murtaza and Shah Nawaz, were in Kabul organizing a group called Al-Zulfikar to carry on the struggle by violent means. There was the hijacking of a passenger plane, there were bomb attacks, and Mir promised to "turn Pakistan up and down." Zia tried to link mother and daughter Bhutto to these violent acts, but never produced any evidence. Indeed, both women suffered greatly on account of the two brothers. Benazir was locked up in solitary cells where she received inadequate treatment for an ear disease that could have killed her.

Nonetheless, Benazir writes about her brothers with reverence. Shah, a spoiled and handsome playboy—Swiss school, frequent attendance at Regine's in Paris, flat in Monte Carlo—"was so generous you never knew what he would do. . . . He had empathized with the poor since childhood. He had built a straw hut in the garden at 70 Clifton and slept in it for weeks, wanting to feel the deprivations of the poor."

Shah was interested in intelligence work: "Just remember you have a little brother who can help you if you give him a high post in intelligence." It was not to be. During a family holiday in Cannes he died of poisoning. His Afghan wife, who sounds like an even worse brat than her late husband, was recently found by a French court to have been criminally negligent in letting Shah die. The marriage, by all accounts, including Benazir's, was not a happy one. The exact cause of his death is still mysterious, except to the Bhuttos, who are all convinced that he was murdered by Zia's agents. Or, as Benazir suggests, "had the CIA killed him as a friendly gesture towards their favourite dictator?" But whatever the cause of his death, it is clear that Shah was playing dangerous and nasty games.

Which makes Benazir's sentimental description of his funeral sound nauseating: "I wanted to take him past the lands where he had hunted with Papa and Mir, past our fields and ponds, past the people he had tried to defend in his own way. The people, too, deserved the chance to honour this brave son of Pakistan. The Martyr's son has been martyred." Note the "in his own way." Zia ruled Pakistan in his own way too. But he was evil; he was not a Bhutto. The Larkana Benazir has taken control. But there is more to come:

> In every generation, Shiite Muslims believe, there is a Karbala, a re-enactment of the tragedy that befell the family of Prophet Mohammed PBUH [Peace Be Upon Him], after his death in 640 AD. Many in Pakistan have come to believe that the victimization of the Bhutto family and our supporters was the Karbala of our generation.

Many in Pakistan probably do believe it, but, more significantly, so does Benazir—or at least everything points to that conclusion. Power still has magic in Pakistan; people want to be near it, touch it, feel it. When Benazir was paraded through Pakistan, from morning until late at night, perched on top of a truck, lit by a spotlight, proud, aloof, every inch the aristocratic leader, people fought each other to touch the vehicle. Many treat her like a divine ruler. It is to be hoped that she knows better. Honor has been served; she has restored power to her family. But her cause is to restore democracy. That cause would be ill-served by perpetuating the dynastic myths of Larkana.

1989

ST. CORY AND THE EVIL ROSE

Imelda Marcos today has a mellow beauty in which the radiance has the quality of emotion. When she speaks—of her husband, of her children, of her life—her voice becomes so full of feeling the very air seems to throb, and the great splendid eyes deepen, darken, and dazzle with tears. She has adjusted, she has accepted, she has signed, and she is happy, but whatever the effort may have cost her shows in a deepened glowing of her charm. The loveliness has become poignant.

The fresh-flowers look is what Ferdinand and Imelda Marcos have brought to Malacañang.

Mrs Marcos has been busy with mop and broom too. . . . Whatever her other images—as cultural patroness, as social workers, as a great beauty—she knows that the basic one is her image as housewife: she must show she can run a palace as efficiently as she did her home.

"I do not want to be known as having some friends I prefer to others. . . . Nor do I want people to think I'm a social butterfly going from one party to another."

These little nuggets were culled from a collection of articles written between 1964 and 1970 by the most celebrated writer in the Philippines, Nick Joaquin, under his journalistic pen name Quijano de Manila. The collection, entitled *Reportage on the Marcoses,* was published in 1979, and reprinted in 1981. He is also the author of a gushing hagiography of the Aquino family entitled *The Aquinos of Tarlac,* written in 1972, revised and published in 1983—"The Philippine pageant as only Nick Joaquin can tell it."

The point of digging up these embarrassing quotes is not to ridicule Joaquin; he was not the only one to sing in both camps for his supper— Isabelo Crisostomo, the author of an adulatory book on Imelda Marcos, has just published an equally admiring biography of Cory Aquino. Joaquin's political effusions have never been held against him in the Philippines, as far as I know. Indeed, to many Filipinos, switching sides is a perfectly respectable way to get on in life. Joaquin's early writings on the Marcos couple are useful reading for several reasons. They remind us just how popular the First Family of the Philippines was in those days. Adoration of a new leader did not start with Cory Aquino. They also illustrate the extent to which Philippine politics is a matter of showbiz, of images—the housewife with mop and broom, the beauty queen, the social worker. At the end of 1986 I asked Mrs. Marcos what she thought of Benigno Aquino as a politician. "Ninoy," she said, "was all sauce and no substance." "Sweetheart," said Mr. Marcos, "that is the essence of Filipino politics."

There is a Filipino word for this: *palabas.* It literally means ostentatious show—the ostentatiousness of the village fiesta, sometimes combined with the solemn sentimentality of Hollywood melodramas. The way Marcos cloaked the most extraordinary skulduggery in earnest legalisms was a form of *palabas,* of ostentatious playacting. Perhaps fortunately, much of Marcos's so-called dictatorship was *palabas,* more bark than bite, as were many of the flamboyant gestures to oppose the "brutal dictator." In 1985 I was on the same plane to Manila as Senator Jovito Salonga, an opposition politician returning after years of exile in the U.S. He was accompanied by a crowd of fellow oppositionists: Senator Lorenzo Tañada, leaning on his stick, grinning from ear to ear; Ninoy's brother, Butz Aquino, chatting up the air hostesses; José "Pepe" Diokno, just out of a hospital in the U.S.

"I shall return! I shall return!" shouted several members of the entourage, echoing the words of General MacArthur, as the plane banked toward Manila. "I am prepared to share the brutal fate of Ninoy," said another man, his face flushed with emotion. Salonga, a quiet-spoken Protestant, looked a little embarrassed by it all as he was escorted off the plane by his friends, who, as one put it, were "protecting him from the dictator's bullets." The group was greeted in the arrival hall by a hysterical mob of press people and more oppositionists, one of whom told the television cameras that "neither wind nor rain can wipe out the blood of the martyr." This is what Filipinos mean by *palabas*.

Carmen Navarro Pedrosa's biography *Imelda Marcos*—an updated and, I think, inferior version of an earlier book entitled *The Untold Story of Imelda Marcos*—is full of *palabas*. Indeed, it reads like a showbiz biography, which, given the style of Philippine politics, is perhaps appropriate. Imelda, after all, is a showbiz figure, albeit a rather tawdry one—her movie connection was George Hamilton, not Laurence Olivier, or even Robert Redford. The central thesis of the book is itself a showbiz cliché: the poor, small-town girl hits the big time, wipes out her sordid past by building a palace of dreams, and then, at the very pinnacle of fortune and fame, everything comes crashing down—the dream palace of diamonds and gold turns into a handful of dust. Well, perhaps not quite all dust.

With her perfect pitch for schlock, Pedrosa comes up with some marvelous images. This description of the very end, for instance:

> Marcos was said still to hope he could stay, clutching at straws in the wind even as gunshots echoed in the distance. His children pleaded and cried while Imelda in the meantime went about saying good-bye and handing out money, in a zombielike fashion. Friends said that minutes before they flew to exile she was fully made up, her hair perfectly coiffed, and that she was still wearing the white gown she had donned for the morning's inauguration. She was said also to have sung "New York, New York" all the way to Hawaii.

Oh, for Vivien Leigh, Clark Gable and David O. Selznick. And yet it all rings horribly true. The Filipinos' knack for turning even the most serious events into comic melodrama—as happened often during the February 1986 revolt—is their charm, their strength and their weakness. Desperate to be taken seriously by outsiders, they can make it so very, very hard. In this respect, among others, Imelda is a true daughter of the Philippines.

The untold story of Pedrosa's original book was Imelda's unfortunate childhood. Imelda was the daughter of Vicente Orestes Romualdez and his second wife, a shy convent girl called Remedios, who died when Imelda was only nine. In a family of distinguished lawyers and politicians, Vicente Orestes did not shine. A nervous, rather weak man, he was broke much of his life. What comfort he could provide went to the children of his first marriage, who, according to Pedrosa, resented Remedios and her offspring so much that they could no longer live in the same house. In 1937 Imelda's family, minus the father, moved to the now legendary garage next to the main house in Manila. They slept on boards propped up by milk crates. No wonder the relationship between Imelda's parents was a disaster. As Pedrosa puts it in her inimitable style, "for nine years Imelda saw her mother cry." A few faithful family servants helped out the distressed family. One, called Siloy, once "bought a new pair of shoes for Imelda after he saw how worn her old pair was. In later years this pair of shoes would be multiplied three thousandfold." It is this kind of addition to the original text that mars Pedrosa's amusing book. The empathy of the earlier work too often turns into snide knowingness, now that we all realize what an evil princess Imelda really was.

Even though a little simple, Pedrosa's idea that Imelda's status as "a poor relation of the rich Romualdezes . . . would fuel her lifelong obsession to achieve fame and fortune" is probably correct. This obsession still strikes me as pathetic rather than evil, even though the Marcos couple robbed their country blind. It is the pathos of the showgirl who will do almost anything to be accepted by princes, and ends up by making a spectacle of herself. It is the basic impulse behind *palabas,* the song-and-dance of the dispossessed colonial trying to please, exploit or cheat the master.

"Meldy," as she was then commonly known, started her career in show business by singing to exhausted GIs after they landed with MacArthur near Tacloban, her home town on Leyte. She became known as "the Rose of Tacloban," and rode on a float in a victory parade as "Miss Philippines." In the early 1950s she worked as a singing shop girl and then as a clerk in a bank, where she was made to sing by colleagues in exchange for dinner invitations. She ran for the Miss Manila contest, lost and broke down in tears in the office of the Manila mayor, who adjudged her the winner after all. Exactly what passed between the beauty queen and the mayor is still food for gossip in Manila coffee shops. Not long after that she met the young senator Ferdinand Marcos, who had an eye for beauty queens, and Miss Manila manqué no longer needed to look back. It was all the way up. Today Manila, tomorrow the Philippines, and then . . . the world—meaning, to a Filipina, primarily the U.S.

Again Pedrosa finds the right image. After meeting the Lyndon Johnsons on her first official visit to America, and after Marcos had gone to sleep,

> [Imelda] tiptoed out of her own suite and sought out her favorite brother, Benjamin [later ambassador in Washington]. Taking his arm, she led him to a dark corner by a window overlooking a spectacular view of New York. . . . She asked him to look down below. "Kokoy, that is the world beneath us. Think of it. What we came from, and now the world . . . the whole world beneath us."

Show business, of one kind or another, became Imelda's only concern, the only thing she took seriously. Some of the most bizarre and striking legacies of Imelda's rule in Manila are not so much the grandiose hotels and cultural centers built to impress the world—Filipino wits called it her edifice complex—but the white walls erected to block the slums from outside view. They were part of Imelda's "beautification" campaign. It seems typical of the woman that, instead of using her wealth and power to do something about the poverty, she would simply build walls, so she, and, just as importantly, foreign visitors, would not have to see it. She also beautified her own past. The Quonset hut in Leyte where she spent much of her childhood became a grand palace with wall paintings depicting Imelda's life and a holy shrine for the infant Jesus. The Manila house with the famous garage was pulled down, and the grandest house on the same street was bought and stuffed with art and antiques. Foreign guests were told that this is where Imelda grew up.

Imelda's efforts at diplomacy were another form of beautification. Philippine embassies and chanceries had to be refurbished or moved to the best addresses, so that, in Imelda's words, "these Westerners cannot look down on us." Her own diplomatic trips were partly shopping sprees, partly photo opportunities played up in the Philippine press as triumphs of foreign policy. She tried to push her daughter, Imee, as a marriage candidate for Prince Charles, or at least an Agnelli (to her credit, Imee defied her mother and married a Filipino basketball player). She threw exorbitant parties at home for her favorite friends—and what a circle it was: King Hassan of Morocco, Cristina Ford and, typically, that connoisseur of pomp, Kurt Waldheim. She purchased herself a regal crown to wear on grand occasions—when told that this was really not done in European circles, she is said to have simply turned the crown back to front.

It is easy to laugh at all this, just as it is tempting to giggle at the tackiness—a mixture of the grandiose and the primitive—during the guided tours of Malacañang Palace, now a museum. One must realize, however, what one is laughing at, for the tackiness is as much a product of centuries of colonial rule as of the tasteless avarice of two parvenus. Imelda was deeply conscious of the Filipino "little brown brother complex," and her regal pretensions, preposterous though they may have been, were a clumsy and irresponsible attempt to impress, to gain the little brown sister some pride. We should not forget that for a very long time many poor Filipinos loved her for it.

Popularity, patronage and opportunism, more than brute force, enabled the Marcoses to undermine the institutions of democracy in their country. Their rule became so personalized that it was hard to imagine the Philippines without them. It was typical that when the Marcos downfall finally came, it took place in front of American TV cameras, indeed on American talk shows. In a way they were defeated by showbiz as much as by People Power. Meeting them for the first and only time, in Honolulu in 1986, I was not entirely surprised that their conversation, when not about war medals, communists and beauty, revolved largely around Ted Koppel and General MacArthur—a television star and a showbiz soldier.

It is hard to imagine somebody more different from Imelda Marcos than Corazón Aquino. In one of her confused campaign speeches before the 1986 "snap elections," Imelda told her audience that "our opponent does not put on any makeup. She does not have her fingernails manicured. . . . Filipinos are for beauty. Filipinos who like beauty, love, and God are for Marcos." Pedrosa describes early on in her book how Ninoy Aquino's attacks on Imelda's showiness and extravagance were deeply resented in Malacañang, especially the "innuendo that these qualities were traceable to an impoverished childhood." She quite rightly points out that "since Aquino represented the Philippine social élite to which the Marcoses aspired, the attack added insult to injury" (Pedrosa is not one to eschew clichés):

> The colorful, swashbuckling senator was a true blue blood; what's more, he was married to Corazón Cojuangco—heiress to a fabulous sugar fortune. The Cojuangcos represented the crème de la crème, at the top of Manila's Four Hundred. They were archetypes of Marcos's and Imelda's ambitions.

No wonder that believers in class struggle feel deeply ambivalent about Cory Aquino. "The millions of Filipinos aching for change," writes Pedrosa about the 1986 campaign, "now only had eyes for Cory, with her quiet charm, her intelligence, and her simplicity. She was the real heiress, the woman born with a silver spoon in her mouth. . . . If she did not show her wealth, it was because she did not need to."

Cory outclassed Imelda, and she is indeed a very different person, but her role as the savior is not devoid of *palabas* either. At times St. Cory of the February Miracle seems as theatrical as the evil Rose of Tacloban. Naturally the villain is far more interesting than the saint. In the same year that Imelda hammed it up for MacArthur's boys in Leyte, Cory was at a New York convent school, where, according to a former classmate quoted in Lucy Komisar's *Cory Aquino: The Story of a Revolution,* "she was always talking about Our Lady and her faith in religion." To be blunt, Cory, compared to Imelda, is a bore. This is even reflected in the prose of the two biographies. Pedrosa's is flashy, funny and often silly, especially as far as her trendy left-wing politics are concerned (but this hardly matters in a showbiz biography); Komisar's is pious, earnest, not funny at all, but in some instances equally silly. About Cory's attempts to unify the opposition before the 1986 elections, for example: "Her unhappiness at their refusal to let her seek unity between the two groups brought tears to Cory's eyes, and she wiped them with her handkerchief. The day before the convention, she ran into a woman law professor who gave her some pointers on how to be more assertive in dealing with men." Or this: "A few days later, Cory told Tañada and Ongpin that she wished she could be regarded as a person in her own right rather than as just Ninoy's widow. Ongpin advised her to be more assertive." These sound like notes from a feminist consciousness-raising session. Feminism really was hardly the point of Cory's running for president; the fact that she was Ninoy's wife was.

Switching roles from the self-effacing housewife to the political savior was a confusing and sometimes manipulative exercise. When she was first asked about running for office, Cory modestly replied that she was just a widow and mother: "There are many, many Filipinos more intelligent than I and who are recognized political leaders. I speak for just one person—Cory Aquino." What, then, made her into the ideal candidate? Nothing but Ninoy's death. Her widowhood became political. Encouraged by her advisers, Cory turned her suffering and her religious devotion into political emblems. And, sure enough, it worked. She had terrific press:

> Corazón Cojuangco Aquino. This woman in yellow, one could say, is the same woman of other times. There was Judith of the Bible. And in medieval times, there was Joan of Arc who led the French in battle against the conquerors, keeping faith in the voices who spoke to her in the garden. Cory, our beloved Cory, kept her faith in God and in her people to go about her husband's work.
>
> *The Philippines,* published by the Philippine Ministry of Tourism

> We voted in the past for Presidents for all sorts of reasons, but those who voted for you in the last elections did so because they also LOVED you.
>
> "Love Letter to a President," Luis D. Beltran in the
> *Philippine Daily Inquirer,* August 1986

When our leader-by-example exhausts all options given a democratic process, she is labelled weak and indecisive. Let us remember that it was never Cory's own Will to become President, but
rather God's and the Filipino people's.

Letter in the Philippine Daily Inquirer, August 1986

During the campaign, Cory would sense Ninoy's presence helping her, pushing her on during the difficult moments in the campaign. . . . "It's what we Catholics call the communion of saints,"
Cory said, "I pray for him, as I believe he prays for me."

Weekend, magazine of the Sunday Express, March 1986

Having Ninoy and God on her side is one of Cory's greatest political assets. To many Filipinos it gives her rule moral legitimacy. For the
time being, at least, she has the religious authority to hold her country
more or less together. But does it help to strengthen democratic institutions in the Philippines? Or could the effect be the reverse, as some
Filipino commentators—albeit often for self-serving reasons—argue?
After all, St. Cory's rule is no less personalized than that of Marcos. As
Komisar quite correctly points out, in her description of the 1987
plebiscite on the new constitution: "The constitution wasn't the
issue—Cory was." A major weakness of Komisar's biography is that
this central question of personalized rule versus democracy is hinted at
but not addressed; the issue gets lost in the biographer's understandable admiration for Cory personally. The closing sentence of the book
is typical:

She had proved to her countrymen and to an astonished world
that a political neophyte with little besides courage, tenacity and
innate good sense could embark on a moral crusade and defeat a
dictator who had controlled the country through brutality and
bribes for twenty years.

Cory's speechwriters could not have put it better.

Reading some of Komisar's descriptions of Cory in action, one cannot help feeling a little worried about Philippine democracy. Before the
election even took place, Cory did not want Salvador "Doy" Laurel—
her subsequent vice president—to run, because he did not meet "the

standards required to run on a platform of moral leadership." While trying to make up her own mind whether to run for president, "she had a recurring dream that she had visited a church and looked into a casket she thought held Ninoy's body. But it was empty. She believed that Ninoy had been reborn in her."

After being swept into Malacañang by People Power, the Church and members of the armed forces, Cory abolished such institutions as the parliament, which she called "a cancer in our political system which must be cut out," and the constitution. Both had been much abused by Marcos and his cronies, to be sure, but need she really have done away with them? She feared that her reform program would be blocked by remnants of the KBL, Marcos's old party. This was probably unfounded. In February 1986 Cory Aquino was in such a powerful position that she could have got most of the Marcos politicians on her side, on her terms—as I said earlier, switching sides is a respectable way to get on. Komisar quotes an interesting exchange between Cory and one of her advisers, Cecilia Muñoz Palma, who told the president, "We have to preserve the institutions, while we do not like the people who are there, if we will abide by our promise to the people that we will effect reforms through the constitutional legal process in place. We could do it." No, said Cory, she had to abolish the legal body, because that is what the people wanted her to do. Did they really? Is it not more accurate to say that she could have got away with anything, however undemocratic, because she was St. Cory, whom the people LOVED?

1987

THE BARTERED BRIDE

I heard the story from Francisco ("Frankie") Sionil José, the foremost Filipino novelist in English: a group of American and Filipino friends at a smart dinner party were discussing the U.S. bases in the Philippines. One of the Americans mentioned the increasing number of AIDS cases among American sailors. "That's what you guys get for screwing us," said a young Filipina, quick as a flash.

The image is apt. It is hard to discuss what Filipinos call the Fil-American relationship honestly without resorting to sexual imagery. Screwing, literally and figuratively, is the operative word. Filipinos' accounts of their national history leave the overwhelming impression of a people that has been screwed by powerful foreigners (and their local mimics) for centuries. The picture of a beautiful woman in native dress being raped by the alien conquerer has become a cliché of Filipino iconography. You come across her everywhere, in movies, cartoons, novels, and on posters displayed in street demonstrations.

Power often contains a sexual element, but the Philippines is somehow special. It is hard to think of the Dutch subjugation of the East Indies or the Spanish conquest of South America mainly in terms of screwing; exploitation, certainly, large-scale killing, yes indeed, but not screwing. Is it perhaps because of a masochistic streak in Filipino behavior, a willing submission to superior might, which is degrading and at the same time almost voluptuous? As an American character in F. Sionil José's novel *Ermita* observes to his Filipina girlfriend, "Filipinos get screwed because they like being screwed." One of the best descriptions of the Fil-American relationship I have read is a 1984 *Playboy* magazine article about the U.S. Navy base in Subic Bay, by the American novelist P. F. Kluge. An unforgettable passage described the ramshackle pleasure town called Subic City, "Home of the three-holer":

And now, here you are, and it looks like a Mexican town, something the Wild Bunch might ride into, everything facing a main street, with jeepney after jeepney of sailors tumbling out, the smell of barbecue mixing with diesel fumes, cute, lively, incredibly foul-mouthed girls saying hello and asking what ship you're from and offering head, and the jukeboxes from a dozen bars playing all at once, and the song you notice is Julio and Willie doing "To All the Girls I've Loved Before," and you climb to King Daryl's, where dozens of girls await just you, and you take a chair right at the edge of the balcony, with a King Shit view of the street, and you have a beer in one hand and a pork-satay stick in the other, and a woman between your legs, which are propped up against the railing, and you know you have come to a magical place, all right, a special magic for a nineteen-year-old Navy kid, the magic of a place where anything is possible. And cheap.

Offering head to whoever happens to be king of the mountain seems to have become second nature to many Filipinos. To be down there, between the legs of the Spanish friar or Uncle Sam, or Ferdinand Marcos, or whoever, has become the natural place to be. But screwing has another meaning as well: that of betrayal. Philippine history is also a story of betrayal; those who offer head so willingly usually end up being screwed in both senses of the word, the bitter and seemingly ever recurring experience of a submissive people that expects too much in return.

How did this gifted, humorous people get into such a sorry state? Stanley Karnow's highly engaging *In Our Image: America's Empire in the Philippines* offers us many pointers. The United States, after a bloody campaign to take control of the Philippines, was on the whole a benevolent and enlightened master of what was its only major colony. José likes to remind one of the days, not long ago, when "Bangkok was a backwater, Jakarta a big village, and Singapore a sleepy colonial outpost, while Manila was the richest and most cosmopolitan city in Southeast Asia." Why, then, has the Philippines, which had everything going for it, turned into such an unholy mess?

The first encounter with the West, in the shape of Magellan, who arrived in the Philippine archipelago in 1521, went well enough. A tribal chieftain called Humabon was converted to Christianity on the spot. Magellan named him Charles, in honor of the Spanish king. But soon disaster struck: Humabon asked Magellan to go and punish a rival chieftain called Lapu Lapu. Lapu Lapu, a fierce-looking character with feathers in his hair, didn't take kindly to this, and his men hacked Magellan to death. Jeane Kirkpatrick tactfully reminded newspaper readers of this event in 1986, just as Marcos was digging his heels in, as a warning to Washington not to get involved in native squabbles. As for Lapu Lapu, his portrait now hangs in the presidential palace in Manila. He had been forgotten for centuries until, as Karnow notes, "contemporary Filipino nationalists revived his memory in an effort to endow the Philippines with a historical continuity that never quite existed."

A famous Filipino historian, Teodoro Agoncillo, once said there was no Philippine history before the end of the nineteenth century. What he meant was that there was only Spanish history, written by Spaniards, mostly about Spaniards. There are no great pre-Spanish monuments, and few pre-Spanish heroes, except, of course, Lapu Lapu. The nineteenth-century Filipino elite, educated in Spanish, was quite literally the product of Spanish screwing, the so-called mestizo offspring of friars, soldiers and local girls, whose charms had also attracted many a Chinese trader. The great national hero José Rizal, a reformer who pleaded for equality with Spain in the 1890s, was, according to the historian Gregorio F. Zaide, a mixture of Negrito, Spanish, Chinese, Japanese and Malay—"a magnificent specimen of Asian manhood."

To seek equality with the alien power is of course not the same as overthrowing it, although it could be dangerous enough. Another national hero, Father José Burgos, a mestizo and not, as Karnow calls him, "a full-blooded Spaniard," was publicly garrotted by the Spaniards for allegedly instigating a rebellion. What he actually wanted was emancipation of the native clergy.

There is, however, a revolutionary tradition in the Philippines which occasionally finds common cause with the mestizo elite, but usually does not. It is a tradition of peasant revolts, led by messianic figures, usually many shades darker than the mestizos. In Vigan, formerly the Spanish capital of the northern Luzon, I visited the old house of Father Burgos. There was a display of pictures of a peasant revolt, sparked by the imposition of a Spanish government monopoly on a locally brewed alcoholic drink called *basi*. The pictures showed bands of small, dark men fighting the government militia, identified in the captions not as Spanish troops but as mestizos. This ethnic divide still exists, although it is easy to make too much of it in a country where most people, like Brazilians, are a mixture of something. José, himself a dark-skinned man with native "Indio" features, is fond of saying that "the higher you go up in this country, the whiter it gets." A look at Mrs. Aquino's cabinet would seem to prove his point.

It was the mestizo elite that, so to speak, offered head to foreign powers, in exchange for which service they could rule their darker brothers and sisters. This is the way it has been, and, so many say, this is the way it still is. Hence the sense of betrayal. According to Filipino nationalists (often a code word for leftists), the educated mestizos, called *"ilustrados,"* betrayed the revolution against Spain by cutting a deal with the Americans, after the Spaniards had been driven out by the U.S. Navy in 1898. As soon as the old one was deposed, the new king of the mountain was appeased.

Things are, of course, never quite so simple. General Emilio Aguinaldo, who fought the Americans bravely for three years after Commodore Dewey's navy blasted the Spanish ships away, was a typical *ilustrado*. And, even though he cooperated eagerly with the Americans after his surrender, he wore a black tie until the day of Philippine independence in 1946, on which occasion he ceremoniously took it off. His house in Cavite is a showcase of Filipino ambiguity. The ceiling is decorated with the Philippine flag as well as the American eagle, and pictures of Filipino heroes and American presidents hang side by side, like old friends, or, more appropriately in the Filipino context, relatives.

Karnow quotes Aguinaldo's foreign affairs adviser, Pardo de Tavera, to illustrate the *ilustrado* mentality. Partly educated in Europe, Tavera was a nationalist and a liberal who believed in universal education, civil liberty and capitalism, all encapsulated, as Karnow says, "in that magic term of the time: progress." Not the sort of thing admired by left-wing revolutionaries, or, for that matter, right-wing autocrats. But what truly damns a man like Tavera in "nationalist" eyes is his approach to the Americans. He wrote to President McKinley, who seems to have spent much of his time on his knees asking God what to do about this new colony, which he had barely heard of before hotheads like Roosevelt (Theodore) and MacArthur (Arthur) urged him to acquire it. "Providence," wrote Tavera, "led the United States to these distant islands for the fulfillment of a noble mission, to take charge of the task of teaching us the principles that . . . have made your people the wonder of the world and the pride of humanity." To MacArthur he wrote that "all our efforts will be directed to Americanizing ourselves" in the hope that "the American spirit may take possession of us," infusing the country with "its principles, its political customs and its peculiar civilization."

Although it is Karnow's thesis that these principles never took hold in the Philippines, some of the political customs and at least the forms of the peculiar civilization certainly did. Teodoros became Teddys, Juans became Johnnys, Corazóns became Corys, and Franciscos became Frankies. American public education was to change the Spanish-speaking elite into an English-speaking one within a few decades.

In *The Aquinos of Tarlac,* Nick Joaquin, who was educated in English and Spanish, lamented the fact that "the cultured Filipino of the 1880s . . . intellectually at home in several worlds . . . had a latitude unthinkable in the 'educated' Filipino of the '20s and '30s, for whom culture had been reduced to being knowing about the world contained between Hollywood and Manhattan." Hence the fact that half the educated male population today seems to bear the title of attorney-at-law. Or the fact that on prominent display at the biggest department store in Manila is a large oil painting of Ronald and Nancy Reagan in formal Filipino dress. Or the fact that thousands of Filipinos apply every year to work for the U.S. Navy, and that many thousands more are waiting to emigrate to California. Or that Filipino cities all look like East L.A., with minimarts, discos, hamburger joints and honky-tonks. Amid the jumble of street signs and slogans, my favorite discovery was a sign over a funeral parlor that said, "Funeraria Rosaria: Home of the Superior Casket." Now here is a people that has clearly taken that peculiar culture onboard. Filipinos appear to love it—although to some, of course, it might seem more like rape.

But, if so, the Americans were peculiar rapists. The U.S. conquistadors remind one of Jimmy Swaggart, praying while they sinned. They were at once racist and at times unspeakably brutal, and benign, generous and idealistic. Karnow uses contemporary American journalism and popular songs to illustrate the mood in the U.S. It was from the start one of profound ambivalence. An 1898 Finley Peter Dunne column in the *Chicago Tribune* is an especially effective example:

> "I know what I'd do if I was Mack," said Mr. Hennessy. "I'd hist a flag over th' Ph'lippens, an' I'd take in th' whole lot iv thim." "An' yet," said Mr. Dooley, " 'tis not more thin two months since ye larned whether they were islands or canned goods."

Mack was, of course, President McKinley—the one who went down on his knees, prayed, and realized that "there was nothing left for us to do but take them all, and to educate the Filipinos, and uplift and civilize and Christianize them, and by God's grace do the very best we could by them, as our fellow-men for whom Christ also died."

No doubt that was sincerely meant, in the best tradition of Yankee generosity. But it took about 200,000 Filipino lives to convince the natives. And not all Americans were as high-minded as Mack. Teddy Roosevelt is quoted by Karnow as saying, "All the great masterful races have been fighting races. . . . No triumph of peace is quite so great as the triumphs of war." These feelings were echoed by ordinary soldiers, one of whom stated that "I am in my glory when I can sight some dark skin and pull the triggers," while another observed that he would like to "blow every nigger into nigger heaven." A brigadier general named Jacob ("Hell-Roaring Jake") W. Smith hoped to turn one of the Philippine islands into "a howling wilderness." This is like Curtis LeMay's wish in World War II to bomb Japan "back into the Stone Age."

But once the fighting was done and many "goo-goos" found their rightful places in nigger heaven, the Americans were indeed benevolent. They quickly set up an education system that was second to none in colonial Asia. American soldiers repaired roads, built hospitals, vaccinated children against smallpox, and a U.S. Army band entertained the locals every afternoon in central Manila to such inspiring tunes as "There'll Be a Hot Time in the Old Town Tonight."

Karnow rightly compares the American colonial record favorably with that of European nations. There is a more interesting comparison, though, which he does not draw, and that is with Japan. American colonial history, such as it is, began around the same time as Japan's. Both countries, for obvious reasons, were opposed to European imperialism, yet at the same time emulated many of its trappings, down to the white topis and classicist architectural bombast. Their colonial conquests came in the guise of anticolonialism; they were, in a sense, the first modern "liberation" movements, and, like so many such subsequent movements, they were marked by a peculiar savagery.

This might be explained by a racist element that did not yet exist in earlier European adventures. The British, the Dutch and the French did not arrive in their respective colonies to liberate anybody, nor were they burdened with racial or even nationalist zeal. They simply wanted to trade. Their empires grew out of that, though not always peacefully, of course. By the late nineteenth century it was too late for empires to grow: they had to be conquered.

The racial theories, the White Man's Burden and all that, came around about the same time, a product of Social Darwinism. They had an enormous impact on Japan, obsessed with national survival in the jungle of struggling nations, and, as one can see in the statements of Roosevelt and MacArthur, many Americans were infected by the same virus. Trade was an added benefit, but it was not the only purpose of American or Japanese colonialism. "In their own eyes," says Karnow, the Americans "were missionaries, not masters." The Japanese, who felt rejected by the Western world they had wished to join as equals, went on a similar mission, but in their case—at least according to the propaganda—it was to spread the superior virtues of the Japanese race. Conquerers with missions (including the Spanish conquistadors spreading Christianity with the sword) have by and large caused more mischief than traders.

It has been suggested that American savagery in the Philippines, as well as in the campaigns at home against Indian tribes, helps to explain the brutality of the Pacific War. In fact, American brutality came to a speedy end in the Philippines, not just for moral reasons, but because the Americans, unlike the Japanese forty years later, quickly realized how counterproductive it was. Besides, as Karnow points out, it got bad press at home. And though Darwinist theories were used to justify the conquest of the Philippines, it is hard to see their relevance to American behavior after Pearl Harbor.

Karnow draws a different parallel: between the Philippine war and the Vietnamese struggle for "liberation." He attributes the Vietnamese success to a combination of national cohesion—bolstered by a shared history, national heroes and so on—and a revolution promising a better life to the dispossessed peasantry. Aguinaldo's mestizo elite, in contrast, fought for independence, but not for social reforms that would benefit the masses. And, unlike Vietnam, the Philippines had little national cohesion, solidarity or identity, which made it hard to find any common cause. There is some truth in all of this, but one important point is, I think, missed—a point that cuts to the core of Philippine politics today. Was Ho Chi Minh's or General Giap's success in mobilizing the people a question of national identity, or was it to a large extent something more mundane, like political coercion? Do the subjects of a communist state really have much choice when they are ordered to fight? The same is of course true of many communist reforms: they are forced on the people. Aguinaldo may not have been a great agricultural reformer, but he was more of a democrat than Ho Chi Minh.

The constitution of the first Philippine republic, promulgated in 1899, was a remarkably sophisticated document, and the new state, whose executive powers were checked by a strong legislature, was remarkably liberal. It may be that a more authoritarian leadership—especially if it had been backed by a foreign power—would have had more success fighting off an invasion, just as there are many people today who would like the Philippine government to be more authoritarian in pushing through social reforms. It may also be true that Aguinaldo and his fellow *ilustrados* would never have reformed their feudal society. It can even be argued, as many do, that in a democracy run by an elite whose interests are contrary to those of the masses, reforms will not be carried out. But the Filipinos never really had the chance to prove themselves as a nation, for their efforts to do so were preempted by the Americans. It seems questionable to me, in any case, that Aguinaldo's defeat by the U.S. had much to do with the lack of cultural unity or historical heroes.

It fits right into Karnow's general thesis, though. He believes that the American mission to transplant its values and institutions to the Philippines, or anywhere in Asia, was a dangerous illusion. As he puts it, "A noble dream, it proved in later years to be largely an exercise in self-deception." This, in Karnow's view, is because of deep cultural differences. I have my doubts about this argument as well. The idea that every country can be just like America and every capital another American town is naive, to be sure, but the aborted effort of Filipinos to establish their own democratic republic, partly based on American institutions, proves that there is nothing in Filipino culture innately hostile to a liberal democracy. Karnow rightly says that Filipino politics are based on personal relationships—between landowners and peasants, political bosses and clients and so on—rather than impersonal institutions, but this is less a cultural peculiarity than the normal condition of any preindustrial society.

The Americans were a destructive force not because their ideals could not be transplanted, but because they robbed Filipinos of the chance to be their own masters. By making them dependent on American tutelage and largesse, they perpetuated the old colonial setup and deprived the Filipino elite of responsibility, the effect of which has lasted to this day. The Filipinos submitted to foreign domination, but not from choice. Indeed, as Karnow describes in detail, one of the worst instances of betrayal was the American promise to Aguinaldo in 1898 that the Philippines would be left alone once the Spaniards were ousted.

It is, of course, true that the Americans tried to remake the Philippines "in our image," which included lessons in democracy. But the reason these lessons didn't stick has less to do with incompatible Filipino values than with the gap between ideals and colonial reality. How could Filipinos become responsible democrats if the democratic tutors behaved like feudal patrons, fostering dependence while preaching the virtues of independence? This is where the cultural and political signals got seriously confused—again a situation that has lasted more or less to this day. For when the Americans act like masters, Filipinos talk about freedom from the American yoke; but as soon as the Americans threaten to cut their charges loose, Filipinos feel betrayed, as though the patron is forgetting his obligations. By the time the Filipino elite was actually offered independence, the Fil-American relationship had already become much too cozy, the psychology of dependence too deeply entrenched, the special privileges too convenient. Sergio Osmeña, who became president just before coming home with Douglas MacArthur in 1944, is said to have observed that "the Filipinos wanted independence only when it seemed to be getting farther off, and the minute it began to get near they would begin to get very much frightened."

As far as other Asian "client states" are concerned, the problems with democracy have less to do with the incompatibility of American values and local traditions than with America's ambivalent policies. South Korea and Japan are good examples. After World War II, there was great eagerness in both countries, especially among leftists (the only real opponents of Japanese authoritarianism), to accept America's help to set up liberal democracies. At first they even got the blessing of General MacArthur—not a man generally known for his liberal views. But by the late 1940s fear of communism was such that the noncommunist left was purged along with the communists, and reactionary regimes returned to power, secure in their knowledge of American support. Realpolitik alternated with idealism in a way that has bewildered American allies ever since Aguinaldo sailed to Manila onboard a U.S. Navy ship. Masters or missionaries? Liberation or the White Man's Burden? Anticolonial colonialism: President McKinley was not the only American unsure of what to do in Asia.

In a way, American foreign policy has always been a hostage to its own propaganda. Moral arguments must be harnessed to convince the home front of the justness of America's cause. Great expectations are raised abroad only to be abandoned in sudden shifts of policy. The national interest can get hopelessly mixed up with the national mission to spread the gospel of freedom and democracy, and the two, alas, don't always dovetail neatly. Sometimes the national interest suffers, sometimes the mission; either way, people end up feeling betrayed.

Nonetheless, despite the demands of realpolitik, America has been a relatively generous superpower. So much so that it strikes many Americans as extraordinary when such generosity is reciprocated with surly resentment instead of gratitude. For someone like Imelda Marcos, indulged by at least four American presidents, to feel betrayed by America must appear perverse. But it has to be said that some Filipinos had ample cause to think they had been screwed by Uncle Sam.

When MacArthur returned to repossess the Philippines from the Japanese, he found a Filipino elite, led by Benigno Aquino Senior, Cory's father-in-law, and José P. Laurel, father of Cory's vice president, that had dealt with the Japanese in precisely the way the American and Spanish masters and missionaries had been dealt with before: collaboration in exchange for patronage. Once again the Filipino elite had offered head. The strongest resistance to the Japanese came from the darker-skinned people, the traditional rebels recruited in the poor rural areas, in this case the guerrilla army of the leftist *Hukbalahap,* or Huks. They had helped the Americans free Luzon, but when that job was done they were seen as a communist threat to the established order. The Huk leader, Luis Taruc, was jailed on charges of preventing the country "from returning to a normal way of life." The normal way of life was, of course, a meager existence for the peasants whose cause the Huks championed under the domination of the old landlords, the very people who had collaborated with the Japanese.

As Karnow rightly observes, MacArthur "aborted change in the Philippines by reinstalling the traditional dynasties, whose primary aim was to protect their vested interests." Could he have done otherwise, a man in a hurry to restore order in a chaotic country in ruins? Perhaps not. But what was truly unforgivable in many Filipino eyes was his swift abandonment of the Philippines to become the proconsul in Tokyo, where, again in Filipino eyes, the great American Father, their very own compadre, proceeded to make the old enemy rich and powerful again. This offended the old custom of *utang na loob,* obligation earned through favors. Hadn't Filipinos died for the U.S.A.? So, did most Filipinos feel well and truly screwed by the old Lion of Luzon? No, no, no, said Cardinal Jaime Sin, archbishop of Manila, interviewed by Karnow in a fascinating television documentary about the Fil-American relationship: "Nobody can say anything against MacArthur here. You'd get stoned. That man saved us. He promised to return, and he did return."

If only he hadn't, if only America had left its old colony alone, things might have turned out better in the end. For if the Americans are often confused about their motives and aims, the Filipinos have an even harder time disentangling sentimental and cultural expectations from national interest. We hate you, we love you; Yankee go home, but please not just yet. As President Quezon once said, "Damn the Americans, why don't they tyrannize us more!" There are many countries where men have come to power with the help of the CIA, but only in the Philippines can one imagine a local boy being elected—and, what is more, being hugely popular—*because* he is backed by the CIA. This was the case with Ramón Magsaysay ("He's Our Guy"), elected president in 1953. The agency could not have wished for a better front man. He was an earthy, dark-skinned man of the people, quite different from his rich mestizo predecessors. He didn't even have a Spanish name. Although hardened foreign correspondents like to dismiss him as nothing but a CIA creation, many Filipinos remember Our Guy wistfully: if only we could have another Magsaysay; if only he were still with us. He died in a plane crash in 1957.

Marcos, too, was a change from what he called the old oligarchy. But, unlike Magsaysay, he was not made by the CIA. He was a brilliant young upstart from the gritty north who first gate-crashed the privileged world of the Filipino elite and then proceeded to strip some of its most prominent members of their assets—only to redistribute the new wealth among his friends. He also seemed serious about land reforms, and even dared challenge the traditional power of the Catholic Church. Here, at last, was a popular nationalist who would tackle some of the country's fundamental problems. Now more than a few people think wistfully of his early years too: if only he had done what he promised to do.

But instead he created a mirror image of the old colonial system, in which he was the only patron, the super compadre, the don of dons. And American eagerness to keep the bases (the country's biggest employer after the Philippine government) meant that Marcos, just like his predecessors in the colonial era, could make himself and his friends fortunes by squeezing the old White Chief. He became so adept at this, and Washington was often so clumsy, that it was not always clear who was screwing whom. In addition, he stole from his own country's coffers. The extraordinary insouciance of Marcos's kleptocracy can be understood only as an example of colonial psychology: Why should he be responsible for anything but himself, his family and his friends? America would always be there to protect him and clear up the mess. After all, he was America's loyal friend, and he fought communists. Isn't that what America wanted?

But, as we know, even Marcos came to grief, the beginning of his demise shown live on Ted Koppel's TV show. There they went, the president and his First Lady, lifted out of their palace in an American helicopter, the First Lady singing "New York, New York." And then the Marcoses, too, feel screwed, as they told *The Washington Post* in April 1989. They were "kidnapped" by the Americans, they said, after having been betrayed by the American press. "I grew up around everything American," said Mrs. Marcos, in between singing old Irving Berlin tunes for visiting reporters—"American food, American music . . . U.S.A., red, white and blue . . . We were not just friends, allies, we were one in spirit with America." But, then, "America did us in. . . . Before the kidnapping, we were clean, we were good-looking. I was 'beautiful,' I was 'great.' And after the kidnapping, I was—everything was rotten."

I daresay that, underneath all the lies and all the playacting, this emotion was sincere—as sincere as is humanly possible with show folks like the Marcos couple; as sincere, at least, as President McKinley's intention to civilize and Christianize and do the best by the little brown brothers in . . . what was the name of that place again? It was sincere and deeply humiliating, in the way that squabbles over money in a whorehouse are humiliating. Mrs. Marcos's tears were like the tears of a hooker who feels she has not been paid enough for her services.

Much of this really has to be seen to be believed. Karnow is an excellent sketcher of characters, and what characters they are!—Teddy Roosevelt, Douglas MacArthur, Manuel Quezon, Imelda Marcos, "Ninoy" Aquino. In the world of Filipino politics—one is tempted to say Filipino life—everybody becomes an actor, playing roles, often confused, always *bella figura.*

Frankie José in some ways exemplifies the turmoil of Filipino intellectual life. He talks about the need for a "truly nationalist revolution," though he loves America, where several of his children have settled. He sympathizes with young people who disappear into the mountains to join the communist New People's Army, though he has little sympathy with communism. Yet in some circles he is regarded as a communist, while more progressive types accuse him of being a "CIA agent"—for his association in the 1950s with the Congress for Cultural Freedom. This is nothing special in the Philippines: most people are suspected of being either communists or American agents. That José is accused of both says something about the man: he is the kind of free spirit who would be intolerable to any revolutionary regime, whether of the right or the left.

José's radicalism is not so much the product of Marxist analysis as of a moral rage: what V. S. Naipaul calls colonial rage, against the humiliation of subservience, the indignity of a history of failure. This is the theme that runs through all José's novels, including his major work, the so-called Rosales saga, four novels dealing with Filipino history from 1872 to 1972. The entire saga can be read as an allegory for the Filipino in search of an identity.

The heroine of José's novel *Ermita* is a prostitute. As if that metaphor were not strong enough, she was born as the result of a rape, inflicted on her rich mestizo mother by a Japanese soldier during the sacking of Manila in 1945. Ermita, the name of the heroine as well as the title of the novel, screws her way to the top, ending up with that most desirable of things, a rich American husband. But in the kind of denouement José likes, she rejects the American and goes back to her real love, a Filipino she grew up with. His real name, incidentally, is Mac—short for MacArthur. She doesn't actually take to the hills, to join the revolution, as does the hero in José's best-known novel, *Mass,* but she does, as a Manila intellectual might put it, find her identity as a Filipina. In José's moral universe, the two are closely linked: revolution is a matter of pride, dignity, identity. "What we need," says José, tapping his nut-brown head, "is a revolution in here." What we need, he means to say, is to stop being prostitutes.

Colonial rage usually boils over into self-hatred. A young student in *Mass* sums up the author's feelings:

Listen, our history . . . is a history of failed revolutions. Always, in the end, someone was bought or someone turned traitor. We are a nation of traitors. . . . We delight in seeing the downfall of others, even friends. We betray for money, for revenge, for envy . . . but most of the time, out of sheer cussedness.

In *Ermita,* a former historian called Cruz, now "prostituting" himself for a multinational company, tells Ermita that

we are witnessing the slow demise, the gradual self-destruction of this nation. And we don't need a foreign colonizer to do this. We are blissfully doing it ourselves. . . . Our entire educational system—and I am its product—is valueless. It is our creation. We cannot blame it for the fatal flaw in us. Maybe we deserve the darkness that is coming.

José's rage seems at odds with the seemingly indestructible carnivalesque jokiness of the Filipinos. Yet it reflects a dark current that runs through their history, occasionally erupting in messianic zeal and violence. José is an urbane, witty, cosmopolitan man of the world, a pillar of the local PEN club, a gourmet and a connoisseur of art. He is not a communist, and voted for Cory Aquino. But his spirit is with the rebels in the hills, in whom he thinks he sees the latest incarnation of his Indio ancestors, still waiting to exact their blood debt from the mestizos who betrayed them.

1989

THE SEOUL OLYMPICS

In September 1988, for the second time since its opening in 1987, I visited the Independence Hall of Korea, a huge patriotic monument south of Seoul, and I was struck by the same thoughts as during the first visit: Was my revulsion a sign of decadence, of Western flabbiness? Were Spengler and Toynbee perhaps right? Is there something to the idea of the rise and fall of national, even racial vigor? Intellectually, one rebels against such notions. But still the place overwhelms by its sheer force; it has the fascination of Leni Riefenstahl's documentaries. One notes the kitsch, the absurd mysticism, the sentimentality, the brutal aesthetics, but one cannot deny the power.

Unlike before, the place was virtually empty. People were either at work or watching the Olympics on TV. I examined at my leisure the great Patriots Memorial, the Patriotic Poems and Quotations, and the Grand Hall of the Nation, an enormous temple with large stone groups of patriots, nude, Nordic-looking and vigorous, their lantern jaws and outstretched arms pointing towards a glorious future. The effect of histrionic power was heightened by Wagnerian music and sounds of drums and neighing horses. The hall commemorates the struggle against Japanese colonialism. The style owes a great deal to Arno Breker and Stalin's socialist realists. The purpose, according to the official guide, is "to awaken Korean national consciousness and promote patriotism." The method is quasi-religious.

Inside the exhibition halls I read some of the anthropological information. On the physical characteristics of Koreans (in English): "Their arms are rather short. Their heads tend to be flat in the back and their fore-heads are rather broad, suggesting large brain capacity."

In the history section there was a nineteenth-century stone with an inscription that read: "Western barbarians invade our lands—if we do not fight, we must appease them. To urge appeasement is to betray our nation." A rebellion by the Righteous Army against the Japanese in 1907 was said to have "sent a signal to the world that the Koreans were prepared to unite to fight for their national sovereignty, justice and world peace."

At the end of the exhibition, as a kind of climax after all the heavy oil paintings of battle scenes, pictures of Japanese atrocities and relics of Korean martyrdom, we get to the Olympic Games. There is a model of the Olympic stadium, there are photographs of Korean medalists at the 1986 Asian Games in Seoul and, in a panoramic film entitled *Korea, My Motherland,* we see a thousand young tae kwon do fighters in identical martial gear punching the air in unison while letting out a piercing battle cry. This is followed by images of steel furnaces, followed by more pictures of Korean athletes winning gold.

"Welcome to '88 Olympics, and the Land of Ginseng," says a ginseng-root drink commercial: "Ginseng for over forty centuries has symbolized power and youth throughout Asia."

KOREA'S ECONOMY OUTPOWERS JAPAN'S AT TIME OF TOKYO OLYMPIC GAMES IN 1964, said a headline in the *Korea Times* on the day before the opening ceremony.

"We must say we are proud that the miracle-maker of the East, Korea, has done it again," said a columnist called Rhee Chong-ik in the same newspaper, commenting on the games.

Power, miracle, power, power! One cannot escape it: these are the expressions of a country that is either superbly confident or racked by anxiety. Whenever one assumes it to be the former, evidence of the latter tends to break through. When a Greco-Roman wrestler called Kim Young-nam won Korea's first gold medal, the *Korea Times* was in ecstasy: "He did it. He turned the entire nation wild with enthusiasm, quenching their thirst for the gold." But whenever I felt the inclination to sneer at this thirst, I was held back by my own anxiety: How will countries that lack the thirst, that scoff at notions of national vigor, that take the good life for granted, be able to compete with people who are so hungry for achievement and recognition, for power and gold medals?

Many times during my stay in Seoul I was reminded of an athlete who was the antithesis of all this power and glory: Eddie the Eagle, the bumbling British amateur ski jumper, who had earlier endeared himself at Calgary by his clownish performances in the Winter Olympics. Part of his charm was his complete indifference to finishing last. He exemplified Baron Pierre de Coubertin's Olympic ideal (which, incidentally, was far from the ideal of the highly competitive ancient Greeks): just to take part was enough; winning was irrelevant. Apparently, Eddie got on the nerves of his more pugnacious rivals—particularly, I believe, the East Germans. The Koreans would not have understood Eddie either. To them he would have seemed typical of Western decadence. And perhaps they would have been right. Is there not something flabby and complacent about the British indifference (some might even say attraction) to failure? Or is it a sign of higher civilization? Or perhaps both?

British athletes did not do very well at the 1936 Berlin Olympics. Germany did best, and both Italy and Japan did better than Britain. Duff Hart-Davis's book *Hitler's Games* quotes a letter to *The Daily Telegraph*, written by one Revd F. Brompton Harvey, who observed that "the failure of Englishmen in the Olympic Games should give a jolt to our national complacency. . . . What are the reasons for this decline in athletic prowess—in skill and will to win?" The answer, in the reverend's opinion, was democracy, which encourages mediocrity and does away with virility. "And we need not wonder if this failure in manly sports on the world stage is interpreted by our rivals as another proof that England has 'gone soft.' "

———

Sports of one kind or another have a long history of being used to fend off decadence. Richard D. Mandell, in *The First Modern Olympics,* a study of the games held in Athens in 1896, writes that sport "was an integral part of many educational schemes advanced by Greek philosophers to improve or reform their society." The Romans, with the exception of a few philhellenes, found sports bad for the character—particularly when indulged in without clothes on. But gory gladiatorial spectacles, which were sports of a kind, were approved of. According to Mandell, some Roman moralists recommended this type of blood sport as a way of accustoming effete youths to the sight of carnage.

Medieval knights were kept out of mischief by staging jousting tournaments. And through the ages the common people found their pleasure in games of various kinds. But sports as an exercise in national character-building, the philosophical foundation of the modern Olympics, came much later. That belongs to the nineteenth century, when national consciousness was, to use a twentieth-century expression, raised all over Europe.

There were two distinct European sporting traditions: sports, specifically athletics and team games, as a way to test individual skills and character; and sports as a mass spectacle, to forge unity and promote a cultish kind of beauty, often involving pagan rites—torchlight parades and so on. As one might have guessed, the former was Anglo-Saxon in origin, the latter German. The British were cricketers and athletes; the Germans preferred gymnastics, or, as they called the art of body contortions, *Turnen*. *Turnen* was an expression of Germanness (*Deutschtum*). The word *Turnen* was coined by the so-called *Turnvater*, Friedrich Ludwig Jahn (1778–1852).

The *Turnvater* was a patriot spurred into action by Napoleon's occupation of Germany. His *Turnbewegung* was part of an effort to unify the German nation. Clubs were formed, and eventually great festivals were held on special Turndays, when turners demonstrated their loyalty to the Second Reich in the form of mass calisthenics. Turners were contemptuous of the kind of sports enjoyed by decadent Anglo-Saxons. The turners, writes Mandell, "claimed that sport was an alien infection that might damage the integral structure of robust German culture." Jahn, apart from being responsible for the physical torture of generations of continental children (my father's back never quite recovered from his childhood contortions), has left his mark on sports to this day: he was the inventor of the rings, the pommel horse and the parallel bars.

Turnen was closely linked to a wider movement in Germany, a neo-classical cult of physical beauty called Nordische Freikörperkultur (NFKK), which reached its apotheosis around the time of Hitler's Olympics in 1936. Body culture involved much healthy nudity and well-oiled heroic posturing. Leni Riefenstahl's films, of the Berlin Olympics especially, but also *Triumph of the Will,* about the Nuremberg rally, are the perfect documents of this sort of thing. Riefenstahl, inspired by generations of German romantics, was big on harmony with nature, in woods or on lonely mountaintops, preferably at dusk. When the young men in her films are not harmonizing with nature, they march, perform great physical feats or indulge in healthy horseplay, yodeling with pleasure as they beat one another with twigs in the sauna bath. Riefenstahl's employers liked these young men to be blond, but the filmmaker herself was as much drawn to the physical perfection of Jesse Owens as to "healthy SA men" of the Third Reich.

The groundwork for Hitler's, Stalin's, Sukarno's, Mussolini's, Kim Il Sung's and, yes, South Korean monuments, in stone or in the flesh (the difference is not always easy to detect), was laid by eighteenth-century neoclassicists, such as the artist Jacques-Louis David (1748–1825). This propagandist for the French Revolution reacted against the effete rococo style of the ancien régime. Riefenstahl's marching men in their high boots (or athletic singlets), and their expressions of steely determination, are the heroic neoclassical images come to life. The aesthetic, then, was not uniquely German in origin. But the link with mass sports events was certainly German. And the perculiarly Teutonic link with the Olympic idea is suggested by the title of a book first published in 1924 but reissued in an expanded version in 1936: *Mensch und Sonne, Arischolympische Geist* ("Man and Sun, the Aryan Olympic Spirit"). It was written by one Hans Süren, the inventor of a special rubber penis-holder. Süren liked to be photographed in the nude, slapping punch-bags or engaging in other such manly gestures. His inspiration, he wrote, was Hitler's *Mein Kampf.*

The British concept of sport during the nineteenth and early twentieth centuries was less absurd than Germany's nudism and synchronic calisthenics, but no less patriotic. English games go back to two sources, often linked: village festivals and upper-class schools. Cricket was played by village boys in the sixteenth century and was later taken up as a gentrified adult game. The special national ethos of cricket was, how-ever, like the Olympics, a nineteenth-century phenomenon. "Mark me," wrote a hearty headmaster of Uppingham School, quoted in John J. MacAloon's study of Coubertin, *This Great Symbol,* "cricket is the greatest bond of the English speaking race, and is no mere game." Sports, at exclusive schools as well as in workingmen's clubs, were an expression of "muscular Christianity." Sport built character—specifi-cally, the character of empire builders.

The British empire was built on the belief in racial superiority. Just as the Germans did later, British sports enthusiasts often identified themselves as the true heirs of the ancient Greeks. And, just as the Greeks confined their Olympics to athletes of pure Greek blood, En-glishmen in the 1890s talked of holding an "Anglo-Saxon Olympiad." This scheme, wrote the main promoter, J. Astley Cooper, "ought to act as an antidote to the debilitating effects of luxury, wealth and civilisa-tion, for, should it be carried out in its full conception, the honours which it affords should be those for which the flower of the Race would chiefly strive."

The seminal work on Victorian English sports was *Tom Brown's School Days.* The book begins with a description of Tom's native village in Berkshire. In an aside, Thomas Hughes laments the loss of native village loyalties: "We were Berkshire, or Gloucestershire, or Yorkshire boys," he writes, addressing his young readers,

> and you're young cosmopolites, belonging to all counties and no countries. No doubt it's all right, I dare say it is. This is the day of large views and glorious humanity, and all that; but I wish backsword play hadn't gone out in the Vale of White Horse, and that confounded Great Western hadn't carried away Alfred's Hill to make an embankment.

Here we have a quintessentially nineteenth-century sentiment. Rail-ways, Empire, cosmopolitanism, large views and glorious humanity—I dare say it's all right, but . . . what about native values? What about moral discipline? How about community spirit? This is where sports came in, to restore such morals and values. When Tom first goes to Rugby, alma mater of many a moralist, from Hughes himself to Salman

Rushdie, he helps to win a football match for his house against "the School." The hero is a sixth-form boy known as Old Brooke. On the day of victory Brooke gets up to give a speech to the boys of the house. His theme is why the much smaller house beat the school:

> It's because we've more reliance on one another, more of a house feeling, more fellowship than the school can have. . . . We've union, they've division—there's the secret—(cheers). But how's this to be kept up? How's it to be improved? That's the question. For I take it, we're all in earnest about beating the school, whatever else we care about. I know I'd sooner win two School-house matches running than get the Balliol scholarship any day—(frantic cheers).

Union versus division: this was the overriding obsession of nineteenth-century pedagogues—and authoritarian leaders. The Germans turned to turning, the British to the public school spirit, and the French . . . ? They were of two minds. Some admired the German spirit. But after the bitter defeat by the Prussian armies in 1871 this became a rather indefensible position, and so a large number of Frenchmen, including Pierre de Coubertin, turned to England—in the baron's case, specifically to Tom Brown's school.

Coubertin, a restless aristocrat in search of good deeds, was deeply shaken by the French debacle in 1871 and sought to put some backbone into the French, or, as he put it, to "rebronze" them. Following the ideas of Hippolyte Taine, another Anglophile, Coubertin believed in Progress, the kind of progress celebrated in world's fairs, the ethos of which is akin to that of the Olympics. The conditions for Progress were Harmony and Patriotism. These values, so essential to rebronzing the demoralized and enervated French, were to be found in British public schools, particularly at Rugby, where Coubertin literally worshiped at Dr. Arnold's tomb. Coubertin, himself a product of a strict Jesuit college, where sports would have been the last thing on the curriculum, admired the likes of Old Brooke, who would rather win a football match than get a Balliol scholarship. Thus the sporting baron began his crusade for *la pédagogie sportive*. And thus the Olympic idea was born.

In fact, Dr. Arnold's muscular Christianity stressed Christianity more than muscles. Coubertin's patriotism was more secular. Olympia, he said, was "consecrated to a task strictly human and material in form, but purified and elevated by the idea of patriotism." Like many nineteenth-century men, he loved ceremonies and hated politics. Olympia, to him, was a "cult centre." Men who dream of perfect harmony always hate politics (but they are usually deeply moved by pagan rites and torchlight parades). Ever the true aristocrat, Coubertin believed in patronage, dispensed by a noble elite that chose its own members not for their politics or the interests they might represent, but for their devotion to the "idea" of Peace, Harmony and Progress. Voting, interests, ideology—these divide men. Religious or pseudoreligious ceremonies, service to common ideals, and great rallies—not to mention great leaders—bind men together. What Coubertin hoped to achieve with his Olympic idea was to emulate the union of Old Brooke's house on a massive scale, first in France and then throughout the world.

It is of course a deeply antidemocratic idea. And there are few less democratic institutions than the International Olympic Committee, which appears to operate a bit like a Freemasons' lodge—there is the same addiction to ritual, the same secretiveness and pomposity. This is not to say that Coubertin himself was a protofascist. But antidemocratic ideas, however well-intentioned, are ripe for the plucking by more cynical manipulators. Coubertin believed that pseudoreligious incantations about Peace and the Brotherhood of Man could solve political conflicts. He took his own slogans about sports transcending politics seriously. He really thought that by holding vast jamborees, we would all learn to understand and respect one another, and that this would lead to world peace.

Coubertin was an internationalist under attack from French nativists, who were equally interested in staging jamborees but who favored pageants involving French games, French ceremonies and French traditions such as revived medieval French student festivals. Coubertin's enemy was Charles Maurras, the reactionary royalist who loathed Dreyfus, democracy and all foreigners, though not necessarily in that order. While Coubertin saw no contradiction between promoting patriotism through the competition of nations and the ideal of international brotherhood, Maurras saw the contradiction all too well. But he was all for it. Let the races mix at international competitions, he thought, and they will learn to hate one another. True Frenchmen, when confronted by the barbarian Americans and other unspeakable peoples, would recognize the superiority of France.

So while Coubertin was an enemy of the Action Française, Brown Shirts and analogous fascist movements, his political naïveté contributed to their cause. The removal of politics can be the first step toward totalitarianism. Those that seek to solve political problems by turning to cults or romantic ideals of harmony are the first to end up as victims of tyranny. There is an interesting link between Coubertin and Marxism-Leninism. Communist countries are the most successful Olympic contenders and the true heirs of Coubertin's ideals of Patriotism, Peace and International Brotherhood. In this, as in so many other ways, communists are the last Victorians.

The baron's saddest defeat was perhaps perceived by himself as a victory. He was too ill to attend the Berlin Olympics in 1936. But he had praised Germany's efforts in staging the grandiose games, and the Nazi organizers praised the old baron in return.* After the German team had entered the stadium for the opening ceremony and 100,000 arms were raised in the Hitler salute, after the last words of *"Deutschland, Deutschland über Alles"* and the "Horst Wessel Song" had been sung, silence was requested, and the frail voice of the baron spoke his recorded message: "The most important thing at the Olympic Games is not to win, but to take part, just as the most important thing in life is not to conquer, but to struggle well." Hitler in his uniform, Goering in a flamboyant white outfit, Speer in an impeccable suit and Goebbels, with a wide grin, applauded these noble sentiments with glee.

———

In Seoul I visited a man who had won glory at Hitler's games, a bluff Korean called Sohn Kee Chung, gold medalist in the marathon. Sohn

---

*Hitler's games should, of course, never have been held at all, but the president of the IOC, a Belgian aristocrat in Coubertin's mold called Henri Baillet-Latour, insisted that Nazi politics were a domestic matter of no concern to the IOC. When the subject of the Nazi persecution of Jews was raised, the Belgian remarked that "the IOC does not go into such details." Baillet-Latour has been praised in *The New York Times* by George Plimpton as "one of the great heroes of Olympic history." Well, no doubt he is.

remembers Hitler as seeming "hard as a rock." His handshake "was like an iron fist and his eyes were very clear. He seemed to stare though me and seemed very powerful and strong." Those being the days of Japanese empire, Sohn ran as a subject of the Japanese emperor. When he received his gold medal, the Japanese national anthem was played. Sohn bowed his head. In respect? Or, as he now claims, in shame? Sohn, said a young Korean interpreter at the Seoul games, is not a sincere patriot. Perhaps that is why he was allowed to enter the Seoul stadium carrying the Olympic flame, but not to complete the final lap: Sohn may be a great Korean, but he had run for the Japanese.

Sohn struck me as a sad figure, perhaps the perfect example of a pure athlete manipulated by political forces beyond his control. And yet, in his apartment, cluttered with trophies, this hero of the Berlin Olympics still insisted, more than once, each time more vehemently, that without the Olympics we would have wars. But what about Hitler and World War II, I asked. "That," he answered, "was the fault of politicians."

The greatest promoter of Japanese marathon running before the war was an odd professor called Hibino Yutaka. In his photograph he looks like a stern moralist, dressed in a kimono, Japanese fan in the right hand, Homburg hat in the left. Like Coubertin, Hibino believed in sports as a national tonic. After the Olympic games in Paris in 1924, he traveled all over Europe demonstrating his own new concept of the marathon. Hibino also wrote a book, *Nippon Shindo Ron* (*The National Ideals of the Japanese People*), published in English in 1928, just as he was attending the Amsterdam Olympics. It is one long hysterical paean to the Japanese emperor, whose power is unique in the world, divine and always benevolent; only absolute obedience to his sacred power will lead to perfect harmony and peace. Hibino, as did many men in his time (and as do many Japanese and Koreans still today), saw the family of nations in terms of a permanent Darwinist struggle:

National success in this contest waits upon unity of purpose in the hearts of the people. If unity of purpose in the hearts of the people is strong and vigorous the nation may face a myriad of foes without anxiety. The subjects of our Empire have never been lacking in this respect. May this immemorial jewel of our national glory be ever exalted in unparalleled effulgence, a lasting wonder to the startled gaze of foreign peoples.

It would be interesting to know whether Coubertin ever met his fellow amateur from Japan, and what he would have made of his ideas. More to the point, however, is the similarity in tone between Hibino's writings and some of the sentiments expressed in South Korea today—particularly the bit about the startled gaze of the foreign peoples, but also the yearning for unity and national glory. This can be explained through Korea's painful past, always at the mercy of stronger powers, who are blamed to this day for dividing the country in two. But bitter feelings are often inflamed for political ends, by the government and by the opposition.

It was perhaps unfair to watch the opening ceremony in Seoul with Leni Riefenstahl's films and books by prewar chauvinists fresh in my mind. Yet, with all the banners bearing Coubertin's slogans, the uniformed athletes marching behind their national flags, the parades of folk dancers, the sacred flame, the thousands of children drilled to form gigantic flags and Olympic symbols, the chatter about Peace and Progress, one realized how profoundly old-fashioned South Korea (not to mention the North, of course) still is. This is one of the few countries that combines a capitalist economy with the militant patriotism and obsession with folk culture more often seen in communist states. And more than once I imagined Friedrich Jahn watching the proceedings in Seoul with great approval from his great stadium in the sky. Much heavy weather was made in the Korean press about the bad behavior of American athletes who would not march in line (the Soviets gave the Korean riot policemen, dressed in natty white for the occasion, no such trouble). I found myself applauding American rowdiness, just as I applauded the Japanese in their events when the entire Korean audience was baying for Japanese blood.

It might seem perverse to call South Korea old-fashioned when its image in the world press is that of a superdynamic steel-and-glass economic miracle. But this is not necessarily a contradiction. Industrialization, nation-building and "internationalization" formed the background in nineteenth-century Europe to world fairs and the Olympic ideal, but also to world wars and totalitarianism. South Korea is not on the warpath, nor is it totalitarian, but it is still struggling with democracy. One often hears in Seoul that a political miracle followed the economic one, and that the Seoul Olympics will make Korean progress even more miraculous. Well, perhaps. It depends on what one means by progress. Politics are not the result of miracles, and international rallies have nothing to do with democracy—or with peace.

The ideals of unity and patriotic harmony were not only, as is so often assumed, the natural aspirations of a people cast adrift by rapid industrialization. They were an integral part of political propaganda. Park Chung Hee, the father of Korea's economic miracle, enforced a military dictatorship in the name of harmony to achieve economic progress. Dissent was called unpatriotic. Dissenters, for their part, called the government unpatriotic for making deals with foreigners. Both sides claimed a monopoly on patriotism. The Seoul Olympics were used by Park's successors to lend legitimacy to yet another dictatorial regime. One of the major promoters was Roh Tae Woo, then a minister without portfolio, now president of the republic. Now that South Korea finally has achieved a more liberal political system in which politicians are taking over from military strongmen, the ritualized patriotism of the Olympic Games may be good for what Korean columnists, students and scholars call "the Korean identity," but not so good for the budding democracy.

The gradual opening up of Korean society is not helped by a process of nation-building that is not only anachronistic, but encourages xenophobia instead of openness. Nation-building can be good for sports—which explains, perhaps, why the U.S. is one of the few noncommunist nations to do well: it is in a constant state of nation-building. And the dynamism, optimism and faith in progress of South Koreans are exciting, even inspiring. South Korea indeed astonished the world by organizing the largest games ever, under great provocation from belligerent northern neighbors and some of its own students. That the games went off smoothly for the most part—some unpleasantness about drugs and boxing decisions aside—testifies to Korean efficiency and goodwill.

But the pressure on the Korean athletes was extraordinary. Not to win a gold was regarded virtually as a national disgrace. Several Korean winners of silver and bronze medals actually apologized for their failures. I watched the Koreans in action in several sports, among them women's volleyball. They played Japan. The stands were filled with rival tribes, preparing for war: Japanese tour groups waved their flags and banners, while Koreans stamped their feet and banged their drums, the men howling, the women ululating. Every Korean point put the entire Korean tribe into a frenzy. But when it became clear that the Japanese were going to win, the audience went very quiet, then began slinking out of the stadium, as though embarrassed to witness defeat.

Korean chauvinism was often hysterical, particularly when it involved Americans or Japanese. During the games, many ordinary Koreans went out of their way to be polite and helpful to foreign visitors, but there was a mean-spirited edge to comments in the Korean press. When the Japanese brought over for the first time since the end of the war an entire Kabuki theater troupe, the *Korea Herald* ran a headline saying COARSE KABUKI SHOW FAILS TO IMPRESS. The play, the story went on to say, "stirred up bitter memories of the Japanese samurai culture, or Japanese militarism . . . which clashes with Korea's time-nurtured consciousness of literati." I thought of the images I had seen in the papers of Korean athletes being drilled in boot camp, wearing full military gear, and screaming "Fight, fight, fight!"

There had been a disgraceful incident in the boxing ring. When the decision went against a Korean boxer, several people, including his coach and a security guard, jumped into the ring and beat up the hapless New Zealand referee. The Korean television cameras quickly averted their gaze, but NBC did not—rightly so: it was good TV. Why did the Korean security guard shed his blazer to indulge in some punching of his own? His honest answer was "The Korean man, he win, so I pissed off." The immediate reaction in Korea was to blame the referee. "He was bribed by the Americans to get at us Koreans," was one comment I heard. But things clearly had got out of hand, and the papers called the rowdy behavior a national disgrace. "Referee number ten, Korean men number ten," was the opinion of my taxi driver, who had a more balanced view of the matter than many.

But that was not the end of it. NBC was accused by, among others, members of the ruling Democratic Justice Party of being anti-Korean, even of insulting the "Korean identity." One wonders whether NBC's Bryant Gumbel even knows what the Korean identity is, let alone desires to insult it. But perhaps that was the problem: he should have been more informed about Koreans. I had lunch with a Korean government spokesman who did little else but talk about the crass attitudes of Americans. The American press, he said, had ignored the deep significance of the opening ceremony. They willfully refused to understand Korean culture. The Europeans, they were quite different. The Germans, especially: they understood the symbolic depth of the ceremony. Well, I thought, with an element of spite (I must confess here that the Dutch defeat of Germany during the European soccer championship made me as happy as a Korean watching the Japanese go down): they would, wouldn't they?

Some American commentators put the anti-American mood down to a clash of cultural values. Tony Kornheiser, for example, writing in *The Washington Post,* pointed out that Koreans were hurt because American journalists refused to obey the unspoken rule that they should look only at what Koreans chose to show them. If press censorship, self- or government-inflicted, is a cultural value, then let us help change the value or shut up about democracy in South Korea.

The rhetoric from the left, if one can call it that in Korea, was even more aggressive. When Carl Lewis appeared impatient with reporters on his arrival at the Seoul airport, the *Hangyoreh Shinmun* berated him the next day for his "shallow-hearted and haughty attitude," which

clearly betrays the twisted racism among American black people, looking down upon the Asian people more than the white people. . . . Champions from Africa, where he should find his "roots," say that "the black people are not free as long as Mandela is in prison." Carl Lewis is a degenerate American.

The tone of the article betrayed two things: the anxiety behind the swagger and the politics of this paper, which was set up by antigovernment activists as a result of more liberal press laws.

What is disturbing about South Korea is the way both government spokesmen and antigovernment radicals often sound like members of Action Française. Sometimes I felt that Charles Maurras, even more than the woolly Baron de Coubertin, would have felt at home in Seoul. This is not a matter of being for or against the Olympics. The radical students seducing the TV newsmakers with their daily demonstrations of firebomb-throwing are every bit as antidemocratic as the authoritarian generals who wanted the Olympics to give them face. They blame the division of their country on American imperialism. And they believe that America deliberately prevented North Korea from sharing the Olympics. The division of Korea is a political problem, which radicals think they can solve by violence, by prayer meetings, and by marching to the DMZ to meet the North Korean delegations to discuss peace and unification. Like Coubertin, they proclaim that, by cutting out politics and staging mass meetings, peace and brotherhood will naturally follow.

Perhaps the Korean belief in miracles *is* cultural. Korea is, after all, a nation of mass prayer meetings and new religions, the birthplace of the Reverend Moon, and a hospitable destination for the likes of Billy Graham. Russell Warren Howe, in his otherwise egregiously ill-written, misinformed book *The Koreans,* is probably right to call Korean culture shamanistic. Filipinos often seem to be waiting for a national messiah, but Koreans have a tendency to take a messianic view of the nation itself. One of the more amusing spectacles at the Seoul games was the peddlers of many different sects and creeds lying in ambush outside the main entrances of sports arenas. I shall restrict my quotations to only two of the many pamphlets pressed into my hands by beaming proselytizers. One was from one Presbyter Park Tae-sun, of the Sun Kyung (Fairland) Development R&S Institution:

> To All Mankind!—We proclaim that the Republic of Korea is the country where mankind was first created and civilization was cradled, and the parental country of all mankind. All mankind now participating in the '88 Olympic Games! We advise you to realize the fact that the Republic of Korea having about 5000 years [*sic*] long history, is your parental country.

The Kingdom Gospel Evangelical Association had this to say:

> The reason why the kingdom of God where our human body can live eternally comes true herein [*sic*] the Republic of Korea is that the Taegukki, Korean National Flag has the figure of glorious God, and the Republic of Korea has seen the Second Advent of Jesus Christ really coming to it. Now, all the world should recognize the fact that the republic of Korea is the right place where the heaven of eternal life shall be realized.

One suspects something wrong happened on the way to modern nationhood in Korea. An unfortunate synthesis must have occurred between West and East. The West, usually via Japan in the 1920s and 1930s, gave Korea half-baked German notions of Blood and Soil; it also exported, mostly from America, the equally half-baked notions of vulgar evangelism. Korea contributed an emotional legacy of historical bitterness and a propensity for shamanistic rites. These are precisely some of the ingredients that went into Independence Hall, and were encouraged by the Olympic games. No doubt the sense of victimhood, of being ignored or worse by other powers throughout history, has contributed to the modern zeal to gain recognition, to win gold medals, to beat the Japanese, and ultimately, who knows, even the Americans. The Koreans got twelve gold medals, an astonishing number, and for that they should be congratulated.

But as one casts one's eyes on the list of the most successful sporting nations—East Germany, Bulgaria, Romania, the Soviet Union—gold medals are not necessarily the marks of great national progress (of any kind), let alone of civilized and open societies. South Korea wants—no, craves—to be recognized as a great nation and a democracy. Less zealotry, less reliance on shamanistic incantations, and a greater willingness to let bygones be bygones would carry South Koreans a long way toward that goal. If that spells a little decadence, then so be it.

1988

THE LAST DAYS OF HONG KONG

Everything you need to know about a new life abroad. . . .
It's all in the pages of The Immigrant.

Advertisement for a new Hong Kong periodical, 1989

May 1983: it was exactly seven months after Mrs. Thatcher stumbled and fell on the steps of the Great Hall of the People in Beijing that I arrived in Hong Kong to take up a job. The prime-ministerial fall, which preceded a fierce quarrel with Deng Xiaoping about the future of the British colony, was regarded in Hong Kong as a dark omen: a few days later the stock market crashed and the Hong Kong dollar slumped to a point not seen since the riots of 1956.

As usual in Hong Kong, the market bounced back, some canny speculators made a killing, and corporate towers of silver- and gold-tinted glass sprouted up in a Babylonian frenzy that lasted until the end of the decade. Still, I thought, as I arrived on that hot spring morning, this place must be feeling jittery, not to say fragile, not to say terrified of the likely prospect of being handed over to a communist regime. It was still only a prospect, to be sure, for the deal was yet to be concluded, but Deng had made no bones about Beijing's firm intention to take back what it saw as rightfully its own.

On the afternoon of that same day, I was taken by an old friend to a barbecue party attended by a group of what the white people call "expats" and the Cantonese call *gweilos,* or devil men—a collection of nice, suntanned young Aussies, Brits, an American or two and the odd Chinese girlfriend for local color. The talk was of parties, boat trips, restaurants and absent friends. Partly out of boredom but also out of genuine interest, I asked my new acquaintances how worried people in Hong Kong were about the not too distant future. There was a moment of rather awkward silence, as though I had asked the wrong thing. Then I realized it was simply the result of a misunderstanding.

"Worried?" asked an Australian PR man in Bermuda shorts. "Us worried? 'Course not. Lots of opportunity here. Why, Bob, he's opening a new hairdressing salon. And Kevin is doing great in advertising, and Ann's just got a huge pay rise at the bank. No, no worries, mate. Every day I wake up, I'm glad to be in Hong Kong, and the moment that ends I'll move somewhere else."

It was a valuable lesson in Hong Kong anthropology: it had not occurred to my PR friend that I might be referring to 6 million Chinese and not to our cozy bunch of expatriates. It was also clear that people were not in the habit of measuring time much beyond the immediate here and now, that you avoided thinking of the future (or, for that matter, the past) until, well, until you moved somewhere else.

I found this extraordinary insouciance both refreshing and perplexing. It came in different forms: "Give Hong Kong back to China? Oh, no, dear boy. That will never happen. You see, it's simply not in China's interest to take Hong Kong back. Too much money to be made." This was said to me by a charming old hand who had lived in "Honkers" for almost thirty years. We were having lunch at the Hong Kong Foreign Correspondents' Club, where there was no dearth of such old hands to sort out the ignorant newcomer on the Chinese mentality, not to mention China's interest. Such experts were always ready to explain that the Chinese are by nature indifferent to politics. Making money is all they really care about. And the Hong Kong Chinese, they're a clever lot. No need to worry about them. They'll manage to make some kind of deal. Anyway, it's in China's interest to let them be.

Perhaps I am being unfair. How were these people to know that only one year later, on September 26, 1984, a declaration was signed in Beijing by representatives of the Chinese and British governments that formally sealed Hong Kong's fate? The formula was one country, two systems: Hong Kong was to be a Special Autonomous Region under Chinese sovereignty, allowed for fifty years to retain its own legislation, judiciary and socioeconomic system. There was no mention of a bill of rights, and freedom of speech would not extend to criticism of the Chinese government.

But even then the propensity for wishful thinking was extraordinary. On the day of the announcement, the British editor of the *Far Eastern Economic Review,* the most authoritative local newsweekly, wore a Union Jack T-shirt and arrived at his office to celebrate the good news with a bottle of champagne. He wrote an editorial firmly in support of the agreement, and put the "dark voices prophesying doom" sternly in their places. Hong Kong, he said, would help put "China back on to its traditional search for peace, stability and prosperity—the Confucian Golden Mean . . ."

Perhaps he was not to know that Hong Kong was the victim of a cruel confidence trick often termed a "conspiracy of euphoria." Everything would stay the same. Lots of money to be made. Stability and prosperity. Democracy with a fully elected legislature. (Just how it was to be elected was never made clear.) The Confucian Golden Mean. All this, and more, was promised by officials from London and Beijing who kept on grinning fiercely in the hope that this would keep the locals quiet.

But things didn't stay the same. Hong Kong is hardly stable, though still relatively prosperous. Hong Kong is run by a British governor appointed by Her Majesty's government, who presides over a legislative council, none of whose members are directly elected. Democracy never materialized, and probably never will. Instead we have had a succession of grotesque financial scandals; a string of broken banks that had to be bailed out; a calamitous collapse of the Hong Kong dollar, which had to be pegged hastily to the U.S. currency; a serious shortage of labor; forced repatriation of Vietnamese refugees; a judiciary compromised by corruption—and, on top of all that, the Beijing massacre. And still the incantations ring daily in our ears, albeit with an increasing tone of desperation: it is not in Beijing's interest to change Hong Kong; everything will be all right; democracy will come, though perhaps at a slower pace; stability and prosperity; etc., etc.

Fifty thousand Hong Kong people a year know better. They are already boarding the planes, bound for Sydney, Vancouver, Singapore, New York. They have seen the future and they are moving somewhere else.

—

Opinions on the decor were as mixed as the drinks at last week's opening party for Hong Kong's newest nightclub. "Sort of 50s," offered one reveller, "but with a bit of '60s and '90s as well," she concluded.

South China Morning Post, January 1990

The first time I visited Hong Kong, in 1974, you could still see vestiges of the old colonial city. Portly Indians played cricket with British bankers and civil servants in the middle of the Central District, between the Hong Kong Club and the Supreme Court building. The highest buildings in Central were the Bank of China and the Hilton Hotel. The waterfront was a collection of ramshackle warehouses still redolent of opium dens and mysterious Oriental skulduggery. I remember walking up Queen's Road Central and striking up a conversation with two beautifully dressed Asian girls who emerged from an expensive jewelry store. They spoke in exquisite French. They had come from Saigon on a shopping trip.

I have no idea where those girls are now, but I know that the Hong Kong Club, a charming Victorian building resembling a square Wedgwood bowl, is gone, the cricket ground is gone, the Bank of China stands in the shadow of a brand-new I. M. Pei building, and the Hilton Hotel is so dwarfed by new skyscrapers that you hardly notice it anymore. The physical change in Hong Kong has been so devastatingly fast that if you put two pictures side by side, one from 1974 and one from 1990, you would hardly believe they were of the same city. It is as if midtown Manhattan had been built in the last ten years, with nothing left to remind you of the 1950s, let alone the nineteenth century. Hong Kong looks like a city without a past.

"Cities," wrote Lewis Mumford, "are a product of time."

They are the molds in which men's lifetimes have cooled and congealed, giving lasting shape, by way of art, to moments that

would otherwise vanish with the living and leave no means of re-
newal or wider participation behind them. . . . By the diversity of
its time-structures, the city in part escapes the tyranny of a single
present, and the monotony of a future that consists in repeating
only a single beat heard in the past.

Mumford's convictions would have been shaken by Hong Kong, for
little is left behind in this city of immigrants, so many of whom ended
up moving somewhere else. There are hardly any museums in Hong
Kong, precious few libraries, no great historical buildings, and no monuments to speak of. Well, perhaps there are two. One is the terrace of
the Repulse Bay Hotel, rebuilt after the original hotel was pulled down
some years ago. The other is a well-known tourist trap called the Tiger
Balm Garden. This extraordinary piece of moralizing kitsch—plaster
models of Chinese deities, folk heroes, wild animals, and torture scenes
in a Buddhist hell—is a monument left behind by a rich Chinese businessman named Aw Boon Haw, the inventor of, among other things,
Headache Cure Powder, Chinkawite Wince Mixture and, of course,
Tiger Balm. Aw Boon Haw was born in Rangoon and died in Honolulu. His theme-park fantasy of Chinese folk culture is a monument
to the enterprise of an overseas Chinese, a permanent drifter, the emi-
grant who made good.

There is, perhaps, another reason for the jangled sense of time in
Hong Kong, the lack of any feeling of continuity besides the hurried
mentality of the immigrant on the make, and that has to do with a more
ancient Chinese approach to cities. The Chinese were never in the
habit of building cities as monuments. There is no Chinese Rome, or
London or Paris, a repository of centuries of civilization, to be handed
on and added to from one generation to the next, cherished as a precious heirloom, meant to last forever. Mao Zedong may have been one
of the great vandals of all time, but long before the Chairman was born,
travelers in China remarked upon the nonchalance with which Chinese let the vestiges of the past rot away. Instead of preserving the old,
people would rebuild in the same style. Hence a pagoda erected during
the Tang Dynasty, but entirely rebuilt in, say, 1912, would still be regarded as ancient, for it is not so much the age of the bricks as the style
or even the site that counts.

It is also true that Chinese connoisseurs tended to make a fetish of the ancient, which explains why China has the oldest industry in fake antiques in the world. But fake, to a Western ear, has a pejorative sound not entirely appropriate to the common Chinese view that a good imitation can be admired in its own right.

Instead of eternal cities, China had eternally shifting cities. With a new dynasty often came a new capital, whose layout was based on geomancy and other signs of auspiciousness. These seats of administrative power sometimes lasted about as long as the dynasties that built them were blessed with heaven's mandate. Thus once great cities—Changan, Kaifeng, Hangzhou—are now provincial towns, with only a few monuments, frequently rebuilt through the ages, as reminders of past glory.

Most Chinese capitals were in the north or center of China, in the heartland of Chinese civilization. None was ever in the deep south, long considered a swampy region filled with ghosts and other undesirables. Trade is what made the southern coastal cities tick, not bureaucratic power. But commerce and cosmopolitanism were not highly valued by Chinese governments: on the contrary, merchants were strictly controlled, and contacts with outsiders were limited, if not forbidden. Mandarins, in the name of the Son of Heaven, ruled China, and they kept the businessmen firmly under their long-nailed thumbs. In its entire history, China had truly cosmopolitan cities only twice: between the eighth and thirteenth centuries, during the Tang and Song Dynasties, and again from the latter years of imperial China to the beginning of what is still called, without irony intended, Liberation.

Changan, the capital during the Tang Dynasty, was a center of trade with central Asia. Official control was relaxed, and business was good. Then, in the fourteenth and fifteenth centuries, the imperial government put the lid back on. As William Skinner observed in *The City in Late Imperial China,* the impact was especially severe on the southeastern coast, which is precisely where foreigners arrived in the nineteenth century to prize China open again. They were led in this enterprise by the English and Scottish opium pushers, who settled in a rocky little pirates' lair called Hong Kong. Once more, Chinese merchants, stifled and disdained for centuries by the supercilious mandarins, were able to escape their official leash and, protected more or less by foreign laws, were free to make money in Amoy, Fuzhou, Tianjin, Shanghai and, of course, Hong Kong. It wasn't long before Shanghai became the most cosmopolitan city in Chinese history.

Some Chinese were very rich as a result, many were better off than before, and many remained miserably poor. The pursuit of wealth and happiness led to the usual things—well-organized crime, well-stocked brothels and well-greased palms—but also to the richest cultural life the Chinese had seen for centuries and, despite wars, famines and terrorism, the freest marketplace for ideas Chinese had ever known. One of these ideas was Marxism.

Naturally, when a new breed of Chinese mandarins took upon themselves heaven's mandate in 1949, all this had to go—except the Marxism, of course. Destruction is easier than one sometimes thinks. Whenever I enter the battleship-gray headquarters of the Hong Kong & Shanghai Bank to cash a check, and watch in wonder the silent efficiency of this modern capitalist beehive, Hong Kong appears, for a moment, indestructible. But in Shanghai, once the government put its mind to it in 1952, it took exactly two months to turn the great metropolis into what one observer described as a dead city. (Pol Pot worked even faster, but then Phnom Penh is not Shanghai.) Businessmen were systematically humiliated, persecuted and above all squeezed of their assets, which, according to the correct line of the day, they had "stolen from the people." One of the many curiosities of China after Mao is that you can still hear, in remote villages of the poor northwest, traces of the Shanghai dialect, spoken by the children and grandchildren of businessmen booted out of their city thirty-eight years ago.

Hong Kong might not be treated in quite the same way. But when people speak blithely of China's interest, they do well to remind themselves that China plucked its interest from a thriving business city before, by plunder. It is also useful to remember that however well-meaning or, to use a favorite word in this part of the world, sincere China's mandarins may be, and however much they speak of Open Doors and Reforms, their understanding of commercial enterprise is more akin to that of the imperial mandarins than to the views of Milton Friedman, or even John Kenneth Galbraith. The traditional instinct is not to let the flowers of business bloom by encouraging the free pursuit of riches, but to control and to squeeze. Many Hong Kong businessmen are already paying their dues by donating vast sums to the motherland to curry favor with officialdom. The more they pay, the more will be demanded, for this only confirms to the mandarin mind that business is there to be fleeced.

Hong Kong and Shanghai are the products of peculiar historical events over which a feeble, decadent, insular China had little control, and the humiliation of being forced by foreigners to concede extraterritorial rights on Chinese soil is still keenly felt in Beijing. When Mrs. Thatcher, still flushed with her victories over the "Argies," stumbled into Beijing in 1982 to convince Deng of the validity of the nineteenth-century treaties, Deng answered with expletives that were, I believe, deleted from the record but would have made even the Iron Lady blush. Hong Kong was promised autonomy nonetheless, which sounded very well on paper, but before reaching for their bottles of champagne, people might have paused to contemplate the fact that virtually throughout their history the rulers of China did everything in their power to deny their cities precisely what Hong Kong has been promised.

The freebooting, vice-ridden, cosmopolitan, mercenary, wonderful urban bitch goddesses—Berlin, New York, Shanghai, Hong Kong—are never much liked by those who live in the hinterlands, but the hatred, awe and envy inspired by Hong Kong are often extreme. Intellectuals in Beijing usually express a disdain for its empty materialism, its lack of culture and the rough-and-ready manners of its mainly Cantonese inhabitants. To most ordinary Chinese, Hong Kong is a wealthy Xanadu, so far away it hardly seems real. To millions of Southern Chinese it is the place they would rush to, if only they could. And, if they are lucky enough to live close by, they watch Hong Kong television and ask their friends and relatives who have made it to Xanadu for money, electronic gadgets, anything they can carry. To provincial communist cadres, Hong Kong is a place for freebies. You see them walking about in groups, in their badly cut suits and pudding-bowl haircuts, gawking with open mouths at the shops, the buildings, the restaurants, hoping perhaps that one day all this will be theirs. To the mandarins in Beijing, often men from China's poor interior, Hong Kong represents everything they loathe: it is southern, urban, subversive, wicked, rich, relatively free and, above all, full of foreigners and their polluting foreign ways.

Of course it would be in Beijing's interest to keep its hands off Hong Kong. But if the men who rule China today were to follow their instincts, they would stamp on the bitch goddess after having picked the last meat off her carcass. Few tears would be shed over Hong Kong's demise, for it was never a Chinese heirloom to be cherished, but rather a monument to a past that still hurts. Why then, you might well ask, hasn't China pounced before? What has kept the mandarins so long from booting the Brits out and grabbing what is theirs?

There is a possible answer to this, which sounds paradoxical, but isn't. The reason for Deng's decision to take back Hong Kong was, I believe, the result of his Open Door policy. Mao never wanted Hong Kong back, for the colonial city was hidden from sight, a Chinatown that was in China but not of it. The vice, the subversion, the spiritual pollution never penetrated China enough to be a threat. This began only once China's door was ajar, and Deng realized that the only way to impose control was to turn Chinatown back into a Chinese town, subservient once again to the mandarins in Beijing. Yes, he wants Hong Kong to make money, but he also wants to suppress some of the very ideas and institutions that produce the wealth: Deng's dilemma in a nutshell.

Alas—and after thousands of years of subservience, who can blame them?—most Chinese need little encouragement to fall into line with officialdom, particularly when the spirit of patriotism is invoked. And, with the unfailing accuracy of an experienced acupuncturist, Beijing has time and again managed to prick the one raw nerve in this hardbitten community of refugees and their offspring: patriotism—the need for a shared sense of the past, the need to feel Chinese.

—

Chinese authorities yesterday claimed that Mr Lee Cheukyan, the Hongkong pro-democracy lobbyist who was detained in Beijing, had confessed to supporting 'counter-revolutionary organizations'. Mr Lee, a senior official in the Christian Industrial Committee, was allowed to return to Hongkong on Thursday after he was 'educated' by police in the mainland capital, Radio Beijing said.

South China Morning Post, June 1989

There are few more melancholy sights than Martin Lee, QC, standing on a platform in the rain, manfully singing "We Shall Overcome" with a crowd of 300 fellow crusaders for democracy in Hong Kong. His cause is just, his criticisms of London and Beijing are unfailingly correct, his methods are always peaceful and polite, which makes it all the sadder that he appears to be fighting for a lost cause. Hong Kong was promised direct elections by various representatives of the British government, who were, however, always carefully vague about the practicalities; Beijing doesn't want direct elections to take place, or only to such a limited degree that they will be virtually meaningless. According to the 1990 Basic Law, less than half the legislature will be directly elected by as late as 1999. Although Beijing has made it clear that the Basic Law can no longer be changed, London still promises that something might be worked out. The people of Hong Kong, who have seen too many promises made and broken, maintain a sullen silence.

Martin Lee is not a professional politician: he is a highly successful barrister. And he showed little interest in politics until six years ago, when he realized that without elections Hong Kong would be bereft of an accountable local government, without which the future so-called Special Autonomous Region would have no protection against the whims of Beijing's mandarins. He is, of course, absolutely right. And if you ask many Chinese in Hong Kong, they agree that he is right. Indeed, he is a very popular and much respected figure. And yet, there he is, with the long-suffering face of a sensitive camel, bravely singing songs to no more than a few hundred people.

The reasons for his failure are complex, but they are mostly to do with fear and a crippling sense of futility. The problem is not that the Chinese people are by their nature uninterested in politics. That is a self-serving myth propagated by mandarins in Beijing, in London and, indeed, in Hong Kong itself. But the myth has been sustained for so long in Hong Kong that it has become self-fulfilling; and it also accounts for an astonishing political naïveté, as well as a deep suspicion of politics among the worthies who still help to run Hong Kong today.

One of these worthies is the glamorous Dame Lydia Dunn, director of Swire's, one of the oldest British trading houses, appointed member of the Legislative Council, campaigner for the right of Hong Kong people to live in Britain, wife of the former attorney general, winer and

diner of every titled and famous face in town. She is, despite her anglicized name, completely Chinese, although one can hardly tell from her
almost faultless Knightsbridge drawl. Perhaps to remind people of her
Chineseness, she likes her official photographs to have Chinese screens
in the background. She is, in short, a typical product of Empire, an honorary native member of the colonial club.★

Dame Lydia, like her fellow worthies, native or British, never believed in democracy for Hong Kong, but, again like many others, she
was so shocked by the massacre in Beijing that now she at least pays lip
service to the necessity for some democratic reforms. Her shock was in
itself the result of naïveté, for, she admits, she had had no doubt that
China was on the right track and that Hong Kong's future was assured.
What, then, I asked her, about this democracy business?

"Well," she purred, "you see, the problem with the Chinese people is
that they are simply too individualistic for a democracy. They have no
discipline, which is really most awkward if you have to work for the
common good. The Japanese, of course, are quite, quite different. They
are a disciplined race, and so they can have a democracy."

I was too baffled to argue with her. But I should not have been surprised by this complete incomprehension of democratic principles, for,
when it comes to politics, the tycoons and civil servants of capitalist
Hong Kong are really not so different from the mandarins in communist Beijing. Thus, in Gerd Balke's fascinating little book of interviews,
Hongkong Voices, we hear Simon Li Fuk-sean, former High Court judge
and drafter of Hong Kong's Basic Law, expound the following theory:
"As a society the people in Hongkong are politically immature. By not
having universal suffrage we keep out a lot of people who make absolutely no contribution to society in Hongkong, are totally ignorant of
any form of government, and are exploited by unscrupulous politicians." Instead, says Li, only professional people with "interests to protect" should be elected by their peers to run Hong Kong, for "they, and
not the parasites, deserve representation."

For years the likes of Dame Lydia and Simon Li, as well as such local
tycoons as Y. K. Pao, who made his fortune in shipping, or newspaper

---

★When honored with the title of Dame, she chose to name herself Baroness of Knightsbridge.

editors like Louis Cha, have warned Hong Kong people not to rock the boat, not to push for "divisive" politics, which would only upset Beijing. After all, wrote Louis Cha in an editorial in *Ming Pao* on June 1989, the communists "are Chinese. There are good Chinese and bad Chinese, but most Chinese are good." And, as Clive James described so well in *Flying Visits,* whenever there was a good party in China for a visiting British worthy, there was Y. K. Pao ("Powie"), grinning and hand-wringing like an oily comprador. No wonder such people have been so easy to intimidate. Louis Cha said it all in one sorrowful and all too typical sentence: "We felt we were doing our best to serve the country."

The worthies are still doing their best. When, some months ago, the Hong Kong Arts Center wanted to screen a documentary film about China, footage of the Beijing massacre was censored, because, as a local official put it, "we have to pay attention to the shifting political sensitivities of the Chinese government." One of the main galleries in the Arts Center has been named after Y. K. Pao. His son-in-law, an Austrian worthy called Helmut Sohmen, is chairman of the board.

No wonder, with an establishment like that, that Martin Lee has a hard time, and that few people in Hong Kong wish to stick their necks out when the tycoons and mandarins refuse to stick out theirs. Far wiser, if you have the chance, to take to the planes and move elsewhere.

———

We are Chinese by race. We love our country with Chinese blood flowing in our bodies. But we don't like the communist system.

Martin Lee, Hong Kong, February 1990

In the past Hongkong people thought that they were colonial citizens. But after the signing of the Sino-British Joint Declaration, we knew that Hongkong would go back to China after 1997 and that Britain would not take care of us any more.

Letter to the *South China Morning Post,* February 1990

Martin Lee faces another, perhaps more intractable, obstacle than the cowardice, connivance and bullying of mandarins: the perennial question of many immigrant communities, especially the overseas Chinese:

Where do they feel they belong? It is an important question, for there never was enough identification with the colonial Chinatown, ruled by benevolent British patriarchs, to stimulate the majority of people to engage in politics. This suited the patriarchs in the past, but it suited their subjects as well, for they were pleased enough to have escaped from political mobilization back home. As long as they were left alone, they were content to let the British mandarins govern. The recent half-hearted talk about democracy from the patriarchs themselves—who feel they must give their Chinese subjects some hope, even if only on paper, now that the British are gearing up to leave—must sound decidedly hollow to the Hong Kong Chinese and devious to the Beijing mandarins, who had counted on a neat transfer of power from one authoritarian government to another. That is what they meant, after all, by Hong Kong's staying the same.

To develop a political identity, people must feel a sense of continuity, of a shared past, but also more importantly, of a shared future for which they can be responsible, as citizens, not subjects. This is precisely what is missing in Hong Kong. For once, Dame Lydia hit it right on the button: "Apart from lunatics, condemned prisoners and small children, Hong Kong people must be the only people in the world who seem to have no right to decide their own fate." Political deals are negotiated over their heads, and their more critical representatives are dismissed and sometimes insulted in London and Beijing—Martin Lee's protest activities have been branded as "counterrevolutionary," and he claims to have been told in Beijing that, even if he were elected after 1997, he would not be allowed to be part of any government.

So who in this colony (tactfully called "territory" in the local press) do the Chinese residents think they are? Where do their loyalties lie? Ethnically and culturally, there is no question that they feel Chinese, sometimes defensively, sometimes aggressively so. The Chineseness of the overseas Chinese found its most popular expression in the kung fu movies featuring Bruce Lee, a native of San Francisco, who rose to stardom in Hong Kong. In one of his early films, entitled *Fists of Fury*, ethnic pride is the main theme of the story, set in Shanghai in the early 1930s.

Lee plays a member of a kung fu school whose master is murdered by a gang of evil Japanese, who add insult to injury by stamping on the master's picture and offering a calligraphy which reads "The sick people of Asia." In the rest of the film, Lee redresses the insult by showing the evil Japanese what's what—and not just the Japanese but also the white people, in the form of an odious Russian, whom the Chinese hero, his magnificent torso bared to the waist, hacks and kicks and pummels so convincingly that there can be no question left in anyone's mind about the superiority of Chinese manhood.

The usual racial slights are rather crudely rehearsed, including the infamous sign outside the Shanghai park: "Chinese and dogs not allowed." When Lee's entrance is barred by the most grotesque-looking Indian the casting director could find, he demolishes the sign with a high kick and, while he is at it, demolishes a bunch of Japanese in kimonos too. The most evil character of all is, however, neither Japanese nor Caucasian but a Chinese collaborator called Wu, whose toadying to the wicked Japanese comes to a symbolic climax when he is forced at a geisha party to "walk like a Chinese"—that is, on all fours, doggy-style. Naturally, Lee knows how to deal with Wu: he beats him to death and hangs him from a lamppost.

Once in a while racial defensiveness breaks into racist aggression, not only in fantasy but in fact. The hostility toward the Vietnamese refugees, huddled in their ghastly prison camps in Hong Kong, is a case in point. To be sure, their arrival in large numbers poses a problem for a small, congested place like Hong Kong, but to hear Cantonese schoolchildren protest in front of TV cameras against sending Vietnamese refugee children to local schools because "they stink," and to hear civic leaders virtually begging the British to send the refugees back to Vietnam, is to fast lose one's sympathy for the plight of the Hong Kong Chinese themselves. And to observe, as I did recently, Cantonese accusing the Vietnamese of being "noisy" is to enter the realm of absurdity, for whatever the Cantonese virtues may be, silence is not one of them.

To be Chinese, then, is not the same as to be a citizen of China, but the relationship with the motherland is complicated, vague and wide open to political manipulation. "China," wrote a Chinese-American in a Hong Kong magazine, "is a cultural entity which flows incessantly, like the Yellow River, from its source all the way to the present time, and from there to the boundless future. This is the basic and unshakeable belief in the mind of every Chinese. It is also the strongest basis for Chinese nationalism. No matter what government is in power, people will not reject China, for there is always hope for a better future a hundred or more years from now."

China, in other words, is both real and utopian. To engage in politics in Hong Kong, indeed in all overseas Chinese communities, almost always means politics in China. The average Chinese restaurant owner in San Francisco or Vancouver may not have been interested in American or Canadian politics ("as long as he was able to make money"), but when it concerned the struggle between the nationalists and the communists he became passionately interested, for it involved the future of China. When that future is at stake, the ethnic, cultural and political merge in a sometimes combustible mix.

That moment arrived in the spring of 1989, when the students in Beijing occupied the heart of the Chinese empire. It was a sign for the Hong Kong people to show that they were more than rough-and-ready Cantonese traders; that they, too, cared for the motherland; that they, too, were Chinese to the core. It was in many ways Hong Kong's finest hour: people supposed to be greedy money-grubbers donated millions of dollars to the Beijing students; people supposed to be indifferent to politics took to the streets. At one rally attended by rock stars, TV comedians, professionals, workers, indeed *le tout* Hong Kong, almost a million turned up—one out of every six persons in the colony. Martin Lee, who spoke at last to a mass audience, must have hoped his hour had finally come. It was as if every person in Hong Kong had a glint in his or her eye—a glint of hope, of joy, of patriotism. But then the tanks of the People's Army rolled, and soon the whole thing collapsed.

But not before a moving and dignified demonstration of grief swept over Hong Kong, which for several weeks was draped in black (the Western color for mourning, incidentally—the Chinese traditionally wear white at funerals). Even the procommunist press expressed its solidarity with the students and its disgust with the massacre. Every taxi in town flew a black ribbon; the New China News Agency, the unofficial Chinese embassy in Hong Kong, was surrounded by mountains of wreaths and banners decrying the "butchers of Beijing"; slogans in the streets compared Beijing 1989 to Nanking 1937. "Chinese must never kill Chinese" was another popular phrase (as though non-Chinese were more legitimate victims). There was even a banner hanging from the almost completed Bank of China building, decrying the butchery, and its architect, I. M. Pei, vowed not to engage in any more projects for the motherland.

Grief was followed by confusion. To be Chinese was no longer a simple matter. This was neatly demonstrated in June when the British foreign secretary, Sir Geoffrey Howe, turned up in a maladroit attempt to calm things down. He was greeted by a kind of battle of songs. On one side of town, in Victoria Park, where a hideous old bust of the queen-empress has found its last resting place, protesters gathered to demand the "right of abode" in Britain, as the country of refuge. They played a tape of Dame Vera Lynn's "Land of Hope and Glory" and made speeches, often in English, about Hong Kong people not wishing to be second-class citizens, and displayed banners that said "Shame on you, England!" and "Howe can you sleep at night?" Dame Lydia Dunn flew to London to plead Hong Kong's cause. Newspaper ads appeared in the English-language press, pointing out that "There is no point in being almost British." The full-page ad was accompanied by a photo-graph of a Chinese boy in a British school uniform. The text deserves full quotation:

> The coins in his pocket bear the impression of the Queen. On Saturdays he plays football. His school flies the British flag. He doesn't think about freedom because he takes it for granted. He was raised in the British tradition in a British colony. He is one of the millions of people for whom Hongkong is home. And who want to continue living here. All they want is some form of insur-ance. And the only form of insurance that will mean anything to them is the right of abode in Britain. Otherwise, being almost British is like being homeless.

But another ad, asking for the same thing, made the point of emphasiz-ing that "we wish to stay in Hongkong, as it is our home, and we are proud to be Chinese."

The demand for insurance was understandable, even right; but why the stuff about the queen on the boy's coins, why the reference to foot-ball, and what did pride in being Chinese have to do with anything? A conversation with Dame Lydia, or any of her peers, titled or not, tells one why. Those who understand the irony of playing Dame Vera's song—and not many in Hong Kong do—are trapped between colonial dependence and old-fashioned Chinese patriotism.

There was, however, another set of songs being sung in Hong Kong that week. Members of the Hong Kong Federation of Students gathered in one of the busiest shopping areas of Hong Kong island and sang the Chinese national anthem. They handed out leaflets in Chinese saying that the right of abode in Britain would benefit only a small, rich elite, that it was humiliating to ask for help from the colonial masters, and that the duty of the masses was to stay in Hong Kong to struggle for a democratic China. "China and Hongkong are one family," read the headline of their pamphlet, "and helping the motherland is the way to help Hongkong."

Near the turnstiles of the ferryboat to Kowloon, a group of young people had set up a booth, representing a kind of mini-Tiananmen Square: the Internationale blasted from a loudspeaker, lurid cartoons of the blood-soaked Chinese leaders were displayed, and recorded speeches by the Beijing students were endlessly repeated. And in another ad, placed in a Chinese-language newspaper, a hundred showbusiness personalities renounced their right of abode in Britain, for "We Stand Upright and We Don't Beg."

And what, while Dame Lydia was begging the British for the right of abode, did her fellow worthies at the top of the Hong Kong heap say? Well, they didn't all say the same thing, of course, but the predominant message was twofold: not to rock the boat any further in China, and to kick the Vietnamese boat people out as quickly as possible. The replica of the Statue of Liberty, or rather the Hong Kong replica of the replica that was crushed in Beijing, had to be removed from Victoria Park, for, as one prominent Hong Kong businessman, Vincent Lo Hong-sui, said, "China will become skeptical about the people in Hong Kong if they continue to organize what Beijing has already criticized as counterrevolutionary activities."

What we saw, then, was a fine irony: those least emotionally involved with China were most inclined to appease the Chinese leadership, while the young patriots wanted to fight on. They, and Martin Lee, are still the only ones fighting—albeit for slightly different aims, since Lee confines his ambitions to a directly elected government for Hong Kong. Even as I write, in February 1990, 3,000 students are marching to the New China News Agency to protest against the inadequate Basic

Law, whose final draft was recently imposed by the Chinese on a joint drafting committee, causing one of the Hong Kong representatives to return home in tears. On the eve of the lunar New Year, in February, I visited a "democracy booth" set up by the young patriots, to find out more about their views on democracy. I didn't find out much, but bought a coffee cup engraved with the spirited, though not especially democratic, slogan, "I am Chinese. One country. One heart."

And the British? They have done their best to appease the spokesmen of local bigotry and have forced the first group of Vietnamese to return to the country from which they risked their lives to escape. And they have appeased the worthies by offering the worthiest—50,000 of them, to be exact—the right of abode in Britain. This has already unleashed the British variety of bigotry, in the shape of right-wing Tories led by Norman Tebbit, who has vowed to fight against the admission of even one Chinaman from Hong Kong to the green and pleasant isle—an attitude shared, alas, by the Labour opposition, worried about losing working-class voters.

So far there has been surprisingly little overt hostility in Hong Kong toward Britain. There is a general but vague feeling of having been let down, certainly, but little outrage—a sign, perhaps, of the lack of emotional involvement with that country. Whatever most Hong Kong Chinese might feel they are, they don't feel British—always excepting, of course, that small number of worthies, who appear, ad nauseam, in the social pages of the *Hong Kong Tatler.*

Perhaps to feel truly outraged at Britain, it helps to be British, for the most outraged criticism of the British government for not doing the right thing by its colonial subjects has come, by and large, from the British themselves, and particularly from those Englishmen who feel most outraged by the likes of Norman Tebbit. These tend to be patrician in background and inclination. It is no coincidence, for example, that the magazine which has done more than any other British publication to voice concern over the shabby treatment of Hong Kong is the *Spectator.* And the most trenchant, not to say outraged, critique of British government policy was written by William Shawcross, a gentleman of impeccable patrician credentials who has done more than any other writer to concentrate our fickle attention on the suffering of refugees.

Everything Shawcross says in his polemic *Kowtow!* is correct. Yes, "Circumspection, prudence, kowtowing, have been the watchwords of our behaviour." Yes, "We have been afraid of [China's] force, not confident of our strength." All this is perfectly true; but how much strength does the old lion still have? And how much of this strength is it still willing to use for the sake of a lot of foreigners reputed to eat monkey brains? Is there not a hint of outrage in these polemics at the fact that Britain is no longer a great power that can set right the world's wrongs?

George Hicks, an Australian observer of the Hong Kong scene, has argued in a collection of articles, *Hongkong Countdown,* that by formally committing the British to govern Hong Kong until 1997, Beijing has London over the barrel. For to ensure a smooth transfer of power, with a minimum loss of face in both decaying imperial capitals, London doesn't feel it can do much to thwart the wishes of China's mandarins. Nonetheless, this shouldn't let Britain off the hook, and the patricians are surely right that history can still make demands on the present, and Britain, even though it is now a somewhat seedy power of the second rank, is morally obliged to feel responsible for the fate of 6 million people being handed over to a harsh regime. For better or for worse, however, the estimable William Shawcross and the noble *Spectator* are less representative of the New Britain than is Norman Tebbit, who hates patricians, doesn't care much for foreigners and, to use his kind of language, doesn't give a toss for the legacy of Empire.

—

The Police Commissioner, Mr Li Kwan-ha, yesterday expressed concern at the marked increase in violent crime in Hongkong, which he said was caused by uncertainty about the future among young people.

South China Morning Post, January 1990

—

Vietnamese boat people are being forced to draw lots to decide who will attempt suicide in a bizarre plan aimed at winning international sympathy, it was alleged yesterday.

South China Morning Post, February 1990

—

The Twenties' atmosphere of the Champagne Bar lured those who could physically manage yet more champers, and those with real stamina stuck it out until way after midnight—now that's an opening!

Hong Kong Tatler, February 1990

"Hong Kong," exclaimed an Italian China hand, "feels like Shanghai in the twenties!" My friend is fond of exclamations, it is true, but one sees what he means. There is a whiff of *The Last Emperor* about the slim young Chinese boys, dressed to the nines in retro styles, their hair slicked back like wet black silk, languidly sipping champagne in the neo–art deco hotels that are at the height of fashion. There is something distinctly devil-may-care about the Priscilla Chois, the Rawley Chaos, Pansy Hos and the Dickson Poons dancing the nights away at their Venetian masquerades, their fifties parties and their Marie Antoinette balls, while the young Brits from the banks and trading houses have fun ruining their dinner jackets in custard-pie fights. There they all are, you might think, tuning their fiddles in anticipation of the great conflagration.

And yet decadent is not the right way to describe late-imperial Hong Kong, for decadence suggests a bored dissipation of wealth acquired over the ages, indeed the squandering of heirlooms. Hong Kong really lacks the cultural richness for true decadence. And the squanderers are too busy making more money to throw away. In fact there is a raw, not to say vulgar, vitality in the way the gilded youth enjoys its excess; not so much divine decadence as nouveau riche flashiness. There is something Gatsbyish about Hong Kong high life. Instead of bored dissipation, there is a frenzied scramble for wealth and a childish desire to show it off before it is too late, before it is time to move on, to the next party, somewhere else.

The brain drain is already so serious that people with special skills have to be paid more and more to stay on. At the same time, people must pay more and more to leave, legally or not. Doctors feel they can no longer afford to work in public hospitals. Policemen may be more tempted to take bribes. There is a flourishing trade in fake passports, fake IDs, fake travel documents. A former principal of the Hong Kong College of Language and Commerce, who also ran an immigration consultancy business, was arrested early in 1990 for having forged immigration stamps. Corruption, always endemic to Hong Kong, is reaching such proportions that half the legal department seems to be under investigation. Far from dying, then, Hong Kong is becoming a free-for-all, battling against the clock.

Now, more than ever, Hong Kong feels like a city without a past or a future, only a frenzied present. Almost the only institution still talking about big investments in the future is the government itself, just to keep the morale up, to show that not all is lost. A new airport is planned, for example, but quite who will finance such a grand project is still unknown. Before anything can go ahead, there are matters to be considered that have little to do with business. "Sensitivity tests" is what these considerations are called in the charming jargon of the day: How will Beijing react? How will it affect the morale in Hong Kong? Will it give the government face? and so on.

The morale of my own Chinese friends is already such that most of them are actively seeking a way out, even those who, when I first met them some years ago, vowed never to leave. One is trying to get a Taiwanese passport, another might move to Canada, a third is thinking of Singapore. But these friends, sad though their departures are, do not deserve our deepest sympathy. That should go to those who stay behind because they have no choice, and especially to those very few who still fight for political change, however naively or quixotically.

As I prepare my own departure, I often think of an image that captures the melancholy of this slowly breaking city. It is a scene I saw on the television news, almost surreal in its violent intensity: the scene of a great bulldozer crushing a mountain of fake gold watches, all made in Hong Kong, until there was nothing left but dust.

1990

PART III

GHOSTS OF PEARL HARBOR

"Why," so an essay with the intriguing working title "The Japs—A Habit of Mind" begins, "do so many Americans, after witnessing the devastation and the futility of war, continue to think of Japan and the Japanese in terms of war? Why have so many Japanese a similar mental attitude toward the United States? Is this mutually apprehensive habit of mind, to whatever understandable origins it may be due, justified today?"

The essay was written for *Asia* magazine by Franklin D. Roosevelt, former assistant secretary of the Navy, in 1923—eight years before the Japanese took over Manchuria, fourteen years before the invasion of China, and eighteen years before the attack on Pearl Harbor. It is a sad fact that Roosevelt's question has lost none of its pertinence even now. For once again, it is said that the U.S. and Japan are on a collision course—a collision not just of economic interests, but of values, cultures, in some cases even of racial sensibilities.

If the reaction of a famous Japanese novelist upon hearing the morning news on December 8, 1941, did not exactly answer the question, it at least illustrated the problem. The news, so Dazai Osamu noted in his book, entitled 8 December,

> entered my pitch-dark room like a shaft of light. The announce-ment was joyfully repeated twice. As I listened, I felt I had become a new man, as though a flower petal stirred in my breast, cooled by the sacred breath of a deity. After this morning Japan had be-come a new country too . . .
>
> It is remarkable how hostile one can feel towards people whose eyes and hair are of a different colour. I want to beat them to death. This feels quite different from fighting against China. The very idea of those insensitive American savages treading on our beautiful Japanese soil is unbearable. . . . Oh, beautiful Japanese soldiers, please go ahead and smash them!

To Dazai, who was not some third-rate nationalist hack, but one of the great writers of modern Japan, Pearl Harbor came as a relief. The war in China, brutal and apparently endless, was an embarrassment; the war against the "Anglo-Saxon oppressors," the "Anglo-American dev-ils," was a righteous explosion of pent-up feelings of inferiority and frustration, the revenge for countless slights and humiliations, imag-ined or real, personal or national, or, as was usual, a combination of both. The news of great victories, wrote the historian Hayashi Fusao, whose opinions were as candid as they were chauvinistic, "changed our feeling of tension into one of liberation, our sense of fear into one of superiority, joy and pride."

This sort of thing had its counterpart on the other side of the Pacific. It can be found in such American reactions to the attack on Pearl Har-bor as the one, expressed by the commander of an airfield on the scene: "To think that this bunch of little yellow bastards could do this to us when we all knew that the United States was superior to Japan!"

That quotation is from Thurston Clarke's *Pearl Harbor Ghosts,* an ac-count of American attitudes towards the Japanese aggression, then and now. The book's central idea is that "there is no greater disgrace than to be defeated by an opponent you have previously denigrated." Clarke believes that Americans, blinded by racial and cultural prejudice, would not recognize the Japanese threat, but were obsessed instead by treacherous aliens in the U.S. "Blinded" is apt: folk opinion actually had it that slant-eyed people couldn't shoot straight—just as many Japanese believed that large-nosed white men couldn't see properly.

Clarke's main idea strikes me as a sound one. A wounded sense of superiority must account for the overblown rhetoric coming from, among others, Gerald A. Glaubitz, president of the Pearl Harbor Survivors Association. When it was suggested that Japanese veterans should be invited to attend the 1991 commemoration of the attack and offer their apologies, Glaubitz was outraged: "Would you expect the Jews to invite the Nazis to an event where they were talking about the Holocaust?" I don't think even Dazai Osamu had a holocaust in mind when the petal fluttered in his breast on that fateful morning fifty years ago.

But then we are dealing here not so much with history as with legend: the legend, on the one hand, of a desperate nation tossing its last card on the table in a heroic struggle for survival against Anglo-Saxon hegemony, and on the other, of the greatest nation on earth being ambushed by a treacherous foe. Clarke gives interesting examples of post-war American mythmaking. It seems that even men who witnessed the attack have trouble distinguishing what they actually saw from movie versions of the same. It is also remarkable how many witnesses claim to have seen the faces of the Japanese pilots as they swooped down to bomb and strafe, usually baring their teeth in devilish grins, "with the square goggles over the slant eyes," sometimes even waving to the intended victims of their treachery. For one veteran, Richard I. Fiske, a marine bugler on the battleship *West Virginia,* the vision was so powerful that he dreamed of it for years. As he told *The New York Times,* "I can still see that smile."

Now, it is possible that some people actually observed the pilots of low-flying aircraft, but the grins and the waves, not to mention the slant eyes, are just a bit too much. They smack of myth, rather like Hitler eating his carpet, or Japanese soldiers having the hearts and livers of executed POWs for lunch.

Much is made in America of the sneakiness of the Japanese attack. To be sure, declaring war after the first blow had been struck was not a gentlemanly thing to have done, but worse things happened in those days. We also tend to forget that when the Japanese used the same tactic in 1904 to destroy the Russian fleet in Port Arthur, their audacity was widely admired, even in America. Again, Clarke is on the right track, I think, when he explains the sense of outrage in terms of American myth. He makes the interesting point that Westerns might have had an influence: "The Indians too were seen as treacherous and sneaky, having no regard for human life or the rules of war. They too lay in wait behind pink desert ridges, ready to ambush white men." The problem with stressing the horrors of Pearl Harbor, rather than, say, the mass murders in China, is that it makes it easier for Japanese apologists to point at Hiroshima and claim it was many times worse.

Clarke is also right, I believe, to connect the continuing desire for conspiracy theories (Roosevelt invited the attack, Churchill knew all about it, etc.) to injured pride. Underneath the Roosevelt-provoked-Pearl-Harbor-to-get-into-the-war theory, he writes, was a desperate need to explain what happened at Pearl Harbor without conceding victory to Japanese arms or defeat to American errors and overconfidence.

There is, however, more to it than that. For the conspiracy theorists include men of very different stripes. There are, as Clarke says, people who begrudge the Japanese what was, after all, an extraordinary military feat. Just how extraordinary it was can be surmised from the reactions of the men who had been warned, had read secret Japanese codes, saw the planes coming and still couldn't believe that such an operation was possible. "Ridiculous," is what Lieutenant General Walter C. Short, commander of the Hawaiian Department, is supposed to have said after being informed that the Japanese had launched their attack. Then there are the isolationists who hated Roosevelt. And there are former intelligence agents, who can only explain the incompetence and pigheaded politicking of their superiors in terms of a conspiracy. Finally, there are perhaps the greatest conspiracy theorists of all: the Japanese themselves.

Not all Japanese, of course. There are many who think the attack on Pearl Harbor was an act of folly, the epitome of militarist stupidity. The historian Ienaga Saburo, among others, has pointed out that just as the Americans underestimated the Japanese, the Japanese showed little respect for the Americans: How could those ice-cream-fed, jazz-loving, flabby democrats possibly have the guts to stand up to the iron will and fighting spirit of his imperial majesty's forces? (One man who never fell for this line was Admiral Yamamoto Isoroku, the planner and commander of the Pearl Harbor raid.) During the Gulf War a literary critic named Matsumoto Kenichi compared Japan in 1941 to Iraq in 1991. He wrote in the newspaper *Tokyo Shimbun* that "Japan and Iraq went to war for virtually identical reasons"—expansionism in the guise of liberation. But, being a good Japanese liberal, he added, somewhat incongruously, that Japanese government support for the multinational coalition against Saddam Hussein showed that Japanese conservatives had "learned little from Japan's own descent into barbarism just fifty years ago."

But still, many Japanese believe that Japan had no choice but to fight. The reasoning is more or less as follows: Japan had legitimate special interests in Korea and China that were never recognized by the arrogant Western powers, whose own right to rule of Asian empires continued to be beyond dispute. It was perfectly understandable that Japan should wish not only to secure its economic interests in East Asia, but also to protect itself from Western imperialism and Chinese and Soviet communism, with force if need be. Far from being an ignoble exercise, Japanese self-defense was at the same time an attempt to liberate Asia and instill much needed discipline in decadent old China.

These aims were, however, thwarted by Anglo-Saxon discrimination at naval conferences and other international gatherings. Not only did the Western powers refuse to endorse the Japanese demand for racial equality at Versailles and the League of Nations, but the U.S. openly supported Chinese resistance against Japan. As a result, Japanese troops got bogged down in what is usually termed "the Chinese quagmire." Then, when the Americans decided to withhold vital raw materials and supplies from Japan, the Japanese had to secure them from Southeast Asia. When this, too, was resisted by the "ADB" (American, Dutch, British) powers, and when Americans insisted on complete Japanese withdrawal from China, Japan, which had never wished for anything but peace, was forced to go to war for its national survival. Most likely, Roosevelt deliberately trapped the Japanese into attacking Pearl Harbor; but even if he did not, it's quite clear that the Pacific War was the final showdown, which the U.S. had wanted at least since the beginning of the century, and perhaps from as long ago as 1853, when Commodore Perry's naval ships first arrived to force open the Japanese door.

It is not an entirely spurious theory, even though it contrives to shift responsibility for almost everything that happened in this century onto others, particularly America. It is true that the Western powers did not treat Japan as an equal. It is also true that after the Japanese victory in the Russo-Japanese war of 1905 the Americans began to worry that Japan would get uppity. In *American Diplomacy: 1900–1950,* George Kennan, not a noted Japanophile, observed that American policy in the Far East was marked more by self-righteousness than by realism, that too little attention was paid to genuine Japanese interests, that the price of American frustration with Japanese policies in China was the entrenchment of military extremists in Tokyo, and that American immigration policies inflamed Japanese passions unnecessarily:

> I cannot say that Pearl Harbor might have been avoided had we been over a long period of time more circumspect in our attitudes toward the Japanese, more considerate of the requirements of their position, more ready to discuss their problems with them on their own terms . . . I can only say that there was a possibility that the course of events might have been altered by an American policy based consistently, over a long period of time, on a recognition of power realities in the Orient as a factor worthy of our serious respect.

This is an eloquent argument for realpolitik. One might find fault with it, of course—I doubt that a liberal government in Tokyo would have had a better chance had the U.S. recognized power realities created by Japanese cowboys in northern China—but at least Kennan avoids the jargon of racial competition and Kulturkampf, and he admits that the Japanese were not always given their due. It was all very well for Washington to insist in 1921 on Chinese independence and territorial integrity, when the Western powers had left the Chinese little independence and territorial integrity to defend. This was just the kind of hypocrisy that the Japanese—and who could blame them?—managed to exploit. Yet to say that Japanese interests should have been taken more seriously is not to say that America forced Japan into going to war. Robert Smith Thompson has said exactly that, however, in his book *A Time for War.*

Although Thompson doesn't claim, as some Japanese revisionists do, that the Nanking massacre of 1937 was a fiction of Chinese propaganda, he follows the Japanese revisionist line quite closely in most matters. In fact, here and there he even appears to see the events in East Asia from the perspective of Greater East-Asian Coprosperity Sphere propaganda. Chinese resistance is frequently called "terrorism," and the resisters are either "terrorists" or "bandits." There were, to be sure, many ruffians in China, including quite a few in Chiang Kai-shek's ranks, but, at the same time, millions were defending their country against an army of conquistadors.

Thompson's line, briefly, is that Washington made life impossible for the Japanese by fighting a kind of low-intensity war with Japan for years. Economic squeeze was applied, supply routes to Chiang's army were kept open, and those Chinese terrorists were propped up. Years before the attack on Pearl Harbor, Japan was being slowly strangled by Western military bastions which grew stronger by the day. And Japan felt threatened by American readiness to firebomb its cities from the air. This is curious, since the first American attack on Tokyo, the famous Doolittle raid, took place only in 1942 and did hardly any damage at all. However, not only did Japan have to contend with U.S. belligerence, but, according to Thompson, the Tokyo government's grip on power was fragile: "The government was having to use every known device— uniformity of dress, spy scares, mountains of words in the newspapers about Japan's just cause—to stifle domestic dissent. The government could not go backward from the China war; to do so would show weakness and invite revolution."

This seems very odd. Either the Chinese war was popular and the "just cause" message was unnecessary, or it wasn't and a retreat would have been applauded. Either way, I have never come across much evidence of a revolutionary situation in Japan in the 1930s, except maybe among military extremists, whose quarrel was not so much with the general direction of Japanese policies as with the speed and zealousness of their execution.

After years of anti-Japanese provocation, then, "the American players were all in place," the bases in Singapore, Hawaii and the Philippines were loaded, and "On March 30, 1941, [Roosevelt] returned to the White House. He was rested. And he was ready." This apparent readiness to wait for Japan to do its worst, so that America could come in and crush both the Japs and the Nazis, is contradicted by the facts. The Philippines were far from ready, and the defense of Singapore had already been given up as a hopeless cause by the British in the summer of 1939. Indeed, Thompson himself quotes a memorandum from Admiral Stark and General Marshall to Roosevelt in November 1941 which shows the Americans were still playing for time a month before Pearl Harbor was attacked:

> At the present time . . . the United States Fleet in the Pacific is inferior to the Japanese Fleet and cannot undertake an unlimited strategic offensive in the Western Pacific. . . . [But] the U.S. Army air forces will have reached . . . projected strength by February or March 1942. The potency of this threat will have then increased to a point where it might well be a deciding factor in deterring Japan in operations in the areas south and west of the Pacific.

Hardly an ideal situation in which to throw away half the American fleet by inviting the Japanese to come and smash it. Thompson doesn't categorically state that Roosevelt knew of the attack in advance. That, he writes, was "possibly" the case. His main point is that America "provoked" Germany "into its declaration of war and Japan into its Pearl Harbor attack."

Certainly, by the end of 1941 Japan was left with little choice but to forget about the New Order in Asia or go to war with the U.S. We also know that Winston Churchill desperately wanted the Americans to come into the war, and that Roosevelt was working toward that end. The famous note from Cordell Hull, the U.S. secretary of state, to the Japanese government in 1941 was really an ultimatum: get out of China or prepare for war. Churchill never disguised his relief when the Japanese obligingly attacked, and Hitler declared war on America. Quite rightly, he knew then that the war against Germany would be won. But there is no evidence that Roosevelt wanted it to happen quite so soon, and to lose so much of his navy in the bargain.

James Rusbridger and Eric Nave, in *Betrayal at Pearl Harbor,* have tried to shift the conspiracy theory from Roosevelt to Churchill. They use their considerable expertise in the history of military intelligence and code-breaking (Nave was himself an important code-breaker during the Pacific War) to prove that Churchill must have had information on the impending attack, which he deliberately withheld from Roosevelt. The case rests on the premise that the British had access to codes that the Americans might not have broken yet, and that Churchill was given intelligence that Roosevelt never saw, because of office politics in Washington. The book is interesting for cryptography and code-breaking enthusiasts, but the main thesis is not proved. It is hard to prove, since, as the authors rightly complain, Her Majesty's government is absurdly tight about historical documents in its keep. But we cannot be sure that Churchill saw what he was supposed to have seen, and, even if he did, it would not be conclusive. The question, in intelligence matters, is not what raw data you see, but how you choose to interpret them. And, besides, as Dan van der Vat writes in *The Pacific Campaign:*

> The risk involved for Churchill in finding out, not telling, and later being discovered to have known—a very real risk, considering how closely Anglo-American intelligence staffs worked together and the short shelf-life of American official secrets—would surely have been too high even for such a scheming gambler.

At any rate, Thompson's message is less that Japan was a benign, hapless victim of Western conspiracies—although for polemical purposes one is sometimes given that impression—than that America had no business getting involved in these foreign quarrels in the first place. To judge from his sneering asides about Korea, Vietnam, Iraq and falling dominoes, Thompson is an isolationist.

Would isolation have been a wiser course? Was Japan needlessly provoked? I doubt it. Japan's dilemma in 1941 was the result of having tried to conquer China. If the Chinese morass had sucked them in too deeply, the Japanese could only blame themselves for having entered it. It is possible, I suppose, to argue that power realities should have been accepted and that New Orders in Asia and Europe, dictated by the Axis powers, posed no direct threat to a U.S. in splendid isolation. But aside from the dubious morality of leaving Chinese and Europeans to their fates, I don't think American isolation would have been so splendid.

In fact, the reverse of Thompson's view is more persuasive: it was the failure of the U.S., and Britain, to check the military adventures of Germany and Japan earlier that led to the all-or-nothing war. Unfortunately, however, the Western powers, specifically the American, British and Dutch, had a particular problem in Asia: Japan's "special interests" could not be convincingly curbed as long as Western special interests were to remain unchallenged. This is why Japanese policies met mostly with appeasement, why their propagandists could claim they were fighting a war of Asian liberation, and why revisionists can continue to repeat that line today.

—

Why did Japan get itself in such a stew in the first place? Was there some deep cultural flaw that would account for the extremism of its military forces? Was Pearl Harbor the result of suicidal samurai ethics? In short, were the Japanese mad? There was indeed, as a result of incessant militarist and Emperor-worshiping propaganda, a kind of madness in the land. It took several years of living in the U.S. to cure a gentle student like Murata Kiyoaki of his conviction that his highest duty was to die at the front. Murata's description, in *An Enemy Among Friends,* of his student years in California and Chicago is interesting, since it contradicts the conventional view of America, rather popular in Japan these days, as an utterly racist society, where the only good Japs were thought to be dead Japs, or at least Japs behind detention-camp bars. Far from meeting with prejudice, he writes, "I spent seven delightful and fruitful years in America, including the war years." But then, he admits, he might have been oblivious of racial slights, since he himself never doubted his own racial superiority. It clearly was a rum time for all.

Propaganda madness is no proof, however, that the Pearl Harbor attack was either mad or rooted in a perverted samurai spirit. Its architect, Admiral Yamamoto, was, as I have indicated already, under no illusion about the potential might of the U.S. He knew that Japan could not win a protracted war. But, faced with the fact that the army would not pull out of China, that the navy was passive, that the civilians in government were powerless, that the Emperor did nothing but compose melancholy poems, and that war was therefore inevitable, he thought that only a quick and smashing Japanese victory might prompt Washington to negotiate on Japanese terms. He was wrong, but he was not crazy.

Nor was the tactic used in the Pearl Harbor raid—even that!—originally Japanese.

William H. Honan, in his intriguing if perhaps too reverential book *Visions of Infamy,* shows how the British naval journalist Hector C. Bywater imagined in 1921, and in even greater detail in 1925, just what the Japanese might do in a future war with America. There had been a demand for such books since the turn of the century. Many coming-war-with-Japan books stressed American decline and vulnerability, which shows that "declinism" is not a new phenomenon. This taste was shared by Japanese readers, who lapped up such works as *The Future Japan–U.S. War,* by Fukunaga Kyosuke. Of the American books, Homer Lea's (*The Valor of Ignorance,* etc.) were at the vulgar end of the market, while Bywater aimed at the more sophisticated reader.

In his two famous books, *Sea-Power in the Pacific* and *The Great Pacific War,* Bywater described with amazing accuracy what would come to pass: a swift Japanese raid on the U.S. Navy, followed by many island-hopping battles in the Pacific, and ending with a narrow American victory. Honan, like many journalists, puts great faith in the influence of fellow hacks on public affairs, and might have overstated Bywater's impact on the tactics of the imperial Japanese navy, but his books were given much attention in Japan, notably by Yamamoto himself. There were several Japanese editions. One Japanese author even wrote a book-length critique, the main point of which was that Japan, not the U.S., would be the victor.

Honan's conclusion that Bywater's story should dispel the image of the Pearl Harbor attack as characteristic of Japanese treachery and deceit is just, even if his remark that it was "in reality as English as plum pudding and as American as apple pie," is stretching the point a little far.

But, desperate tactics aside, one still has to wonder why the governments of a civilized nation allowed its army to run amok and start a war. The answer concerns not only the question Roosevelt posed in 1923, but also the current debate on U.S.–Japan relations. After all, we are once again living at a time in which books prophesying wars with Japan mean big business, in the U.S. as well as in Japan.

Maruyama Masao, the distinguished political scientist, thought the root of Japan's political problem in the 1930s was what he called "the system of irresponsibility." In *Thought and Behavior in Modern Japanese*

Politics, he contrasted the Japanese political and bureaucratic elite of that time with the thugs who ran Nazi Germany. The thugs, he wrote, may have been thugs, but at least they took responsibility for their actions. They were even proud of their crimes. The Japanese elites, in contrast, consisted of gentlemen who hid behind "unexpected events," behind decisions made outside their bureaucratic competence, behind unaccountable generals and, perhaps most important of all, behind the emperor, who, as "constitutional monarch," disclaimed all responsibility himself.

It is a plausible analysis that is, however, rooted not so much in the ancient Japanese past or some inscrutable Japanese mentality as in a clear constitutional problem. According to the Meiji constitution, which lasted until 1945, the emperor was not only a constitutional monarch, but also the divine patriarch of the nation. But just as the emperor was above politics, so, according to a rescript promulgated in 1882, were his soldiers and sailors. Their loyalty was to him, not to the governments of the day. The rescript was meant to keep the military out of politics. In effect, it encouraged them to ignore civilian politics altogether and to do anything they could justify to themselves as being in the divine imperial cause. Bureaucrats were also beyond democratic control, and so, after years of propaganda denigrating politics and politicians as corrupt, greedy, unprincipled and un-Japanese, a military–bureaucratic alliance could push the country in a direction that was to end in catastrophe.

The point is often made that the Japanese after the war showed less repentance for what they had done than the Germans. But was this really so surprising when the man in whose name their deeds were done was not just left untouched, but was received as "the first gentleman of Japan" by General MacArthur? Not only that, but some of the very same bureaucrats who were responsible for what happened during the 1930s and 1940s came back into power, with American blessing, after the war. It is surprising, in these circumstances, that anyone in Japan should feel guilty at all. It would be even more surprising if, of all the things to feel guilty about, the attack on Pearl Harbor came very high on the list.

In the end everything was blamed on the army. So it seemed both just and wise, when the war was over, for the Americans to write a new

Japanese constitution that took away Japan's right to wage war, or even to maintain an army. Instead, Japan was told to put all its national energy into rebuilding the economy. Then, as a response to the Cold War, the Japanese government was encouraged to undermine the "peace constitution" by starting a kind of unofficial shadow military called the Self-Defense Forces. Once again, for the best reasons, Japanese soldiers and sailors exist outside the mainstream of civilian politics, since constitutionally they are not supposed to exist at all. In effect, Japanese security policy is dictated by the U.S., resulting in rabid nationalism on the right and stubborn pacifism on the left, and silence in the middle.

Faint signals of this are beginning to be picked up in the U.S., but, as with all decoded intelligence, much depends on interpretation. Ignoring the severe limits on Japanese sovereignty, some observers describe Japan as an "amoral" state, an irresponsible nation, without direction or purpose, or, conversely, as a sneaky state bent on conquering the world through unfair trade. The phrase "economic Pearl Harbor" pops up in political speeches. To Edith Cresson, the prime minister of France, Japan is our new "enemy." Japan—here I quote from the 1991 CIA-funded report *Japan 2000,* by Andrew J. Dougherty—"often appears to be in direct conflict with widely and deeply held Western moral imperatives." Every Japanese action, the same report states, is inspired by oppressive ideas derived from Shinto, Buddhism and Confucianism. The common message in these polemics is that Japan is a special case, not to be trusted, because of the war, its sneaky attacks, its unfairness in trade and its peculiar culture with its alien morality.

Stung by the perception that Japan is being ganged up on by Western bullies, and humiliated by a virtually complete military dependency on the U.S., right-wing Japanese politicians seek to inspire their audiences with messages that Japan should now say no to America. The most vociferous proponent of this idea, the writer and politician Ishihara Shintaro, has written that the Pacific War was a battle of cultures, that the American victors wanted to rob Japan of its identity, but that finally the East (Japan) will prevail in the struggle with the West (America).

This kind of rhetoric on both sides of the Pacific is not only inflammatory, it also muddles the debate on actual economic and political problems. Neither half-baked Spenglerism nor ill-informed lessons in Japanese folklore are of much help in discussing the rights and wrongs of industrial and trade policies or collective-security arrangements. It is remarkable how similar the jargon of Kulturkampf is on both sides: the CIA-funded report on Japan actually repeats many of the clichés used by Japanese nationalists to prove the uniqueness of their nation. One result of seeing Japan as a special case, culturally, economically, politically, is the growing sense of isolation in Japan. And that, some seventy years ago, was the beginning of the Japanese road to infamy.

1991

THE WAR OVER THE BOMB

1.

The flight of the bomber called *Bock's Car* on August 9, 1945, from Tinian to Nagasaki was blessed but not smooth. In a Quonset hut at the air base before takeoff Chaplain Downey had prayed for the success of the plane's mission. "Almighty God, Father of all mercies," he said, "we pray Thee to be gracious with those who fly this night." He also said: "Give to us all courage and strength for the hours that are ahead; give to them rewards according to their efforts. Above all else, our Father, bring peace to Thy world."

But things went wrong from the start. A fuel pump wasn't working. So the captain, Major Charles "Chuck" Sweeney ("cheerful Irish grin"), decided to rendezvous with escort planes over Japan and refuel in Okinawa on the way back. The skies were thundery and turbulent. The rendezvous was missed: the planes lost contact and much time. The primary target, Kokura, an industrial city in northern Kyushu, was covered by smoke from a bombing raid on a neighboring city. Fuel was running low, but Sweeney flew his B-29 bomber on to the second target on the list: Nagasaki.

A thick deck of clouds had rendered Nagasaki invisible, too. "Skipper" Sweeney had to think fast. Fuel was running out. Ditching his load in the ocean was one possibility. But he decided against it. "After all," he said, "anything is better than dumping it in the water." He would ignore his orders, which stipulated that the target had to be visible, and drop the "Fat Man" by radar. Then, suddenly, Kermit "Bea" Beahan ("slow Texas drawl"; "crack bombardier"; "ladies' man"), shouted: "I've got it. I see the city. I'll take it now. . . ."*

And so the "Fat Man" went down, slowly at first. It took a while for things to happen. Internal radar fuses had been activated in the bomb to sense its height. Chuck Sweeney was impatient. "Oh, my God," he said to his copilot, Charles "Donald Duck" Albery ("a deeply religious man"), "did we goof it up?" Moments later, the sky lit up, the plane was rocking like a rowing boat in a storm, and Sweeney could relax at last. "Well, Bea," said "Donald Duck" to the bombardier, "there's a thousand Japs you've just killed."

The "Fat Man," a plutonium bomb, exploded about three miles from the center of Nagasaki, above an area called Urakami, sometimes referred to in Nagasaki as Urakamimura, or Urakami village. The pressure generated by the bomb at the hypocenter—the point directly under the blast—was about ten tons per square meter. The heat at ground level reached 4,000 degrees Celsius. People near the hypocenter were vaporized. Others, who were not so lucky, died more slowly, often after shedding their skins like snakes. Some died weeks or months, or even years, later of various kinds of cancer. Altogether up to 70,000 people are thought to have died as a result of the bombing of Nagasaki. About half of them died on the day itself.

The landscape of Urakami, separated by mountains from Nagasaki proper, was marked by Mitsubishi weapons factories and the largest cathedral in east Asia. Urakami was a district with a low reputation. Its population included a large number of poor Roman Catholics and even poorer outcasts. It was as though a bomb had fallen on Harlem, leaving the rest of Manhattan relatively unscathed. Some residents of Nagasaki

---

*These quotes are all from *Nagasaki: The Forgotten Bomb*, by Frank Chinnock. The effects of the Nagasaki bomb are horrifically illustrated by the photographer Yosuke Yamahata in *Nagasaki Journey*.

quietly voiced the opinion that the bomb had "cleaned up" Urakami. In August 1945, there were 14,000 Catholics in Nagasaki. More than half were killed by the bomb. There are 70,000 Catholics living in Nagasaki today. Southern Kyushu is still the only part of Japan with a large Christian minority.

———

The first missionary to reach Kyushu was Francis Xavier, who landed there in 1549. His high hopes for Japan were not disappointed. By the turn of the century about 300,000 Japanese had been converted to the Roman faith. Even Hideyoshi, the "Barbarian-slaying" shogun himself, was seen in his palace fingering a rosary. This did not stop him from crucifying twenty-six Japanese and European priests in Nagasaki in 1597. Like his more ferocious successors, he was afraid that Japanese Christians might help Spanish invaders take over Japan—a fear that Dutch traders did their best to encourage.

After 1612 persecution began in earnest. Christianity was banned. Men, women and children were burned to death while singing praises to the Lord. Priests were suspended upside down in pits of excrement or boiling sulfur, cut open and bled to death, unless they agreed to renounce their faith and trample on images of Christ. A Christian peasant rebellion in 1632 was put down (with Dutch help) so brutally that hardly any of the 40,000 rebels survived. Naturally, missionary work became impossible and priests could no longer attend to their flock.

Even so, small communities of "hidden Christians" hung on, often reverting in time to folk religion: local deities were worshiped in the name of Jesus; a kind of Christian cargo cult developed, with fisherfolk praying for the return of priests in black ships. Only after Americans (in black ships) and Europeans had pried Japan open in the latter half of the nineteenth century did Japanese Christians dare to declare themselves. But they remained an often harassed and poor minority, forced to do religiously polluted work in the meat and leather trades, which were normally reserved for outcasts. The ban on Christianity was formally lifted in 1873. Twenty years later, the Nagasaki Christians managed to collect enough money to start construction of a wood and redbrick cathedral on a hill in Urakami. It was completed in 1925. It was above this cathedral that the "Fat Man" exploded.

Twice a day, the one surviving Angelus bell rings out from the new cathedral. Visiting Nagasaki this summer I walked from the cathedral to Peace Park. It is built on the site of an old prison, whose foundation stones recently emerged during the construction of an underground garage. The appearance of these prison foundations caused a political row in Nagasaki: Should they be preserved as a reminder of the war (among the prisoners were Koreans and Chinese)? A compromise was reached: the car park was completed, and a slab of the old prison wall is displayed in Peace Park, among the monuments and memorials.

——

Compared to the one in Hiroshima, Nagasaki Peace Park is a small and subdued affair. There is the "Peace Statue," a large white figure pointing his right hand at the sky and extending his left hand sideways. According to a booklet on sale in the Peace Park bookstore, the right hand points to the nuclear threat and the left hand symbolizes eternal peace. The folded right leg and the extended left leg "symbolize meditation and the initiative to stand up and rescue the people of the world." In the rest of the park are various sculptures, some of them donated by countries that no longer exist: the German Democratic Republic, Czechoslovakia, the USSR. Two kindly ladies and an elderly man had set up a long table in front of the Soviet "Statue of Peace." They invited "all the people who love peace," including small children on school excursions, to sign an antinuclear petition to be sent to Washington.

But there is much less of this kind of thing than in Hiroshima, which is dominated by memorials to the bomb victims and messages of salvation. The main reason people visit Hiroshima is the bomb. This is not true of Nagasaki. Hiroshima, not Nagasaki, has become the mecca of international antinuclear activism. The Hiroshima bomb came first. It fell in the center of the city. More people died there—and few of them were despised Christians or outcasts. People say: "No more Hiroshimas." They rarely say: "No more Nagasakis."

Instead of dwelling on the bomb, Nagasaki has turned its history of foreign missionaries, Dutch traders, Chinese merchants and Madame Butterfly into a tourist attraction. Nagasaki takes pride in once having been the nearest thing in Japan to a cosmopolitan city. When the rest of the country was sealed off from the outside world between the early seventeenth and mid-nineteenth centuries, Nagasaki kept a Dutch trading post on Dejima Island. Western science first entered Japan through Nagasaki in the form of medical texts, which Japanese scholars learned to read by memorizing Dutch dictionaries. After Japan opened up, village girls acquired Russian by serving Russian sailors as prostitutes, and outcasts acquired foreign languages by supplying the Europeans with meat. Nagasaki had a large Chinatown, now a cute, touristy pastiche of its former self. A celebrated entertainer from Nagasaki, who sings French *chansons* and wears women's clothes, claims to be the reincarnation of a seventeenth-century Christian martyr, thought to have been the incarnation of *Deusu,* the Lord. The most popular souvenirs in Nagasaki include all manner of Christian trinkets, as well as a sponge cake called *castella,* introduced by the Portuguese four hundred years ago.

———

Nagasaki's most famous survivor was a Christian named Nagai Takashi. He became a symbol of his city's suffering, just as a schoolgirl, named Sasaki Sadako, became a symbol of Hiroshima. Sadako was two years old when the bomb exploded a mile from her home. She died of leukemia ten years later, but not before trying to fold one thousand paper cranes, as symbols of longevity. Her monument in Hiroshima Peace Park is covered in thousands of paper cranes, folded by schoolchildren from all over Japan.

Dr. Nagai was a professor of radiology at the University of Nagasaki when the city was bombed. He had contracted leukemia before the war, perhaps as a result of his laboratory work, but radiation from the bomb cured the symptoms. Dr. Nagai was a devout Catholic and a Japanese patriot who exhorted his students to fight their hardest for the nation. He was devastated by Japan's defeat. But then, as he wrote in his bestselling book *The Bells of Nagasaki,* he had a flash of religious inspiration. The bomb, he decided, was "a great act of Divine Providence," for which Nagasaki "must give thanks to God."* He declared that Nagasaki, "the only holy place in Japan," had been chosen as a sacrificial lamb "to be burned on the altar of sacrifice to expiate the sins commit-

———

*I have used the translation of William Johnston, an Irish Jesuit who believes that Dr. Nagai "takes an honoured place among the great prophets of Asia and of the world."

ted by humanity in the Second World War." In this vision, Dr. Nagai added the Catholic victims of the bomb to the long list of Nagasaki martyrs. They were the spiritual heirs of believers who had been crucified for their faith.

> How noble, how splendid was that holocaust of August 9, when flames soared up from the cathedral, dispelling the darkness of war and bringing the light of peace! In the very depth of our grief we reverently saw here something beautiful, something pure, something sublime. Eight thousand people, together with their priests, burning with pure smoke, entered into eternal life. All without exception were good people whom we deeply mourn.

The symptoms of leukemia returned, and Dr. Nagai retired to a tiny hut near the cathedral, where he wrote his many books and was visited by dignitaries ranging from Emperor Hirohito to Helen Keller. *The Bells of Nagasaki* was completed in 1946, but out of fear that accounts of the nuclear bombings would encourage anti-American attitudes, the U.S. occupation authorities only allowed it to be published in 1949. Two years later Dr. Nagai died. His hut is now a shrine, visited by Japanese schoolchildren and tourists from all over the world, who peer through the window at the bone-white image of the Virgin Mary next to his bed.

I asked Father Calaso, a Spanish priest who has lived in Nagasaki for many years, what he thought of Dr. Nagai's vision. He answered that it was "theologically correct. We cannot know why the bomb was good, but God cannot will anything evil." Of course, as John Whittier Treat points out in his excellent book *Writing Ground Zero,* a critical discussion of Japanese writing about the bomb, the Christian idea of martyrdom was not the only response of Nagasaki bomb survivors. Treat contrasts Nagai's Christian idealism with the existential despair of such non-Christian writers as Hayashi Kyoko, who express not just their own "leukemia of the soul" but also their fear that the atomic disease will be carried by future generations. Hayashi's view is radically secular. In a short story entitled "In the Fields," she writes: "These are deliberate wounds precisely calculated and inflicted by human beings. On account of these calculations, the very life that we would pass on to our children and grandchildren has sustained injury."

Nevertheless, the mood of Christian resignation has affected Nagasaki. There are social reasons for this, too. Like many Jewish survivors of the Holocaust who returned to their native countries in Europe, Nagasaki Christians did not wish to dwell on their suffering lest it expose them to the public gaze. They did not want to stand out in a society obsessed with bloodlines and social conformity. It was difficult enough finding marriage partners for your children, if you were a bomb survivor, being a Catholic could only make things worse. So there is something to the cliché that "Hiroshima is angry, while Nagasaki prays." Compared to Hayashi's *Angst,* Dr. Nagai's beatitude makes the past easier to bear. We are told of *Bock's Car's* crew: "Today, they are all deeply religious men."★

2.

Religion was linked to the nuclear bombs from the beginning. Witnessing the first successful nuclear explosion in New Mexico, Dr. J. Robert Oppenheimer famously quoted from the Bhagavad-Gita: "Now I am become Death the destroyer of worlds." President Truman, announcing the bombing of Hiroshima, thanked God that the weapon had "come to us instead of to our enemies; and we pray that He may guide us to use it in His ways and for His purposes." Arthur H. Compton, a member of the Interim Committee for Atomic Bomb Policy, believed that "God had fought on our side during the war, supplying free men with weapons that tyranny could not produce."

What Truman and Compton had in common with Dr. Nagai—but absolutely not with Hayashi Kyoko—was the convenient view that God, not man, was ultimately responsible for the bomb. Opponents of the bomb often express themselves in equally religious terms. Treat quotes a poem from Nagasaki that goes: "In the Cathedral in the ruins of boundless expanse, I stayed one night cursing God." The bomb has been described on many occasions as a transgression of religious taboos, indeed a sin against God. In 1946, the Federal Council of Churches special committee explicitly said so: "As the power that first used the atomic bomb under these circumstances, we have sinned

★Chinnock, *Nagasaki: The Forgotten Bomb,* p. 299.

grievously against the laws of God and against the peoples of Japan." The Roman Catholic hierarchy concluded at the Second Vatican Council in 1965 that "every act of war directed to the indiscriminate destruction of whole cities or vast areas with their inhabitants is a crime against God and man."

Even if one leaves God out of it, it is hard to disagree that deliberate mass murder of civilians by so-called conventional or nuclear bombing is a war crime. But "strategic bombing," including the use of the two atomic bombs, was not an act of God. It was the result of political decisions, taken by human beings acting under particular circumstances. The trouble with focusing on God, sin, transgression and other moral or religious aspects of this strategy is that it makes it very hard to discuss the politics and the historical circumstances dispassionately. This is especially true when politicians, newspaper columnists, peace activists and veterans enter the debate. Too often emotional moralism sets the tone.

———

Many defenders of the atomic bombs, beginning with President Truman himself, have tried to justify their use on moral grounds: i.e., that the bombings saved half a million, or even a million, American lives by preventing an invasion. These probably inflated figures are supposed to make the bombings of Hiroshima and Nagasaki seem like acts of mercy. And opponents tend to boost their moral condemnation by adding evidence of bad faith: i.e., that the bombings were acts of racism, or scientific experiments, or merely opening shots of the coming cold war, or that they served no purpose at all. In other words, it is not enough for some critics to call the attacks on Hiroshima and Nagasaki a sin against God and man; to strengthen the moral case, they must be shown to have been unnecessary and politically reprehensible, too. Many critics find it impossible to accept, for example, that the A-bombing was a war crime that actually might have helped to bring the war to a quicker end. By the same token, political reasons, however justified, are not enough for some defenders of the bomb to feel vindicated. To them, the bombs must show that God was on our side, that only the purest of motives prevailed.

I think this helps to explain the debacle over the projected *Enola Gay* exhibition at the Smithsonian Institution. The fault does not lie with the authors of the original text prepared by the Smithsonian to accompany the exhibition, now published as part of *Judgment at the Smithsonian*. Newt Gingrich was wrong: the script was not in the least anti-American, nor did it "espouse a set of values that are essentially destructive."★ Historians—unlike many veterans, journalists and politicians—have been debating the history of the bomb for years without invoking God or the Devil. And their different views are admirably and concisely reflected in the Smithsonian script. All the controversies about the atomic bombing are touched upon: whether it was an act of racism; whether the bombs were dropped to warn the Soviets, and keep them from invading Japan; whether Truman should have paid more attention to Japanese peace initiatives; and whether there were better ways than nuclear bombing of ending the war swiftly.

—

The Smithsonian consensus—even-handed to the point of banality—is that racist attitudes existed, but that Roosevelt would have used the bomb on Germany if necessary. On the Soviet factor, the Smithsonian concludes that " 'atomic diplomacy' against the Soviets provided one more reason for Truman not to halt the dropping of the bomb." The Smithsonian writers believe it is possible the war *might* have ended without the bombings if the Allies had guaranteed the Japanese emperor's position. And it is not sure whether a warning demonstration— dropping the bomb in Tokyo Bay, for instance—would have sufficed. But despite all these "hotly contested" issues, its conclusion is that "the bombing of Hiroshima and Nagasaki . . . played a crucial role in ending the Pacific War quickly."

Here and there the Smithsonian text is too glib. I don't think Japanese forces kept on fighting because they feared that unconditional surrender would mean "the annihilation of their culture." Japanese forces had no choice. They went on fighting because their supreme commanders feared the annihilation of their power. Still, the projected Smithsonian exhibition would have provided an invaluable opportunity for

★These views were expressed to Fred Barnes in *The New Republic,* March 13, 1995, p. 23.

the Hiroshima debate to break out of academic circles and reach a wider audience. This opportunity was lost when the Smithsonian caved in to protests from such organizations as the American Legion and the Air Force Association. The text was withdrawn and only the Hiroshima bomber is displayed now, without context or explanation, as just another great American plane, like the *Spirit of St. Louis* and the *Kitty Hawk Flyer.* This is a shame, for not only has it discouraged open discussion in the United States, but it has fueled the self-righteousness of Japanese apologists for the Pacific War. If Americans refuse to question *their* war record, they ask, then why should Japanese risk the reputation of Japanese soldiers by questioning theirs?

Of course, none of this has anything to do with intellectual curiosity (the primary function of a museum, I should think), but everything to do with national pride. The American Legion and its intellectual defenders in the press were less interested in an argument than in a celebration. They wanted it to be taken for granted that the bomb was right and just. Barton Bernstein points out in a thoughtful concluding essay to *Judgment at the Smithsonian* that the dispute was not simply about history but about "a symbolic issue in a 'culture war.' " He writes that

> many Americans lumped together the seeming decline of American power, the difficulties of the domestic economy, the threats in world trade and especially Japan's successes, the loss of domestic jobs, and even changes in American gender roles, and shifts in the American family. To a number of Americans, the very people responsible for the [Smithsonian] script were the people who were changing America. The bomb, representing the end of World War II and suggesting the height of American power, was to be celebrated. . . . Those who in any way questioned the bomb's use were, in this emotional framework, the enemies of America. The Air Force Association, the Legion, many individual vets, segments of Congress, and parts of the media accepted, and promoted, that interpretation.

Unfortunately, the editor of *Judgment at the Smithsonian,* Philip Nobile, is no less emotional than the conservatives he deplores. Reading his introduction, I almost felt sympathetic to the American Legion. Nobile not only believes the bombings were a moral outrage, which would be a respectable position. He goes further: he believes that anyone who defends Truman's decision is morally outrageous. To him, the defenders of the Hiroshima and Nagasaki bombings are not just wrong, they are "white male American intellectuals," who seek to "deny" Hiroshima. Paul Fussell, who argued that the bomb saved American lives, including his own, which might well be true, is smeared as the "Robert Faurisson of Hiroshima denial." This is not just nasty, it is dishonest. Faurisson is a right-wing extremist who maintains that the gas chambers never existed. Whatever the merits of Fussell's argument, he never denied that the bomb was dropped or that countless civilians died. To equate Fussell with Faurisson, or Paul Tibbetts, pilot of the *Enola Gay,* with Rudolf Hoess, commandant at Auschwitz, as Nobile does, is to kill the debate. For how can you argue with bad faith? But then Nobile is as little interested in a debate as the American Legion. Like them, he is concerned with moral gestures, not of celebration in his case, but of atonement, repentance, and so forth. He bandies about words like "original sin."

———

Robert Jay Lifton and Greg Mitchell, in their analysis of Hiroshima's legacy in America,[*] are not nasty, just woolly and moralistic. They believe that the bombings were morally offensive, and so the reasons for dropping them must necessarily have been politically misguided, dishonest and irrational. Lifton takes it for granted that the bombs did not hasten the end of the war, since the Japanese would have surrendered anyway, if only Truman had listened to Joseph Grew, the former ambassador to Japan, and promised the Japanese they could keep their imperial system. He thinks that the Potsdam Declaration was mere propaganda, since it did not mention the atom bomb, the entry of Russia into the war or the Emperor, "each of which would have pressed the Japanese towards surrender."

Was this really as obvious as Lifton and Mitchell, as well as many serious critics of Truman A-bomb policy, claim? Some historians,

[*]*Hiroshima in America.*

such as Gar Alperovitz, believe that the Potsdam Declaration was designed to be unacceptable to the Japanese, so that the United States would have time to drop the bomb and demonstrate its supremacy to the increasingly aggressive Soviet Union.* Truman, on the advice of his secretary of state, James Byrnes, withheld a guarantee of the Emperor's status. In *The Decision to Use the Atomic Bomb,* Alperovitz repeats over and over that Truman did this, fully aware "that a surrender was not likely to occur." The implication is that Truman did not want the Japanese to surrender before the bomb was used. On his way to Potsdam, in July 1945, Truman heard the news that the first atomic bomb had been successfully tested at Alamogordo, New Mexico. With the bomb in his pocket, so to speak, he believed that the "Japs will fold up before Russia comes in." Which was precisely what he wanted.

Alperovitz makes his case for the above scenario with mountains of documentary quotes. He shows how Truman's desire to involve the Soviet Red Army in forcing a Japanese surrender cooled as soon as he heard the good news from Alamogordo. That the Soviet Union played a part in Truman's calculations is neither a new nor an especially controversial observation. Most historians agree with Alperovitz that "even those who still wished for Russian help (to say nothing of those who opposed it) began to see the atomic bomb as a way not only to end the war, but perhaps to end it as soon as possible—preferably before the Russians attacked, and certainly, if feasible, before the Red Army got very far in its assault."

But to say that Truman deliberately withheld a guarantee of the Emperor's status at Potsdam so that he could drop his bomb is to assume it was clear the Japanese would have surrendered *with* such a guarantee. Alperovitz has no difficulty finding quotes from U.S. officials who thought so, but there is no reason to believe that they were right, and consequently that Truman was wrong, or merely Machiavellian, to press for an unconditional surrender. There is no evidence that Japan

---

*Gar Alperovitz first set out his ideas in *Atomic Diplomacy: Hiroshima and Potsdam* (revised edition, Pluto Press, 1994). His new book, *The Decision to Use the Atomic Bomb,* goes over the same ground in more detail, as well as dealing with postwar myths about the bomb.

would have surrendered, even with a guarantee of the Emperor's status, and there are good reasons to believe that it would not. As long as the Japanese were not ready to surrender on terms acceptable to the Allies, Truman had no option but to insist on a sharp ultimatum, bomb or no bomb.

What we know is that even some members of the so-called peace faction in the Japanese war cabinet were remarkably casual about the Potsdam terms—and not only because of the lack of guarantees for the Emperor. One of the "moderates," Navy Minister Yonai, said there was no need to rush because "Churchill has fallen, America is beginning to be isolated. The government therefore will ignore [the Potsdam Proclamation].* Even after the bombing of Nagasaki on August 9, half the Supreme War Leadership Council was still determined to fight on. Japan may have been "licked" militarily, as Eisenhower and other Americans said at the time, and later, but this did not mean it would give up. Instead of preparing for surrender, the Japanese government exhorted the population to defend the "divine land," in mass suicide actions if necessary. The press kept up a daily Die-for-the-Emperor campaign. Thomas B. Allen and Norman Polmar describe in their book *Code-Name Downfall* how Japanese schoolchildren were trained to fight the enemy with bamboo spears, kitchen knives, firemen's hooks or, as a last resort, feet and bare knuckles. Children were told: "If you don't kill at least one enemy soldier, you don't deserve to die." Eight hundred thousand troops, including home defense forces, were gathered in Kyushu to resist an American invasion. If it had come to a final battle in Japan, after more months of firebombing and starvation, the human cost to the Japanese—leaving aside the Allies for a moment—would have been horrendous.

———

If saving Japanese lives was not Truman's concern, it didn't particularly bother the Japanese leaders either. The debate inside the Leadership Council at a crisis meeting on August 9 was not about whether to surrender but about whether to insist on one condition (retention of the

*"Japan's Delayed Surrender: A Reinterpretation," by Herbert P. Bix, *Diplomatic History* (Spring 1995), p. 206.

imperial system, or *kokutai*) or four, including the demand that there be
no Allied occupation. There had to be a unanimous decision. Without
absolute consensus, the government would fall, more time would be
wasted and more lives lost. This is the Emperor's own account of the
meeting, which took place in the sticky heat of an underground bomb
shelter. The Emperor sat stiffly in front of a gilded screen, while his
ministers sweated in their dress uniforms:

> The meeting went on until two o'clock in the morning of August
> 10, without reaching an agreement. Then Suzuki asked me to
> break the deadlock and come to a decision. Apart from Prime
> Minister Suzuki, the participants were Hiranuma, Yonai, Anami,
> Togo, Umezu and Toyoda. Everyone agreed on the condition to
> preserve the *kokutai*. Anami, Toyoda and Umezu insisted on
> adding three more conditions: that Japan would not be occupied,
> and that the task of disarming our armed forces and dealing with
> war crimes would be in our own hands. They argued that at the
> present stage of the war, there was enough room for negotiation.
> Suzuki, Yonai, Hiranuma and Togo disagreed. I believed it was
> impossible to continue the war . . .*

And so, finally, after two atomic bombings, the Emperor spoke out
in favor of the peace faction. It had become impossible to carry on the
war. Not only had Hiroshima been obliterated, but on the day Nagasaki was bombed, the Soviet Union had declared war on Japan. Some
have argued that this, rather than the nuclear bombs, forced Japan's
surrender. Perhaps, but the August 9 meeting had been convened before the Soviet declaration of war, and Alperovitz tells us that the Emperor, "on hearing of the Hiroshima bombing," had already "agreed the
time had come to surrender." In the Emperor's own account, he mentions both the Soviets and the bombs: "The people were suffering ter-
ribly, first from bombings getting worse by the day, then by the

---

*The Emperor gave this self-serving account before the Tokyo War Crimes Tribunal
was convened. The text was circulated among General MacArthur's staff but then disappeared, until it turned up in America after Hirohito's death. The full text was published in Tokyo in *Showa Tenno Dokuhakuroku* (Bungei Shunju, 1991).

appearance of the atomic bomb. Because of these factors, and the fact that the Soviet Union had unleashed a war in Manchuria, we could not but accept the terms of Potsdam."* In his broadcast to the nation, on August 15, the Emperor left the Soviet Union unmentioned, but referred to the bombs:

> The enemy has begun to use a new and most cruel bomb to kill and maim extremely large numbers of the innocent . . . if the war were to be continued, it would cause not only the downfall of our nation but also the destruction of all human civilization . . . it is according to the dictate of time and fate that We have resolved to pave the way for a grand peace for all the generations to come by enduring the unendurable and suffering what is insufferable.

The Emperor's decision to accept surrender is called the *seidan,* or sacred resolution. The Japanese war cabinet needed the voice of God to make up its mind. And as the above words show, the supreme descendant of the Japanese gods, in his divine benevolence, would save not only the Japanese nation but all human civilization. As a result of the bombs, the Japanese had been transformed from aggressors to saviors, a magnificent feat of public relations. In fact, official Japanese reasoning was more complicated than the Emperor's speech suggests. The ruling elite of Japan, with the Emperor as its active high priest, was afraid that the Japanese people, exhausted, hungry, and sick of war, might become unruly. The atomic bombs offered a perfect excuse to end the war on terms that would not destroy the elite. Admiral Yonai Mitsumasa, a member of the peace faction, said on August 12, 1945:

> I think the term is perhaps inappropriate, but the atomic bombs and the Soviet entry into the war are, in a sense, gifts from the gods. This way we don't have to say that we quit the war because of domestic circumstances. Why I have long been advocating control of the crisis of the country is neither for fear of an enemy attack nor because of the atomic bombs and the Soviet entry into the war. The main reason is my anxiety over the domestic situa-

*_Showa Tenno Dokuhakuroku,_ p. 121.

tion. So, it is rather fortunate that now we can control matters without revealing the domestic situation.*

———

It is not certain that a warning, or demonstration of the bomb, would have been enough of an excuse for the peace faction and the Emperor to stand up to the diehards. Oppenheimer could think of no demonstration "sufficiently spectacular" to bring about surrender. Assistant Secretary of War John McCloy disagreed; he recommended a demonstration. The least one can say is that it would surely have been worth a try. For 200,000 deaths was a high price to pay for a gift from the gods.

Alperovitz, among others, suggests that an earlier war declaration by the Soviet Union, coupled with an American promise to protect the Emperor, would have been enough to make Japan give in. After all, the Emperor was protected after the Japanese surrender, so why not before? As soon as Japan showed its readiness to accept the Potsdam terms on August 10, so long as the Emperor would be protected, Truman was so eager to end the war that the Emperor's authority was recognized, "subject to the Supreme Commander of the Allied Powers" (SCAP).

Alperovitz finds this change of policy "puzzling." If then, why not before? But there is quite a difference between recognizing the Emperor's authority as a condition of surrender, and doing so under the auspices of SCAP, after Japan was defeated. For now the United States was in control of the institution. The result was not entirely positive. SCAP, that is to say General MacArthur, used his powers to protect Emperor Hirohito not only from prosecution for war crimes but even from appearing as a witness. This had serious consequences, for so long as the Emperor, in whose name the war had been waged, could not be held accountable, the question of war guilt would remain fuzzy in Japan, and a source of friction between Japan and its former enemies.

Alperovitz thinks that Truman's uncompromising position at Potsdam had given "hard-line army leaders a trump card against early surrender proposals. The army could continue to argue that the Emperor-God might be removed, perhaps tried as a war criminal, pos-

*Quoted in the fascinating article by Herbert P. Bix in the Spring 1995 issue of *Diplomatic History,* p. 218.

sibly even hanged." Here I think he is missing the point. The hard-liners, as well as the peace faction, were fighting to preserve a *kokutai,* which was hardly benign. Indeed, it was the very system that brought war to Asia. Herbert Bix, one of the most knowledgeable historians of the Japanese imperial system, has argued—I think, rightly—that even the peace faction wanted to retain an authoritarian system, which would have left substantial power in the Emperor's hands. He writes:

> If Grew and the Japan crowd [in Washington] had gotten their way, and the principle of unconditional surrender had been con-travened, it is highly unlikely that Japan's post-surrender leaders, now the "moderates" around the throne, would ever have dis-carded the Meiji Constitution and democratized their political in-stitutions.*

Although Truman might have looked better in retrospect if he had guaranteed the Emperor's status earlier, before dropping the atomic bombs, such a guarantee alone was unlikely to have pushed Japan toward surrender before August 9. The hard-liners rejected the idea of an Allied occupation, let alone the submission of the imperial institu-tion to a foreign ruler. Indeed, some of the diehards, including War Minister Anami, continued to argue against the surrender until August 14, when the Emperor, once again, spoke in favor of peace. After that, Anami resisted no more, and committed suicide in the traditional man-ner of a samurai.

Those who claim that Truman should have been more flexible tend to misunderstand the role of the imperial institution. Alperovitz writes that the Japanese regarded their emperor as a god, "more like Jesus or the incarnate Buddha," and that the U.S. demand for unconditional surrender "directly threatened not only the person of the Emperor but such central tenets of Japanese culture as well." In fact, the Emperor was never regarded as anything like the Buddha; he was more like a priest-king, a combination of the Pope and a constitutional monarch. Alperovitz quotes, with approval, John McCloy's proposal in 1945 that "the Mikado" be retained "on the basis of a constitutional monarchy."

*Diplomatic History, p. 223.

But Emperor Hirohito already was a constitutional monarch. The problem was his other function, as the pope of Japanese nationalism. His position during the 1930s and early 1940s had less to do with central tenets of Japanese culture than with a political ideology, based in large part on nineteenth-century European nationalism. It was not culture or religion that the Japanese leaders tried to protect, but their own position in the *kokutai*. Without the Emperor, their power would have lacked any legitimacy. Since it was Truman's aim to break their power, he had to break the *kokutai* first.

The question at the heart of Alperovitz's book is "whether, when the bomb was used, the president and his top advisers understood that it was not required to avoid a long and costly invasion, as they later claimed and as most Americans still believe." He has proved that avoiding an invasion was not Washington's only aim. Secretary of State Henry Stimson's statement (to McCloy) in May 1945 makes that pretty clear. The United States, he said, had "coming into action a weapon which will be unique." The "method now to deal with Russia was to . . . let our actions speak for words." And the United States might have to "do it in a pretty rough and realistic way." There is no doubt that at Potsdam Truman saw the bomb as a joker in his pack.

But Alperovitz does not prove conclusively that the Soviet Union was the only reason for dropping the bomb. There were other considerations, which did involve the possibility of an invasion. Truman wanted to end the war swiftly to stop the Soviet advance in East Asia, but also because Americans were getting tired of fighting. Truman worried that the prospect of a prolonged war in the Far East, including an eventual invasion, would put pressure on him to accept a Japanese surrender on less than favorable terms. In other words, before Hiroshima, Truman did think the defeat of Japan, on American terms, might require a long battle. The problem with Alperovitz's analysis is that he pays too little attention to the political situation in wartime Japan. In his famous book *Atomic Diplomacy*, published in 1965, there is only one reference to Prime Minister Suzuki, and none to his die-hard opponents Anami, Umezu and Toyoda. His new tome still only mentions them in passing.

Alperovitz's case that the bomb was not dropped to prevent a final bloody battle rests entirely on the assumption that Truman and his advisers knew perfectly well that the Japanese were on the verge of capitulation before the destruction of Hiroshima. Closer examination of what went on in Tokyo shows that the Japanese were not. So long as there was no unanimity in the war cabinet and the Emperor remained silent, the war would go on. And so long as the hard-liners prevailed, any attempt by members of the peace faction, such as Foreign Minister Togo, to negotiate for peace had to be vague, furtive and inconclusive. Alperovitz makes a great deal of Togo's dispatches in July 1945 to Sato Naotake, ambassador to Moscow, conveying the Emperor's wish to discuss peace terms through the good offices of Moscow. He makes less of the fact that Ambassador Sato told his foreign minister that the mission was hopeless since Japan had nothing specific to discuss. And he makes nothing at all of the other reason for approaching Moscow: important members of the peace faction, including Admiral Yonai, still hoped to forge a Japanese-Soviet alliance against the United States and Britain.★

So I do not believe it was an irrational policy on Truman's part to insist on unconditional surrender. But analyzing rational policies is not the business of a professor of psychiatry and psychology, so Robert Jay Lifton ignores these political considerations, and dwells on such issues as Truman's "denial of death," or James Byrnes's "totalistic relationship with the weapon," or "the formation of separate, relatively autonomous selves" in the personality of Henry Stimson. From this psychiatric perspective, anyone mad enough to drop an atomic bomb, even in 1945, when any means to end the war had to be considered, must be a mental patient. And the policy of a mental patient has to be touched with madness.

———

Lifton and Mitchell claim, like Alperovitz, that since the successful test of the atomic bomb, "Truman and Byrnes began to focus on how to end the war sufficiently quickly that the Soviets would not gain a foothold in Japan." But again the authors do not consider the reasons why. To them it is but one more example of Truman's irrational state of mind, because he was suppressing his feelings and "any tendency to reflect,"

★Japanese historians have paid attention to this, most recently in a discussion in the September 1995 issue of the monthly magazine *Gendai.*

since he had been bad at sports as a child and was afraid of being "a sissy." Even if all these things were true, there were still compelling reasons for wishing to stop Soviet troops from entering Japan. There was concern in Washington about the swift expansion of the Soviet Empire in Eastern and Central Europe. The U.S. ambassador to the Soviet Union, W. Averill Harriman, called it a "barbarian invasion." He believed, quite correctly, that Soviet control of other countries meant the extinction of political liberties in those countries and a dominant Soviet influence over their foreign relations. As subsequent events in China and the Korean peninsula have shown, Truman was right to worry about Soviet power in northeast Asia. It certainly would not have suited U.S. interests, or those of Japan for that matter, if the Japanese archipelago had been divided into different occupation zones, with Stalin's troops ensconced in Hokkaido.

As he did in his book on the "genocidal mentality" of nuclear scientists and strategists,* Lifton uses the phrase "nuclearism," which he describes as "a spiritual faith that the ultimate power of the emerging weapon could serve not only death and destruction but also continuing life." Believers in this faith, such as Truman, feel like "merging with a source of power rivaling that of any deity." They are, in short, possessed. Here Lifton and Mitchell are close to the religious position of Dr. Nagai: the atomic bombs over Hiroshima and Nagasaki were propelled by a force beyond human reason. Having established that, the authors can dispense with political arguments and concentrate on the corruption of American life by irrational forces. They can write that the "nurturing of this deified object [i.e., the bomb], as our source of security and ultimate power over death, became the central task of our society," without contemplating what the world would have been like if the sole possessors of this object had been the likes of Josef Stalin.

3.

Perhaps it helps to be a Nagasaki Catholic to take a more complex view of sin. Loyalty to their own deity must have given some Japanese Christians a skeptical view of Japanese politics when the *kokutai* was at the height of its divine imperial pretensions. One of the most controversial

The Genocidal Mentality, by Robert Jay Lifton and Eric Markusen (Basic Books, 1990).

and interesting Nagasaki Catholics is the ex-mayor Motoshima Hi-toshi. I first interviewed him seven years ago, in Nagasaki, when Emperor Hirohito was dying. Motoshima had just said in public that the Emperor bore some responsibility for the war and, by not ending it soon enough, for the fates of Hiroshima and Nagasaki. A conservative politician, he was disowned by the Liberal Democratic Party and black-balled by various patriotic organizations of which he was a member. He also received threats from right-wing extremists. One year later, he was shot in the back by one of them, and barely survived. This is the "Japanese culture" that remains from the war. It is no longer the main political tendency, but it is still intimidating enough to silence critics of the imperial system and other remnants of the old *kokutai,* which General MacArthur helped to protect.

This summer, Motoshima looked less robust than I remembered him, perhaps because of the assassination attempt, perhaps because of his recent loss of the mayoral election. He began by reading the late Emperor's statement of August 15, 1945, about the "new and most cruel bomb." He tapped the text with his finger and said the bomb did bring the war to an end. But then he made another point. The atomic bombs, he said, had done away with the idea of a good war. He himself had believed in a Japanese victory. Although he had been tormented as a Christian child by teachers who forced him to declare who was holier, Jesus or the Emperor, Motoshima was a patriot. He served in an army propaganda unit. But the atomic bombs had turned war into an absolute evil, like the Holocaust in Europe. He illustrated this view at a recent press conference in Tokyo, by comparing the innocent victims of Hiroshima and Nagasaki to the Jews killed at Auschwitz. The Japanese press made nothing of this. But the Western correspondents were full of indignation: yet another Japanese whitewash, they thought, another sob story of the Japanese as victims.

I asked him about this. Was there really no difference between the citizens of a nation that started a war and people who were killed for purely ideological reasons? Had he himself not said that the Japanese people bore responsibility for the war, as well as their emperor? He answered my question by asking me whether I thought Jewish soldiers in Hitler's army had been responsible for the war in Europe. Clearly, the precise nature of the European Holocaust had rather escaped him. But when pressed by others he has acknowledged that there was a differ-

ence between the atomic bombings and the Holocaust. The United
States was not planning to exterminate the entire Japanese people. The
question remains, however, whether there is a fundamental moral difference between dropping atomic bombs on Hiroshima and Nagasaki
and many thousands of incendiary bombs on, say, Tokyo.

———

Miyazaki Kentaro, the son of bomb survivors, and a historian specializ-
ing in the "hidden Christian" communities in Japan, saw no moral difference. All forms of carpet bombing were a sin. But like the former
mayor, he blamed the Japanese government for starting the war, and saw
no reason to criticize the United States. I also asked the opinion of Father Sebastian Kawazoe, the priest at Urakami Cathedral. Like Motoshima, with whom he went to school, Kawazoe was born on one of the
Goto Islands, in a family of hidden Christians. He had the same straight,
almost rough, manner of speaking as the ex-mayor. He told me most
Catholics had not been keen supporters of the war. But they had to be
careful, for they were always being treated as spies. He, too, saw no
moral distinction between A-bombs and other forms of terror bombing.

I dwell on this point because I think it clarifies our thinking about
the past. If we see the atomic bombs as morally unique, as something
fundamentally different, in ethical terms, from large numbers of incendiary bombs or napalm bombs dropped on civilians, it is difficult to an-
alyze the actions of men, such as Truman, who saw the A-bomb attacks
as a logical extension of strategic bombing.* McGeorge Bundy wrote
about this in his book *Danger and Survival,* in a chapter entitled "The
Decision to Drop the Bombs on Japan."

> Both military and political leaders came to think of urban de-
> struction not as wicked, not even as a necessary evil, but as a result
> with its own military value. Distinctions that had seemed clear

---

*In his article, "Understanding the Atomic Bomb and the Japanese Surrender: Missed
Opportunities, Little-Known Near Disasters, and Modern Memory," in *Diplomatic History* (Spring 1995), Barton Bernstein emphasizes that "in 1945, American leaders were
not seeking to avoid the use of the A-bomb. Its use did not create ethical or political
problems for them" (p. 235).

when the Germans bombed Rotterdam were gradually rubbed out in the growing ferocity of the war.*

This, rather than theological jargon about original sin or "nuclearism," is the nub of the matter. Truman, in response to an American advocate of "the Christian tradition of civilized war," said there was no such thing, that war "has always been a matter of slaughter of innocents and never civilized." This sounds good, a moral *cri de coeur* from a tough-minded, peace-loving leader, but it is disingenuous. For there is a difference between killing innocents in the heat of battle and killing them deliberately, in huge numbers, as a form of terror. Tens of thousands died horribly in Dresden without any apparent military or political justification. The possibility that the carnage in Hiroshima and Nagasaki might have brought the war to a speedier end made these mass killings expedient, perhaps, but no less morally disturbing. This does not mean, however, that it would have been any more ethical to go on fire-bombing Japanese cities, as Curtis LeMay, an opponent of the A-bomb strategy, wanted. More than 100,000 civilians had already died in one night in May, when LeMay's B-29s torched Tokyo with incendiary bombs. Truman's decision to drop the bombs was the climax of a horrible strategy, started by Germany and Japan, that had left much of Europe, parts of China and most of Japan in ruins.

—

It would make sense for the Nagasaki Catholics, who suffered disproportionately from the A-bomb, to be active in the antinuclear peace movement. Actually they are not. Motoshima, who is a campaigner for world peace, is an exception. Father Kawazoe, himself a survivor, said: "I don't take part in the peace movement. It is used by people to expand their own sect. They talk about peace, but you don't know what's behind it." While acknowledging the checkered record of the Christian Church—"60 percent bad, 40 percent good"—he also said: "We Christians have a history of oppression, but we don't make a living out of our suffering. Emphasizing one's own suffering is just a way to win sympathy."

*Quoted by Barton Bernstein in *Judgment at the Smithsonian,* p. 194.

This is a bit harsh on the survivors in Peace Park, who devote their time to telling schoolchildren about the bomb. But as I watched those same schoolchildren, lined up in straight rows in front of the "Peace Statue" and solemnly shouting lines they had memorized about loving peace, I was reminded of demonstrations in the former East Berlin, where the masses marched past their leaders, raising their fists and bellowing slogans about "people's friendship." These peace ceremonies have become ritual gestures to ward off nuclear evil: "People who love peace, please sign your name here."

There is nothing in Nagasaki to tell those schoolchildren why the bomb was dropped, or what led up to it. It is indeed hard to explain why the bomb had to be dropped on Nagasaki. There is no evidence that it hastened the end of the war. Carl Spaatz, the commanding general of the U.S. Army Strategic Air Forces, is quoted by Alperovitz as saying (to Averill Harriman) that he had no idea why a bomb had been dropped on Nagasaki. We will never know to what extent the fate of Nagasaki influenced the Emperor's decision to tell his soldiers to lay down their arms. But some historical context, some indication of what those Japanese soldiers had done to others, would not have been amiss. Instead, all one really hears in Nagasaki is the sound of prayer. And one only needs to walk past the Peace Park monuments, from China, the USSR, Bulgaria, Cuba, Poland, Czechoslovakia and the German Democratic Republic, to see how peace has been exploited.

———

On my last day in Nagasaki, I visited Urakami Cathedral, where Father Kawazoe was celebrating Mass. The cathedral was full, with more women than men. The women wore old-fashioned veils, a custom that has virtually died out in Europe. Almost all these people were descended from families who had clung to their faith through centuries of persecution. It was a moving spectacle, even if one had no special feeling for the Catholic Church. Father Kawazoe was preaching that God's will could not be known, and it was useless to expect favors from Him. God was not like some local deity, whom one could ask for a good catch or an abundant crop. I was puzzled by this. Here was a Japanese priest, in the cathedral of a modern, sophisticated city, talking to people as though they were villagers on Goto Island who had to be weaned from their native gods.

I left the cathedral feeling touched, but also with a sense of sadness and futility. Outside were some of the remains of the old cathedral: a blackened statue of Christ, with a chipped nose and dark stumps where there had once been fingers; and there a damaged Saint Agnes; and there, in the grass, the charred heads of decapitated angels. People used to believe that Armageddon was a prerogative of God, or of the gods. Now we know it is in the hands of man. Hardly a consolation.

1995

WE JAPANESE

Two books published in 1987, one by an American scholar and former ambassador to Japan, the other by a Japanese industrialist, complement each other to a remarkable degree. The ambassador tells us how America gave Japan a break; the industrialist describes how he took advantage of it. Neither puts it in quite those terms, of course. While in *My Life Between Japan and America,* Edwin Reischauer speaks vaguely of "shared ideals" and "world peace," in *Made in Japan: Akio Morita and Sony,* Morita explains the Japanese Economic Miracle as an expression of unique Japanese cultural qualities: devotion to work, loyalty to company, love of learning and so forth. Both men (one hesitates to call Morita an author—his book bears the marks of having been dictated to his collaborators in a hurry, between appointments) plead for understanding for Japanese culture.

But they do so in a way that reminds me of something that happened to a friend of mine about fifteen years ago. A young Chinese homosexual, who was living in the house of a middle-aged French restaurateur, had the habit of coming home late and sleeping late in the mornings.

The Frenchman got so annoyed by this that he woke his friend one day by dousing him with a bucketful of cold water. The Chinese was furious. The main reason for his rage appeared to be his wounded pride. "How could he have done such a thing?" he asked me. "I am Chinese!" He had lost face, as a Chinese. It is hard to imagine a Frenchman reacting in this way. He might be outraged by having cold water thrown in his face, but not because he is French.

Something a little like this can play a part in international relations. "Face" is a fragile thing in East Asia, and cultural sensitivities are easily affronted. It is interesting to see how often the Japanese, for example, plead understanding for their side in trade disputes on cultural grounds. Tariff barriers cannot come down just yet because of traditional social harmony, or the long history of isolation, or delicate domestic sensitivities or whatnot; but never because it would force local businesses into unwelcome competition with foreigners. Even more interesting is how many American experts, scholars and diplomats come to the fore on these occasions to argue the Japanese case. I have never heard of a Japanese expert on America explaining Washington's point of view to his countrymen on the grounds of special American sensitivities. Face, delicate feelings, a long history, all are part of the East. The West is supposed to be as coldly neutral as the machine age it introduced to the unsuspecting world. (Hence, perhaps, the genuine astonishment of many Japanese when Americans yelp in pain when hit in a soft spot, as in 1986, when Prime Minister Nakasone made his remarks about blacks and Hispanics dragging American educational standards down.)

Morita, one of the founders of Sony and perhaps the most effective public-relations man for Japan Inc., appears to be in two minds about Americans. They clearly lack the warm family feelings of "We Japanese" (a favorite Morita expression), they see nothing wrong in hopping from one employer to another, or in firing workers when times are bad. But when they attack We Japanese for obstructing American trade, they are "too emotional" and show signs of a "victim complex." At one point in his book Morita's own emotions get the better of him:

> In Japan we are still the inheritors of an agrarian cultural tradition
> and philosophy, which are influenced by nature and the change of

the seasons. . . . We have thousands of years of history and tradition and that is why we are not pleased when we are treated as newcomers by such a young—even though great—country as the United States.

One might well ask what the four seasons have to do with international terms of trade, but this is one of the most often heard clichés of the great Japanese cultural tariff barrier, that cluster of myths commonly believed to be signs of Japanese uniqueness. These myths are worth examining, for they affect the way Japan wishes to be seen by the outside world, and thus they affect international affairs. Part of the mythology is Japan's unique claim to the guardianship of peace, linked on the left to the unique suffering from American nuclear bombs, and on the right to a celebration of "our one-race nation" (Morita), with its uniquely harmonious industrial relations. As an example of Japan's peaceful nature, Morita points out that there were no wars in Japan during the country's period of virtual isolation from 1603 to 1868: "Japan may have been the only country in the world where complete peace reigned for such a long time." And he goes on to write, "in our labour relations, we have a kind of equality that does not exist elsewhere." This is complete nonsense, but more about that later. Suffice it to say at this point that many heads were cracked before the power of independent Japanese unions was broken. The implication of Morita's claim is clear, however: foreign pressure threatens Japanese harmony.

In the Tokyo magazine *Bungei Shunju,* an associate professor of philosophy called Hasegawa Michiko wrote in 1984 that Japan unleashed its fifteen-year war in Asia because the Japanese "began to subscribe to the characteristically Western world view of dividing nations into friends and foes . . . and of behaving antagonistically towards enemies." After the war, however, "the Japanese determined never again to take up residence in the violent Western-style international community." Hasegawa is regarded as a right-wing Japanese nationalist. The position of the Japanese left can be summed up best by quoting from *Introduction to Peace Education,* a booklet published by the Hiroshima Peace Education Research Center:

Japan suffered incalculable human, spiritual and material damage from the war. We repented our aggression. We are a new people who will never take part in or start another war. . . . In our constitution it is clearly expressed that we negate war and seek eternal peace. . . . However, after the war, Japan, under the U.S. Occupation forces, was dragged into the so-called cold war and forced to rearm against the Soviet Union.

The Japan–U.S. security treaty allowing the U.S. to keep its forces in Japan, the booklet goes on to explain, is "absolutely contrary to the spirit of the constitution."

The security treaty was extended in 1960, when Prime Minister Kishi Nobusuke, a former minister in General Tojo's wartime cabinet, pushed it through parliament. The extraordinary riots that followed cost President Eisenhower his planned trip to Japan and Kishi his job. It was under these or, more precisely, because of these circumstances that Edwin O. Reischauer was appointed by President Kennedy as U.S. ambassador to Tokyo. Reischauer, born in Japan and a noted Harvard scholar in East Asian affairs, was an expert in Japanese cultural sensitivities, and his brief was, in the parlance of the time, to "restore the broken dialogue"—the dialogue, that is, with the Japanese left.

Was he the right man for the job? The Japanese, as Reischauer himself points out over and over again, certainly thought so. And many Americans thought so too. In a typical passage, Reischauer quotes "a certain Ambassador Flake, who . . . told us upon leaving that never in his thirty-five years in the Foreign Service had he seen the morale and spirit of an Embassy rise so sharply as ours did after we came." Even the Japanese emperor was pleased to see the great conciliator:

> At court functions, the Emperor could not conceal his boredom as he gravely murmured to each person in turn, "*Yo koso* (You are welcome)." However, on more than one occasion early in our stay, he suddenly broke his usual solemn round when he looked up and saw that he was shaking my hand and, bursting into a broad smile, would say with enthusiasm, "*Honto ni yo koso* (You really are very welcome)."

Ambassador Reischauer, it is clear, came, saw and conquered. Ironically, the only ones who never much took to him were the Japanese leftists, who rightly saw the so-called Reischauer line (basically the strengthening of Japan as the main capitalist Asian ally against Chinese and Soviet communism) as inimical to their pan-Asian socialist aspirations. These aspirations petered out in time. Today the voice of the left is hardly audible. Many reasons have been given for this. Few have much to do with Reischauer's ambassadorial dialogues. U.S. and, subsequently, Japanese recognition of China took much of the wind out of the pan-Asian cause. And the sharp rise in living standards that began with the economic boom of the 1960s was part of a deliberate political strategy to undermine political activism. The so-called income-doubling plan was hatched when Kishi was still prime minister, but was carried out under his successor, Ikeda Hayato. The South Korean leader Park Chung Hee, though a far more authoritarian figure than Ikeda, did the same thing for similar reasons. Oddly, Reischauer only refers to Park in the most scathing terms.

So the basis for the Japanese Economic Miracle was laid during Reischauer's tenure, which ended in 1966. The miracle seemed to suit the political goal of making Japan a strong, dependable (and, indeed, highly dependent) U.S. ally. Which is why Japan was treated as a special case, like a gifted child who needs to be carefully nurtured. It was part of the comfortable arrangement whereby Washington more or less took care of Japanese defense and foreign policy, while the Japanese got on with getting rich. In effect, Japan could build a partly state-subsidized and state-managed export economy, retaining domestic tariff barriers to an extent unthinkable in Western Europe or the U.S., and still be treated as if it were a free-trading nation. Of course, once a subsidized industry had cornered the Japanese market, the tariffs could gradually come down. One must give the Japanese credit for using the circumstances to their best advantage.

It was during that golden age of the transistor salesman that Morita built his empire. He describes in his book how he appeared in 1969 before a Joint Congressional Economic Committee in Washington. He was asked by a congressman "whether it was possible for us Americans to start a firm in Japan when you started Sony in Japan." "No," said Morita, "it was not possible." Whereupon the congressman said, "But Sony has now established a firm in America. Why is it that America is not allowed to enter Japan?" And Morita said, "The Japanese had a fear complex that giant America's free inroads into Japan would immediately outmarket them. Whatever the reason, as long as they have this fear complex, they will feel resistant toward liberalization." Quite how this fits in with Morita's admonishments that if only American businessmen would learn Japanese and work harder, the Japanese market would be theirs, is never explained.

Naturally, Japan's rather cushy economic deal and its lack of a foreign policy beyond wishing, like any good merchant, to remain friends with everybody, irritated Americans and Europeans at times, but this is where Reischauer could be counted upon to explain Japanese cultural sensitivities to the unthinking and unfeeling barbarians.

Besides speaking Japanese, Reischauer was a youthful representative of Kennedy's Camelot, and was married to a Japanese. Almost as soon as they arrived in Tokyo, Reischauer and his wife, Haru, became superstars for the Japanese press. He saw his job "as being essentially educational, as it had been at Harvard." This meant explaining America to the Japanese, but, more importantly for a Japanese scholar, it meant explaining Japan to Americans. Reischauer often showed impatience with American newsmen who did not show an adequate understanding of things Japanese. The great Japanese public, which adores benign pedagogues, especially when the subject concerns the great Japanese public itself, loved Reischauer. And Japanese officials, who know a soft foreign touch when they see one, loved him too.

There is obviously nothing wrong with promoting mutual understanding. Indeed, it is desirable. But understanding Japanese feelings is held to be synonymous in Japan with seeing things from Tokyo's point of view. Understanding, in other words, implies agreement. Mixing politics and culture, therefore, almost always works toward Japan's advantage. In the 1960s Japan's advantage was held to be America's advantage too—few people had woken up yet to the potential might of the Japanese industrial machine. So, in the mood of his time, Reischauer did a good job. In the 1980s things became a little different, however. And it would have been fascinating to know what the old conciliator thinks now of the trade imbalance between the U.S. and Japan, and to what extent it can be traced to policies laid down in the days of his own Tokyo Camelot.

Alas, not a word. Instead, endless space is devoted to more prestigious (a favorite Reischauer word) matters: awards, distinguished guests, speeches received rapturously, prestigious positions on prestigious panels of prestigious organizations, and so on. When Reischauer vents his spleen about not receiving a Purple Heart—"which I felt I deserved for my close brush with death in the service of my country"—after being stabbed in the thigh by a Japanese lunatic, one is not sure whether he is being facetious. One rather thinks not.

Morita, as a true insider, could have given us an important account of how the Japanese economic system was set up, how the Ministry of International Trade and Industry decided upon policies, how they benefited Japanese companies, and how Sony, as a postwar parvenu, fitted in with more established corporations with closer links to the bureaucracy. But Morita is so busy promoting himself—so much for the stereotypical self-effacing Japanese—and the virtues of Japanese culture that he explains absolutely nothing, except, well, himself. "As I said to Henry Kissinger . . ."; "I was frank with Deng . . ."; "I told President Reagan . . ."; "I pointed out to my friend George Shultz . . ."; "Herbert von Karajan . . ."; "Cyrus Vance . . ." And there usually follows a self-serving platitude about the feelings of We Japanese. Although Morita likes to think of Sony as an exceptional company in Japan—perhaps rightly—it is not always clear which hat he is wearing: that of Morita the man, Morita the chairman of Sony, or Morita the spokesman of We Japanese. As far as the man's exceptional talents are concerned, we are told that these were "handed down to me through the family genes." But he also believes that as a manager he is blessed with "a kind of Oriental sixth sense." This piece of wisdom was actually suggested by William Bernbach, the New York advertising man, and Morita took to it instantly.

Reischauer, too, appears to have imbibed Oriental wisdom in his baby cot. The first sentence of Chapter 1 reveals a great deal about the ambassador's character:

> In my youth, American children born in Japan, especially those of missionary parentage, were called BIJs. We were very proud of the distinction and felt superior to our less fortunate comrades. We tended to know a great deal more about living in Japan than they did and to speak better Japanese.

The BIJ mentality seems to have stuck for life. As has the missionary zeal to teach mankind the morally correct position, as it were. Reischauer takes trouble to inform his readers that, unlike in other foreigners' households, "the fundamental attitude . . . in my own home . . . was one of deep respect for the Japanese." Four paragraphs later he repeats that "I was free from racial prejudice," and that this meant that "I was a generation or two ahead of my time." It is splendid and reassuring to know that the ambassador was not a racist, but there is something annoying about the way he has to ram the point home. It also betrays the peculiar defensiveness of a man who is emotionally committed to two countries which do not always get along well. Reischauer is constantly ready to defend Japan against would-be attackers. This may not have been quite the right frame of mind for a man with the brief to defend American interests in a competitive world.

Reischauer is a little too proud of his own righteousness. Like a considerable number of liberal-minded people at the time, he thought in the late 1930s that Western colonial empires had had their day. In 1939 he wrote a proposal to the State Department that argued that "all the peoples and nations of the Pacific Area are by nature equal as nations, peoples and individuals" and that "all discrimination based upon differences of race" should be ended. These were noble sentiments, with which one can have no quarrel. But to say that "I was light-years ahead of most other people" is an overstatement. "Who could envisage the disappearance of the British, French, and the Dutch empires?" Well, quite a few people, actually. Why does he think Gandhi had so much support in Britain?

The point, however, is not so much that Reischauer is a boaster: modesty may be a virtue, but it is a virtue lacking in many great men. There is a more important flaw in the BIJ's character—a flaw shared by many liberals, especially liberals born to missionary parents. Reischauer is so intent on proving his moral righteousness that he risks losing touch with reality. Or, to put it in another way, reality is rejected when it does not fit into his moral vision. How else can one explain Reischauer's insistence that the U.S. and Japan shared an "equal partnership," when this was—and is—so patently beside the truth? An equal partnership, when the U.S. ambassador to Tokyo "ranked somewhere between the imperial family and the cabinet"? The equal partnership is, of course, a fine ideal based upon another ideal, presented by Rei-schauer as if it were reality. This is that "the two nations shared common basic ideals of democracy, human rights, and egalitarianism, and yearned alike for a peaceful world order made up of truly independent nations, bound together by as free and open trade as possible." We all want peace. And Japan certainly benefits from free and open trade in other countries. But the same common ideals of democracy and human rights? This is an act of faith, by no means always justified by facts.

Not that allies necessarily need to share the same ideals, as long as they share the same interests. It is certainly in the interests of both Tokyo and Washington that conflict between the countries is avoided. But one wonders whether that cause is served in the long run by painting a rosier picture than one ought, and by tolerating political gambits in the guise of cultural proclivities.

Morita's book is political. It is a huge red herring to distract American businessmen wringing their hands at so many Japanese miracles. His cultural explanations for Japanese business success are not only self-serving and disingenuous, but false. It is not true that Japanese companies never fire workers, because "we are part of the same family." Only the largest corporations offer the so-called lifetime employment system, which covers about one third of the Japanese workforce. The rest are employed as seasonal contract workers or work for small subcontracting firms, which have a vital part in Japanese industry. While it is true that large corporations can ride economic crises without letting many workers go, this is at the expense of smaller firms, who no longer enjoy the trickle-down benefits of the big companies. It is they who suffer from the high yen rate, while the large corporations export as many cars and video sets as before. And plenty of workers get fired in the process.

It is not true that "the competition on our domestic markets makes the consumer king." Japanese consumers sometimes pay as much as 50 percent more than people overseas for manufactured goods, and about five times as much for beef or rice (rice farmers are protected from outside competition because they are part of the "Japanese cultural heritage," as well as voters for the ruling Liberal Democratic Party).

It is not true that "today's Japanese do not think in terms of privilege" or that "we have a kind of equality that does not exist elsewhere."

Japanese society is very hierarchical indeed, especially when compared to the U.S. And the historical example of eighteenth-century actors who broke into the upper classes by dint of their success is absurd: actors, like black slaves, were sought after as illicit sex partners, but they were still beyond the pale in class terms—an attitude that persists even today. When Morita's own son wanted to marry a popular singer, he was almost disowned by his father. As an instance of his own egalitarianism—as opposed to American elitism—Morita tells us that he was prepared to pose for pictures with the staff of a Sony lab near Palo Alto. And as for the idea that "money is not the most effective tool" to motivate Japanese workers, but that "family loyalty" is, well, I would like to hear that from a factory worker, not from his very rich boss. (One wonders, incidentally, what could have stimulated a respected journalist like Edwin Reingold to help write this shoddy book, if it was not money— but then, of course, he is a materialistic American.)

But even if all these things were true, they still do not explain why so many foreign products cannot be sold in Japan at competitive prices. Forget about American cars, what about products from South Korea or other Asian countries?

Morita is quite right to say at the end of his book that the "future holds exciting technological advances that will enrich the lives of everybody on the planet." Take telecommunications, for example, a field in which the U.S. is still superior. Professor Chalmers Johnson of the University of California at Berkeley has written a detailed study of how two Japanese ministries are gearing up to set the stage for another Japanese miracle: the future monopoly of the telecommunications market by Japanese corporations. What is to be done about this? Peter Drucker, among others, suggests bilateralism or "reciprocity": tariffs and other penalties applicable only to goods from countries that refuse to import similar goods.

Morita's answer? "Reciprocity would mean changing laws to accept foreign systems that may not suit our culture." Indeed.

1987

SAMURAI OF SWAT

Few Japanese—if any—have forgotten that dark day in October 1964 when Anton Geesink beat the Japanese judo champion Kaminaga Akio to win the Olympic gold medal in Tokyo. The Dutch giant— 6 foot 6 inches, 267 pounds—didn't just beat Kaminaga, he flattened him. And the nation wept, quite literally. Grown men, pressed against shop windows to see the fight on television sets especially provided for this purpose all over Tokyo, collapsed in tears. Geesink told reporters that coping with the Japanese crowds after the fight had been tougher than the fight itself.

Judo was introduced that year for the first time in the history of the Olympic Games by special request of the Japanese hosts. Judo was not just a national sport: it symbolized the Japanese way—spiritual, disciplined, infinitely subtle; a way in which crude Western brawn would inevitably lose to superior Oriental spirit. And here, in Tokyo, a big, blond foreigner had humiliated Japan in front of the entire world. It was as though the ancestral Sun Goddess had been raped in public by a gang of alien demons. The disaster was blamed on Geesink's bulk, of course, but that rather left one wondering about this business of spirit versus brawn.

Sport, like sex, cuts where it hurts most: that soft spot where national virility is at stake. Nowhere is it more sensitive than in Japan, the peripheral nation, always on the outside edge of greater powers, always panting to catch up with the foreign metropolis, Changan, Beijing, Paris, London, New York. And at no time was it more delicate than in the 1960s, when the nation was beginning to crawl out from the shadow of the greatest humiliation of all: defeat in war and subsequent occupation by a superior foreign power. The Tokyo Olympics were supposed to have put the seal on all that. The revival of national virility, already boosted by the accelerating economic boom, was at hand; the Judo Open Weight gold medal was meant to have clinched it; the shame of defeat would be wiped out and Japanese face would finally be restored.

The writer Nosaka Akiyuki described exactly what it was all about in a wonderful novella, published in 1972, entitled *Amerika Hijiki* ("American Seaweed"). A Japanese man is visited in Tokyo by an American acquaintance who had served in Japan during the occupation. For his entertainment, the American guest is taken to a live sex show, where Japan's "Number One Male" is to perform. On this occasion, however, Number One, possibly distracted by the American in the audience, fails. The Japanese host is as embarrassed as the star performer but understands his predicament:

> As soon as those jeeps started racing through his mind, cries of "come on everybody" rang in his ears, and sad memories of brilliant skies over burnt-out bomb sites returned, he was rendered impotent . . .

Strong measures, in such humiliating circumstances, were called for. And in the late 1950s national virility was redeemed somewhat in the spectacular shape of Riki Dozan, a large and very virile wrestler who specialized in beating big, blond Americans—often wearing cowboy hats—to the mat. Riki Dozan was the perfect Japanese macho man: he had fighting spirit to burn. But he always spoke fondly, even tearfully, of his mother, was benevolent to his juniors, and fought fairly. The outsize Americans, on the other hand, fought dirty. But despite the hidden knuckledusters and other weaponry suddenly produced by these dastardly foreigners, Riki Dozan's fighting spirit would invariably prevail. In comic-book versions of his career, this indomitable spirit was inspired by frequent visions of Mount Fuji. Few men in the history of modern Japan have been more popular. That he was actually born a Korean, like so many other Japanese sporting heroes, was something people preferred to ignore. Hence, when he was stabbed to death in a Tokyo nightclub a year before the Tokyo Olympics, only one national newspaper cared to mention this unfortunate blot on his otherwise exemplary biography.

Given all this, Anton Geesink's victory was deeply shocking. Yet to say that he was not respected in Japan would be untrue. Despite the national shame of Kaminaga's defeat and the common air of contempt for big, blond (not to mention black) foreigners, Geesink's power was held in awe. He was a bit like the demon guardians of hell that stand by the gates of Japanese temples, to be approached with a proper sense of trepidation. But as soon as the great judoka's powers began to flag, and he was foolish enough to appear in degrading wrestling exhibitions, awe and trepidation swiftly changed to ridicule. Once Samson is shorn of his locks, the Japanese show little mercy. Geesink's position in Japan was typical of the way in which foreign demons have traditionally been treated by the Japanese: worshiped one day, despised the next, all according to the state of their virility.

Too much foreign virility, however, is not a good thing either. It upsets the natural, that is to say, the Japanese order of things; it upsets harmony, or *wa*. The fascinating story of Warren Cromartie, the black American baseball player, formerly of the Montreal Expos, is typical of the ups and downs to which the foreign demon is subjected in Japan. In 1983 he was offered a three-year contract by the Tokyo Giants to play for $600,000 a year, roughly ten times what most Japanese players made. He was met at Narita Airport by the general manager of the Giants, who stuck out his hand, bowed, and said, "Welcome to Japan, Mr. Cromartie, you are òur Messiah."

Five years later, with a .313 batting average and 160 home runs to his name, his picture was missing from the Giants' Gallery of Stars outside the team's home park. Nor was he asked to endorse products, like his

Japanese colleagues. Nor was his name mentioned by the club's dignitaries in their celebration speeches, after he had helped win the championship pennant. Instead, the Japanese players were exhorted to play better than the imported *gaijin,* or foreigner. And, when the team went through hard times, the *gaijin* would be blamed for his lack of spirit, his greedy materialism, and his selfish ways, which upset the *wa* of the team. In Cromartie's own words, quoted in one of Robert Whiting's two excellent books on Japanese baseball, *You Gotta Have Wa,* "You're an outcast no matter what you do. You go 5-for-5 and you're ignored. You go 0-for-5 and it's 'Fuck you. Yankee go home.' "

The case of Randy Bass, also described in *You Gotta Have Wa,* is even more remarkable. Bass, a left-handed power hitter from Oklahoma, started playing for the Hanshin Tigers in 1983. He, too, was greeted as the Messiah. He even got to do endorsements on Japanese television—as more than one Japanese politician has hinted in the past, the Japanese tend to prefer blondes to blacks. So Bass was doing all right. Then he threatened to break the home-run record, established in 1964 by Oh Sadaharu, who hit fifty-five homers in one season. When Bass got to number fifty-four, with two games left, the Japanese closed ranks. He hardly had a chance to hit another ball, and was forced to walk in almost every inning. The record remained in local hands. *Wa* was preserved. If this was upsetting enough to Bass, worse was to follow.

After going from strength to strength and winning virtually every trophy there was to win, after becoming the most popular *gaijin* player in Japan, after being offered bigger and bigger contracts, after beating Harimoto Isao's single-season average of .383 (eliciting Harimoto's remark that Asian baseball should be for Asians only—Harimoto, like Riki Dozan, was a Korean), after hitting thirty-seven homers in 1987 with a bad back, after all that, Bass's eight-year-old son was discovered to have a brain tumor, and Bass flew to San Francisco to be by his side. While he was still in the U.S., the Tigers decided to drop him. Bass was accused of selfishness, of lacking team spirit, of putting his private affairs before those of his club, of not understanding *wa.* "Foreign players are just not a good example for young people," wrote Harimoto, the man who was often taunted by Japanese young people with cries of "garlic belly," because of his Korean birth.

Cromartie's autobiography, *Slugging It Out in Japan* (written with

Robert Whiting), could so easily have been a litany of *gaijin* complaints, the sort of thing that can make expatriate conversations so deadly. It is actually much better than that, for he is not bitter about the country that provided him with so much anguish as well as cash. His own background gave him an interesting perspective on the *gaijin* experience: "I've always been a *gaijin,* you might say. I grew up in Liberty City, the poor black section of Miami, where most people were lifetime outsiders . . ." And, in fact, the life of the *gaijin* ballplayer had some notable perks, not the least of which were the many opportunities to get laid. Cromartie is discreet on this score, though there are coy references to what "the guys tell me," but he does reveal that he had some "real relationships, not one-night stands." Which means that he actually bothered to get to know people, which is more than many expatriates do. It shows in his observations, which are both sharp and affectionate.

He is careful to distinguish between the many Japanese individuals, players as well as nonplayers, who were friendly and supportive, and the officials and their lackeys in the popular press, who made life a misery for foreigners as well as Japanese. Some of the most moving passages in the book concern Cromartie's friendship with the Giants' former manager and batting star, Oh Sadaharu, the half-Taiwanese who was forever trying to prove to his Japanese compatriots that he had the true samurai spirit in spite of his Chinese blood.

Cromartie's most important insight is one that many complaining *gaijin* tend to overlook, and one which can be applied far more widely than to the sporting world alone: the main victims of the bigoted, exclusive, rigid, racist, authoritarian ways of Japanese officialdom are not the foreigners, even though they are at times its most convenient targets, but the rank and file of the Japanese themselves. The pampered foreigner, brought in to lend power to the Japanese baseball scene, but exempted from any of the rigors of Japanese discipline, is not just a convenient scapegoat to save Japanese face when things go wrong, but also a kind of Antichrist to keep the Japanese in line. If Japanese players should balk at being kicked around, underpaid and overdisciplined, their frustration can be neatly channeled towards the overpaid, underdisciplined, greedy, selfish foreigner. "The Japanese," writes Cromartie, "always complained that we *gaijin* were overpaid. The commissioner of Japanese baseball in fact was always urging a complete ban on foreigners, saying it was degrading to Japanese baseball to have to pay big money to Americans who were washed up in the U.S. The reality, however, was that the Japanese were getting screwed." When the Japanese players finally formed a union to get a better deal out of their very rich clubs, the union's elected chief told Cromartie that "they'd never strike because it wouldn't be fair to the fans." A Japanese writer then explained to Cromartie that professional baseball players were supposed to be "clean, simple, and obedient."

Now, one might say that this simply shows a difference in culture, that the American is not necessarily better off, that loyalty, team spirit and a sense of belonging are more important to a Japanese than his personal interests; but one should bear in mind when saying so that this is exactly how men in positions of power—corporate, bureaucratic or political—justify the manner in which they continue to keep other men and women down.

Cromartie is highly instructive on how obedience is instilled in Japanese baseball teams. It begins with what a much revered Meiji-period gentleman named Tobita Suishu, also known as the "god of Japanese baseball," liked to call "death training." This meant drilling players until, in Tobita's words (quoted in Robert Whiting's *The Chrysanthemum and the Bat*), "they were half dead, motionless, and froth was coming out of their mouths." (He was referring at the time to the training of high school boys.) One such drill, still practiced by all serious coaches in Japan, is the "thousand-fungo drill." In Cromartie's words, "The coaches would take a guy out and hit ground balls to him until he collapsed. . . . The guy would be flat on his back, and the coaches would praise his fighting spirit." A variation was the "Ole infielder's drill," described in *The Chrysanthemum and the Bat*:

> In this drill, a coach will stand the player on the third base line about twenty feet away and begin to hit bullet-hard line shots at him. Thirty minutes later the player's body is black and blue, one or two fingers are bent back, and more often than not, he is on the verge of tears.

When one of Cromartie's teammates, a player named Makihara, developed a sore arm by pitching too many balls, he was sorted out in the following manner:

Every day the coaches would hit grounders to Makihara until he couldn't stand up, yelling insults at him all the while. . . . Then they'd make him run four or five miles. Once, when a coach thought Makihara wasn't trying hard enough, he grabbed him by the neck and hit him over the head with the end of a bat.

The idea of all this is to nurture spirit, or *gutsu*. Old-fashioned Japanese call it *seishinshugi,* or spiritism. They like to think of it as uniquely Japanese, a tradition handed down from ancient times. In fact, like the Darwinist notion, still widely accepted in Japan, that man's destiny is determined by a worldwide racial virility struggle, it has its European counterparts. Spiritism is the old belief that a show of will can overcome any obstacle, that spirit is superior to strength, and collective discipline superior to individual talent. The fact that Japanese players are often too exhausted by incessant drilling to do well in the actual games doesn't mean that they are given a rest. On the contrary, to build up their flagging spirits, the coaches order more drills.

This military or samurai approach to playing sports or, indeed, making cars, can have remarkable results. There was once a schoolboy pitcher called Bessho Takehiko, who won the baseball championship for his school in 1941 by pitching with a broken arm. He was soon to be sent to the war. "I want to play as much baseball as I can before I die," he said. But Cromartie is not the only one to detect deep flaws in this approach. Not only are the players often too tired to give their best, but their morale is sometimes oddly brittle. When human will is driven to a pitch of group hysteria, it tends to snap quite suddenly when faced with adversity. Cromartie often saw his teammates go from overconfidence to listlessness when things weren't going their way. This is also what people observed in a very different contest, when Japan was collapsing in 1945. Far from being a nation of iron-willed people, bent on fighting to the end, the Japanese were going through the motions of the drills they had learned, without enthusiasm, certainly without fanaticism.

Extreme group discipline, though highly effective on an assembly line, does not always work so well in a crisis, for crises demand individual initiative and imagination—the very things spirit training aims to eliminate. The problem with Japanese baseball, as Cromartie saw it, was that the Japanese players always had to be told what to do: "Take an extra base without a coach's express order, and there'd be hell to pay."

Doing one's duty and staying out of trouble—"clean, simple, and obedient"—was more important than winning the games. When things went wrong, the individual *gaijin* could be singled out for blame. And when the more conscientious foreign players, some of whom were actually hired as coaches, tried to improve the Japanese game in the only way they knew how, by encouraging players to think for themselves, they were seen by Japanese managers as a threat and were eventually rejected. No wonder many *gaijin* players were confused: hired to do well, they were sometimes actively prevented from doing so. And, no matter how hard they tried, they would still be told they were only in it for the money.

That Warren Cromartie managed in the end, through sheer perseverance, to be accepted by most of his teammates as one of the guys was a great tribute to him. All the more so since the Tokyo Giants are more than just another baseball team, they are a Japanese institution, which used to pride itself on the purity of its players' bloodlines. As one typical fan remarked to Robert Whiting in a Tokyo bar, "I'm Japanese, so I like the Giants." But Cromartie's very success might have made the club's officials nervous. He might give his Japanese colleagues the wrong ideas. They might start to behave like him. Think what that would do to *wa*.

In fact, there have been Japanese rebels in the baseball world. The most prominent one was a third baseman named Ochiai Hiromitsu. He was so individualistic, so downright cussed in his ways, that the Japanese call him The *Gaijin* Who Speaks Japanese. Cromartie liked the sound of this man and tried to hug him once during a match. Ochiai grunted and pushed him away. Whiting has a good quote from Ochiai on spirit and *wa:*

> The history of Japanese baseball is the history of pitchers throwing until their arms fall off for the team. It's crazy. Like dying for your country—doing a *banzai* . . . with your last breath. That mentality is why Japan lost the war. . . . *Spirit, effort,* those are words I absolutely can not stand.

Just imagine if more Japanese began to talk like that, instead of venting their frustrations, as Cromartie's teammates did, by smoking too many cigarettes and reading sadistic sex comics.

This has been the worry of Japanese officialdom (and Chinese, too) for centuries, and it is at the heart of its dilemma: How to build up national strength by learning from the West, without damaging the spirit of *wa*? Eighteenth-century thinkers were particularly worried that Christianity would, in the words of one Japanese scholar quoted in Bob Tadashi Wakabayashi's *Anti-Foreignism and Western Learning in Early-Modern Japan*, "incite stupid commoners to rebel." How to separate Western techniques from Western ideas that might upset the Eastern order? A formula was imported from China called *Wakon Yōsai*, literally Japanese Spirit, Western Skill. The scholar quoted above, called Aizawa Seishisai, also wrote the following words, which express the sentiments of some modern Japanese exactly:

> Barbarians are, after all, barbarians. It is only natural that they adhere to a barbarous Way, and normally we could let things go at that. But today they have their hearts set on transforming our Middle Kingdom Civilization to barbarism. They will not rest until they desecrate the gods and destroy the Way of Virtue. . . . Either we transform them or they will transform us—we are on a collision course.

If that sounds a bit like the language used by some Westerners who warn us of the imminent Japanese peril, it is no coincidence. For it is the language of moralists who seek transcendental means to order human society. It is, if you like, the religious approach to politics, the idea that international relationships are a contest of absolute values. What moralistic Western critics of Japan have in common with many Japanese conservatives is the worry that the Japanese state lacks a clear moral goal. The kind of people in Japan who believe that foreign traders, foreign intellectuals and, indeed, foreign baseball players, however desirable the skills they bring, are a threat to the Japanese Way also have a religious belief in the hierarchical Japanese order, symbolized by the chrysanthemum throne, which cannot be open to challenge—not by foreigners, and certainly not by the "stupid commoners" of Japan.

In the world encountered by Cromartie, Bass and many other *gaijin* players, this order seems to have been astonishingly well preserved. To be sure, the world of baseball, or any sports, is more conservative than other parts of Japanese life. Yet there is little sign of change in the Japanese order. In the name of *wa,* Japan remains a rather closed society, where most people continue to be bossed around by unaccountable men in power, whether they be gangsters, bureaucrats or baseball coaches. The problem for the non-Japanese world is not that the Japanese, through extreme diligence and discipline, will beat us at trade and, who knows, eventually at baseball, but that the defense of *wa* remains inextricably linked to the virility struggle of nations.

But let us return to the common-sense language of baseball, in *You Gotta Have Wa.* I could not express the problem of Japan and its relations with the world better than Reggie Smith, who was still playing for the Tokyo Giants when Warren Cromartie was greeted as the new Messiah at Narita International Airport.

> To say, like Oh and the others are saying, that Japanese baseball should be played by Japanese or Asians alone and that a real World Series between Japan and the U.S. would be impossible as long as there are American players in Japan, seems to me just racist . . .
>
> The world is getting more international anyway and the Japanese should be thinking "team versus team" or "league versus league." Instead it seems that Japan is still vicariously fighting World War II. It's like the South in the U.S., still trying to hang on to slavery and segregation.

Reggie Smith had once been a Messiah too. But, after one highly successful season, he lost his touch. The Japanese press called him a broken-down jalopy. He began to lose his temper and beat up sports fans who shouted "Nigger!" at him. Not long after, the Tokyo Giants decided to let him go.

1991

AMÉRICAINERIE

A most unusual advertisement appeared in the *International Herald Tribune* in 1993. It was an ad for the Imperial Hotel in Tokyo. The Imperial always was a good hotel. It was also one of the most handsome, until Frank Lloyd Wright's original building was replaced by a glossy high-rise in the 1960s. The advertisement went like this:

> Tokyo, September 1945. The US Occupation had begun and soldiers were all over the famed Imperial Hotel. They even ran our kitchen like an army mess hall, serving up army fare like potatoes and frankfurters. But in the process, they also taught us the highest standards of orderliness and good management. We learned to keep our facilities ship-shape. And to pay scrupulous attention to our guests' every need, big or small. . . . Today, the Imperial is still one of the grandest hotels in Asia. For this, we owe much to US officers who stayed with us nearly 50 years ago—and to all the VIPs and executives who have stayed with us since. All, without exception, have kept us on our toes. They made us what we are. And we love them for it.

Exquisite Oriental irony? A ritual form of self-abasement? Or simply an attempt to flatter Americans in their age of "decline"? Whatever the intention, there is a strong whiff of the past in this advertisement. It conjures up visions of crisp uniforms, patent-leather shoes, deep bows, lipstick smiles, and filthy urchins shouting "Chewingu gummu pureesu."

Ah yes, those were the days, when GI Joe was Number One, the biggest, the richest, the strongest. America, shipshape, efficient, set the tune to which lesser nations danced. MacArthur was the shogun; aviator shades, corncob pipe and squashed cap were his regalia. And Japan lay at his feet, ready to learn and eager to please. But the Americans were not just the biggest and the best, they were also the most generous. Instead of exacting the punishment that was the victor's due, Uncle Sam would remake Japan more or less in his own image. Out with samurai, feudalism, militarism, chauvinism, racialism—welcome Glenn Miller, baseball, chocolate, boogie-woogie, *demokurashee*!

Politically, Shogun MacArthur famously said, the Japanese were twelve-year-olds. But SCAP (Supreme Commander, Allied Powers) was there to set this straight. The Japanese would have to learn everything from scratch. The process would be supported by the so-called Three Ss: Screen, Sex and Sports. The revival of baseball was to be encouraged (hardly necessary, in fact), because it was healthy, American and democratic. A certain amount of physical affection, within bounds, was healthy too—among your own kind, of course. The Japanese should at least learn to kiss their girls in public, just like us. And the movie screen was best of all, to show the way to the yellow brick road, strewn with healthy, democratic American values.

It is easy, in retrospect, to be facetious about America's finest hour, just as it is easy to forget that the Americans really were the most generous of conquerors, and in many cases the most well-meaning of teachers. The question is whether, in retrospect, SCAP and his loyal retainers got it right. Did they teach the right lessons, in the right way? Was MacArthur's Occupation indeed the glowing success story of American tutelage that people of that generation still like to say it was, or are some of the problems with Japan today actually the result of that remarkable time?

Joseph Goebbels was not the only one to have discovered the efficacy of movies as a tool of propaganda. The Japanese, too, had been superb film propagandists during the war. Their best wartime films were, on the whole, better propaganda and better art than similar fare in America, Britain or Germany, because they were more realistic and less strident. Not much effort was spent on demonizing the enemy (partly because of the lack of Caucasian extras). Instead, the emphasis was on brave soldiers toughing it out overseas, and on loyal, patriotic families on the home front sacrificing personal gain for the greater national good. The very real sacrifices and deprivations people had to suffer in Japan were not hidden or ignored: quite the contrary, they were celebrated as examples of heroism, of what made the Japanese *Volk* great.

In her fascinating book on Occupation movie policies, *Mr. Smith Goes to Tokyo,* Hirano Kyoko mentions the regulations issued during the war by the Japanese Ministry of Internal Affairs. There was a rule against "films describing individual happiness," as well as—naturally— "films dealing with sexual frivolity." That some of the most active wartime propagandists were former communists is not really so surprising: the spirit of collectivism and the suppression of individual desires ("greedy materialism") were not uncongenial to them.

The right (perhaps even the duty) of the individual to be happy was, however, precisely what the Americans wanted Japanese films to propagate after the war. Hence the sensation of the first Japanese screen kiss, an episode which Hirano describes well. The kiss was proposed by an American censor to the Shochiku film company. An actress named Ikuno Michiko was trained by her (American) boyfriend to do it properly. When the scene was shot, she allegedly covered her lips with a piece of gauze to avoid direct contact with her costar, Osaka Shiro. The film, *Twenty-Year-Old Youth,* was released on May 23, 1946.

The audiences loved it. Students cheered and shouted *"Banzai!"* when the famous kiss arrived. An eyewitness, quoted by Hirano, described audiences as "gulping, sighing, and yelling." The first screen kiss clearly had a liberating effect, just as the censor (the sweet irony of it!) had intended. And, as is the way in the film business, the first success was followed by a spate of kiss movies. Conservatives were, of course, upset about this affront to traditional morals. And some left-wing critics were just as severe. The Free Film Workers Group said that filmmakers were engaging in irresponsible sensationalism instead of making films with a "truly democratic spirit."

The Japanese leftists and most of the American censors agreed about one basic thing, however: to foster a democratic spirit, "feudalism" had to be rooted out. This led to some of the oddest policies of the Occupation. Since much of the Japanese artistic tradition could be crudely classified as "feudal," much of it had to go. Kabuki theater, for instance, often appears to celebrate feats of samurai valor and sacrifice—loyal retainers committing suicide or wreaking revenge for the sake of their lords, that kind of thing. Whether Kabuki plays really were celebrations of samurai values is open to question—arguably the commercial classes, which formed the main Kabuki audience, took pleasure in watching the human tragedy brought on by such values—but this was too complicated for most censors, so many classics of the Kabuki theater were banned.

The cinematic version of Kabuki was the swordfight movie, long a mainstay of Japanese entertainment. Like American westerns, which they sometimes emulated, these films featured violent heroes. But their ethos was by no means straightforward. The Japanese had discovered the antihero centuries before Hollywood did. The tragic black-hat, who was inevitably defeated by the same superior forces that kept the common people down, was a subversive figure—antifeudal, if anything. Still, swordfight movies, being very "feudal," had to go. Reels and reels of precious film were burned and dumped into a river south of Tokyo.

Even Mount Fuji was "feudal." The famous cone always was the most revered object of Japanese nature worship. And, since the worship of Japanese nature easily slides into worship of the Japanese nation, Mount Fuji was seen as a symbol of imperialist chauvinism, so Mount Fuji had to go too—at least on film. It could not even be shown in a movie about farmers cultivating land on the slopes of the volcano.

I doubt whether the democratic spirit was promoted by these antifeudal actions. But it probably was not damaged either. More serious was the underlying hypocrisy of the American enterprise. Hypocrisy is of course part of any propaganda in political correctness, but occupation PC was hypocritical in a fundamental way. The official American guidelines for a PC cinema in postwar Japan included the following: "Approval of free discussion of political issues" and "Dramatizing figures in Japanese history who stood for freedom and representative government."

These were both fine things. But free discussion, like sexual expression, had its limits. Crimes committed by American soldiers in Japan could not be shown, or even reported. The Japanese papers had to use curious circumlocutions, such as "The criminals were unusually tall and hairy men." War damage inflicted by American bombing raids was not to be mentioned. Hirano gives the example of a famous film by Ozu, *Late Spring,* in which one of the characters compares the serene beauty of Kyoto to the ruined city of Tokyo. The original line "[Tokyo] is full of burned sites" had to be changed to "It's so dusty all over."

Criticism of American Occupation policies was strictly forbidden. A movie entitled *Between War and Peace,* by two leftist directors, Kamei Fumio and Yamamoto Satsuo, showed workers carrying banners that said "Freedom of Speech" and "Let Us Who Work Eat." The scene was banned by the censors for being "suggestive or criticizing SCAP censorship and encouraging labor strikes." The censors of the free world, in short, had to censor references to their own censorship.

Not only was SCAP above critical scrutiny, but a negative picture of the United States was also deemed undesirable. *Mr. Smith Goes to Washington,* the Frank Capra picture, released in Japan in 1941, could no longer be shown in 1946, because its depiction of graft and corruption might give a false impression of American democracy. And portrayals of the extremes of poverty and wealth in America were censored. As Hirano tells us, a montage in *The Great Gatsby* (1949) of young people joyriding, drinking and running speakeasies had to be cut for distribution in Japan.

The race factor, then as now a central issue of political correctness, tied SCAP's censors into intricate knots. During much of the Occupation, fraternizing with the former enemy was forbidden to the American occupiers. Inevitably, however, a great deal of fraternizing went on. But the problems involved in affairs between American soldiers and Japanese women could not be shown on screen. On the other hand, Hirano mentions a film entitled *Sorrowful Beauty,* which raised objections against an interracial marriage. This had to be revised, the censors decided, "on the ground of racism."

Perhaps most serious of all was the matter of the Japanese emperor. Representative government was all very well, but the Emperor, in whose name war had been declared in 1941, had to be protected "from ridicule, vituperation or virulent criticism." This was the official guideline. SCAP, in the best tradition of Japanese shoguns, thought he could rule Japan most effectively with the Emperor as a symbolic figure who was unassailable from below and easy to manipulate from above. So protection was essential. Not only could the Emperor not be called as a witness, let alone be tried as a defendant at the Tokyo War Crimes Trial, but his innocence during the war could not even be questioned. Hirano discusses at length the case of *The Japanese Tragedy* (1946). It is an unusual case, since it concerns a film passed by the censors at first, only to be banned later. *The Japanese Tragedy,* directed by Kamei Fumio, was a montage of newsreels, films, photographs and newspaper cuttings suggesting that Emperor Hirohito was formally responsible for going to war. The point Kamei and other critics of the imperial system sought to make was that, to be democrats, the Japanese had to be weaned from Emperor worship. This could not succeed without a critical analysis of the imperial role during the war.

After having passed the censors, the movie was screened privately for the then prime minister, Yoshida Shigeru, in the presence of Brigadier General Charles Willoughby, head of the Military Intelligence Section. Yoshida was a conservative patriot with Churchillian pretensions. Willoughby, to put it mildly, had little sympathy for the "pinko" New Deal Democrats employed by SCAP. Yoshida complained that the film was too critical. Willoughby agreed. The film was banned. And when Hirano saw *The Japanese Tragedy* in 1984, with Kamei, she was told that "it was around the time that the film was banned that the Japanese people stopped actively discussing the responsibility of Emperor Hirohito as a war criminal." In effect, the greatest test of postwar Japanese democracy had been flunked, not because the Japanese were political twelve-year-olds, but because Shogun MacArthur took away their right to free speech.

By 1952 China had been lost, the Korean War had been almost lost, and SCAP's reign in Japan had been terminated. The so-called Reverse Course, a key phrase in the lexicon of left-of-center Japanese historians, had already taken place. Halfway along the yellow brick road to democracy, Japan had been turned around by Japanese bureaucrats and American conservatives, and remodeled as an anticommunist bastion against Red China. SCAP had helped to slap down the same labor unions it had encouraged earlier. Former war criminals emerged from prison to join the government once again. The left-wing parties were pushed into the margins, where they remain today. And Japanese industry was urged to let rip. Japan would be a pacific exporting nation, while the U.S. took care of war and peace.

But if the course of Japanese politics had been reversed, an equally dramatic reversal took place in Japanese movies. As soon as SCAP left town, the forbidden fruit was swiftly displayed. Films about Hiroshima made it clear just who should feel guilty about the war. Movies about American military bases reveled in American crimes. Scenes of big GIs, usually black, raping innocent Japanese girls became a stock image in Japanese films about the Occupation. And the taste for sensational imagery of the U.S., showing the former enemy in the worst possible light, has persisted to this day.

None of this means that the Japanese are implacably anti-American: it just proves that propaganda can produce the opposite effect from the one intended. People cannot be fooled all the time, and the price of American hypocrisy was a lingering resentment among many Japanese intellectuals, on the left and the right, and a propensity toward self-pity among the general public. Which is not to say that American culture had no positive impact. Glenn Miller, screen kisses and easy manners did much to loosen up Japanese social life. But, apart from the unique case of the first kiss, these were not part of SCAP propaganda. People danced to "In The Mood" because they wanted to, not because it was a lesson imposed on them.

One might well wonder what problems with Japan today have to do with cultural propaganda of almost fifty years ago. They are linked, however, in a confused and confusing manner. One legacy of Occupation propaganda is a myth which has lost none of its tenacity: the myth that economic policies or political arrangements are mainly a reflection of cultural values, of *mentalités*. There was, and still is, a strong belief, for example, that democracy is a Western value fostered by Christianity, and so on. To become a democrat you must be "Westernized," and preferably play baseball and kiss your girl. There is, on the other hand, the belief that the Japanese Economic Miracle can be explained primarily by ancient Japanese traditions, instead of policies decided upon by American Cold War strategists and Japanese officialdom. And there are those who think that the authoritarian nature of Japan's so-called democracy is mainly caused, let us say, by Confucianism, rather than by the monopoly on power skillfully achieved by pork-barrel politicians and bureaucrats who have managed to rig the electoral system.

Culture, some maintain, is why we have to worry today about the mighty Japanese—not because there is something flawed in Japan's political relations with the outside world, but because they are *Japanese,* heirs to the samurai tradition, lacking in universal values and so on. The myth fostered by the Occupation was that if only Japanese values could be changed, which in time they would, then all would be right between Japan and the world. In the meantime, until that happy day when the Japanese could be truly trusted, they would be kept under the protective American thumb.

The confusion was made worse by a number of well-meaning American experts, collectively known as the Chrysanthemum Club, who saw it as their duty to protect the delicate Japan–U.S. relationship by deflecting criticism of Japan. Like professional Pollyannas, they would tell us over and over that, despite appearances to the contrary, the Japanese, given some patience, would one day be just like us. In a 1965 book written with John K. Fairbank and Albert M. Craig, *East Asia: The Modern Transformation,* the late Edwin O. Reischauer, the doyen of Chrysanthemums, wrote that Japan had "passed from the 'investment boom' of the early 1950s to the 'leisure boom' of 1960 and the 'vacation boom' of 1963."

Reischauer was wrong. But the Pollyannas were perhaps right in a way that none of the SCAP's men anticipated. The filmmaker Oshima Nagisa was a teenager during the Occupation. In a book published in 1975, he remembers how hungry the Japanese were for any entertainment, anything from the outside world, where people had money, ate plenty of food, and lived in big houses instead of among the ruins. They wanted to see America, if only in flickering images on a torn and dirty screen. But did these films teach the Japanese democracy? Oshima thinks not. Instead, he believes, Japan learned the values of "progress" and "development." Japan wanted to be just as rich as America—no, even richer. "And if we think about the extraordinary speed of postwar progress and development in Japan, perhaps we should say that the route upon which we travelled was that Union Pacific railway line which we saw in those Westerns several decades ago."

—

Ever since Japan was exposed to the expansive power of Europe and America, Japanese thinkers have been exercised by the cultural problem. Nationalists in the eighteenth century, such as Aizawa Seishisai, thought Christianity explained the strength of the Western world. (Max Weber, incidentally, thought so too. He argued that Protestantism produced successful capitalists, and Confucianism kept them back.) Japan, so Aizawa believed, needed a unifying religious force of its own, something purely Japanese. This turned out to be an official version of Shintoism, with the emperor as the apex of the cult. And so the Japanese were furnished with an unchanging "soul," even as they acquired the techniques of modern life from the West.

The desire to separate the purely native from Western importations is still strong. Prominent political writers, such as Eto Jun, maintain, for example, that the American Occupation robbed Japan of its purity, its true identity, by censoring traditional culture and stifling the imperial cult. He has the ear of quite a few Western journalists and Japanophiles who worry about national identity, too, especially in non-Western countries supposedly "swamped" by Americana. Western romantics have sought to escape for centuries from the messy reality of their own world to a purer universe across the horizon: in Shangri-la, Cathay or the Land of the Rising Sun.

But while the fin de siècle Japanophile Lafcadio Hearn could still dream of the pristine Orient betwixt the cherry trees (and even he lamented the continuing hemorrhage of purity), the modern visitor to Japan, or anywhere in Asia, can hardly overlook the lively cultural mess. What makes Leo Rubinfien's photographs, published in *A Map of the East,* so superb is his refusal to overlook it. Instead, he finds poetry in the hybrid vulgarity of contemporary Asia. The temptation for a Western artist in Japan is to look for juxtapositions: East–West, foreign–native, Buddhas and Coca-Cola. Rubinfien, although he too, according to his own introduction, is given to lamenting what has been lost, avoids this easy choice. His photographs of Japanese picking their way through the urban landscape show everything at once: kimonos, business suits, paper lanterns, jazz coffee shops, skyscrapers, Shinto shrines. It is all here: the architecture, the clothes, the clutter of life, presented without cheap irony. Some of it might have originated in China, or Paris, or

New York, yet all of it is unmistakably Japanese. Categories like East and West, let alone pure and impure, cease to exist, or at least to matter.

This is also evident from the more sophisticated anthropological works on Japan. The search for purity appears to be on the wane—except in Japan itself. The contributors to *Re-Made in Japan,* a collection of essays edited by Joseph J. Tobin, have their hearts in the right place, but, alas, in many cases the blight of Baudrillard has wrecked their prose, even if the authors do not always agree with his ideas. Oddly enough, the dated Parisian jargon of deconstruction has had a more devastating effect in America and Japan than anywhere else. It is distressing to open a promising Japanese journal of criticism, only to find every sentence messed up with *ekurituru* (*écriture*) and *disukuru* (*discours*).

Re-Made in Japan has its fair share of this jargon. Here is Dorinne Kondo on Japanese fashion designers working with the Western styles: "As these questions construct a transnational space, essentializing gestures and geopolitical relations simultaneously refabricate national boundaries." But, once one disentangles the language, there is much of interest in the book, particularly on the artificial separation of East and West. The key term running through most of the essays is "domestication." The Japanese are not passive receptacles of Western influence, but active shoppers in a global bazaar, picking and choosing what they want, before turning it into something of their own. The Japanese version of the English language, for instance, sometimes known as "Japlish," is hardly intelligible to the English speaker. Who in London would know that *sebiro* means men's suit, and was derived from *Savile Row*? But, as James Stanlaw points out quite rightly, "Japanese-English is used in Japan for Japanese purposes." Maybe the same is true of *ekurituru,* but I doubt it.

To balance the domestication of cultural imports, the Japanese have always been active inventors of native "traditions." They did this when China was the main source of imports, and they do it today—in their lavish department stores, for example. A walk through the food halls of Mitsukoshi or Takashimaya reveals two distinct worlds, or perhaps even three: a Western one, offering Japanized versions of Italian or French delicacies, sometimes accompanied by piped European music; a Chinese one, displaying stacks of bamboo baskets filled with steamed dumplings and other delights; and a Japanese one, where, in Millie R.

Creighton's words, "employees dressed in *hanten* (happy coats) and *hachimaki* (headbands) clap and chant the virtues of their noodles, pickles, and bean cakes using the same boisterous sales techniques favored by street vendors of three or four centuries ago." The point of these culinary theme parks is to establish clear cultural boundary lines, however invented they might be. As Creighton says: "Through this dialectic of 'us' and 'other' depāto [department stores] help their modern clientele affirm Japaneseness in a culturally eclectic age."

This is clearly true. Where I think I differ from some of the contributors to *Re-Made in Japan* is in their emphasis on modernity, as though cultural eclecticism were a specific product of the modern age (whenever that may have started). Culture never was pure; traditions always were invented, or parodied. Nancy Rosenberger quotes Baudrillard and Bourdieu to observe that Japanese consumers advertise the status they desire by the products they buy, by simulating "the tastes . . . of the higher classes they aspire to." First, one does not need Bourdieu to tell us this. Second, the phenomenon is not new, or, if one prefers, "modern." Edo-period merchants paid good money to acquire samurai culture. They even paid good money for prostitutes to act as noble beauties of the Heian period.

What has changed—perhaps the real point of this book—is Japan's relative wealth vis-à-vis the rest of the world, particularly the West. In a very interesting essay on Tokyo Disneyland (bigger than the lands of Anaheim and Orlando), Mary Yoko Brannen challenges the Baudrillardian assumption that Disneyland means American cultural imperialism. As she describes the place, it is rather the other way around. The Japanese have turned Disney into a modern Japanese equivalent of nineteenth-century European *japonaiserie*. One might call it *américainerie*. The Western craftsmen and guides, who are not allowed to speak Japanese and, unlike their Japanese colleagues, do not wear name tags, are put on display like exhibits in a Victorian ethnological fair. The theme parks, such as "Meet the World," have been carefully redone to make the Japanese look both normal (to the Japanese) and unique (to everybody else), and the foreigners exotic (in the case of Westerners) and disreputable (in the case of Chinese). She concludes that "the selective importation of Disney cultural artifacts works in the service of an ongoing Japanese process of cultural imperialism."

What would SCAP make of it all? Now Japanese executives land in L.A., New York and Honolulu and buy the flashiest buildings, the finest companies and the biggest studios in Hollywood. GI Joe is still in Japan, to be sure, but he can hardly afford to leave his base. Indeed, the more salacious Japanese weeklies love to recount that his own wife is sometimes constrained to meet Japanese patrons to exchange her favors for yen. Meanwhile, Japanese politicians and popular authors write best-sellers about the Japanese ruling the world. One of the latest, by Watanabe Shoichi, is entitled *This Is How History Begins.* The jacket announces that "Japanese civilization has begun to take over from the white man's civilization," and that "for the next 250 years, Japan will move the world." No wonder people in the West are beginning to feel anxious.

The new fashion for Yellow Peril fiction is one anxiety symptom. There is the pulp end of it, with titles like *The Tojo Virus,* by John D. Randall, about a dastardly Japanese plot to cripple the military, scientific and business computers in America by infecting them with a virus. Or there is *Blood Heat,* about Japanese biological warfare against American civilians. Or *Dragon,* about Japanese nuclear blackmail. Then there is the sophisticated end of the market, with Michael Crichton's best-seller *Rising Sun* (see "Wake Up, America," page 270).

What most of these books have in common is an image of the Japanese that makes them seem omnipotent, sinister, fanatical and sexually threatening. The cover of Steven Schlosstein's *Kensei* reads, "Circulation. Determination. Elimination. The samurai code for total victory in the war on America." Those tired old samurai again. Since these books also play up the idea of American doom, Americans are often depicted as venal, decadent or simple suckers. As a Japanese character in *Dragon* observes to an American opponent, "You've become a cesspool of deterioration, and the process is unstoppable."

More rational, or at least more sympathetic, are the books on how to learn the secret of Japanese power. Miyamoto Musashi's eighteenth-century tract on samurai tactics, entitled *The Book of Five Rings,* has proven a popular book among the businessmen seeking insights into Japanese business strategy. More up-to-date accounts have such titles as *Yen!* or *Why Has Japan "Succeeded"?* or *Japanese Power Game.* The most detailed and by far the best informed of the crop is Karel van Wolferen's *The Enigma of Japanese Power.*

Now there appears to be a third genre: how to cash in on Japanese economic power by joining it. Some, like *Yankee Samurai,* by Dennis Laurie, or *Funny Business: An Outsider's Year in Japan,* by Gary J. Katzenstein, are accounts of what it is like to be employed by Japanese companies. One of the odder specimens of this ilk is by Jina Bacarr, a longtime student of Japanese culture and a spokesperson for the Japan Mutual Food Company. It bears the straightforward title *How to Work for a Japanese Boss.* The book is an amalgam of advice, potted history (from 660 B.C. to 1992 in four pages) and cultural analysis.

But culture is just one aspect of Bacarr's objective, which is "to teach you how to *think* Japanese." She tries to achieve this by combining the down-to-earth and the airy-fairy in a disconcerting way. Her advice on how to do business with Japanese is practical, even though presented in the kind of baby talk to which readers of American business magazines have become accustomed. Chapters open with haikulike personality sketches that read like captions to Glen Baxter cartoons: "As Kurt followed the kimono-clad waitress to his table in the Japanese restaurant, he paid little attention to the beautiful decor and the sound of the small brook running through the restaurant." If much of her advice to aspiring American "salarymen" seems more appropriate to aspiring courtiers, that is because the unfortunate salaryman's chances of success do indeed depend to a large extent on his or her capacity for fawning, dissembling and attending to the boss's whims.

What is distressing about this book is how little we seem to have progressed from the cultural clichés of the Occupation. Bacarr, like so many others before her, has this to say about "the Japanese character": 1. the Japanese are good at copying; 2. Zen, or "the contemplation of the void" is "the root of much of their success"; 3. the Japanese are masters of "group thinking." The Americans, she concludes, "tend to use logic," whereas "the Japanese use a system based on emotions and spiritual values that goes back to feudal times when they were ruled by a class of samurai who . . ." etc., etc.

Of course it would be foolish to ignore culture altogether. Cultural differences exist, and they affect the way we do things. But, if crude cultural distinctions are to be the main explanation for economic and political arrangements, there are only three options when conflicts arise with countries whose cultures are different from our own: they become like us, we become like them, or we go to war by boycotting their trade or, in extreme cases, by taking up arms.

To judge from the latest books, good and bad, there are few takers any longer for the idea that Japan will be just like us. In this respect, the Chrysanthemum Club has lost, and the so-called revisionists who maintain that the Japanese (or East-Asian) version of capitalism is fundamentally different from the Anglo-American system, have won. Quite how Japan differs is a matter of contention, even among the revisionists.

Whatever their differences, however, many revisionists share a portentous tone of gloom. They are the professional Cassandras, as opposed to the Chrysanthemum Pollyannas. Their very language invites visions of catastrophe. On the subject of American decline, they tend to sound like French nationalists after losing the war with Prussia in 1871. It is as though the virility of the nation were at stake. When Michael Crichton began to research *Rising Sun,* he said in his contribution to a June 1992 symposium on political correctness and Japan-bashing, he "was stunned to discover how desperate our situation really is." America, I was told by a revisionist in Tokyo, was now going through its "darkest hour." Karel van Wolferen, not himself an American, warns that American inaction on Japanese trade will invite "calamity." His 1989 op-ed piece for *The Washington Post* bears the headline "Japan: Different, Unprecedented and Dangerous." These are not his own words, but they do reflect the tone of the revisionist debate.

The least one can say about America's relative economic decline is that opinions differ. According to a 1992 *C. V. Starr Newsletter* issued by the Center for Applied Economics at New York University, "Japan's higher growth rate has been slowing down and is now hardly ahead of ours anymore, while the level of Japan's manufacturing productivity certainly remains well below ours."

Views are equally divided on just what, if anything, should be done about Japan's brand of capitalism, whose differences the revisionists have uncovered. Is it a threat? Is the American economy really being ruined by Japanese trade practices? So far, the biggest losers as a result of Japanese mercantilism have been the Japanese consumers, who pay too much. In the U.S. and Britain many people have benefited from Japanese trade, as consumers, as employees and as recipients of investment. Are these benefits outweighed by other, darker factors, such as a dangerous dependency on Japanese capital or technology? Perhaps, perhaps not. What is certainly true is that the present relationship between the U.S. and Japan is that of a resentful and mercantilist power locked into a state of infantile dependence on U.S. security.

Two articles that appeared around the same time, one by Chalmers Johnson in the autumn 1992 *Daedalus* and the other by Joseph Nye in the winter 1992 *Foreign Policy,* offered two different solutions to the problem. Johnson, professor of Pacific international relations at the University of California at San Diego, is often called the doyen of the revisionists. Nye, a Harvard professor of government, is a traditional American liberal. Of the two, Nye favors the more conservative solution. Basically, in his view, GI Joe should stay in Japan. For if Japan were to become a military power, all kinds of unpredictable things might happen, including an East Asian arms race. The best thing, Nye believes, would be for Japan to become a "global civilian power." This would mean a bigger role in UN agencies, including a seat on the Security Council, even though Japan would be unable to implement the military policies it would have to help to decide.

Johnson thinks a greater change is in order. Unlike Nye, Johnson wants to end the Occupation, not just in form, but in fact. The U.S., in his opinion, can no longer afford to be the policeman of East Asia, and the Japanese will resent it more and more. The Cold War, after all, is over, and it is time the Japanese took care of their own affairs. The continued presence of American troops stops them from doing so. Ergo, if the U.S. pulls out, Japan will be weaned from its narrow mercantilism and will become a more responsible, more "normal" regional superpower. Or so we can only hope.

I believe he is right. But it will take some doing, and the process will not be helped at all by the *Amerika Erwache* rhetoric that is currently so popular. For the image of Japan as a fundamentally dangerous nation will impede any moves toward an end to the informal Occupation. Herein lies one of the paradoxes of revisionism. All the revisionists, including Chalmers Johnson, are agreed that if something is not done to stop Japanese mercantilism in its tracks there will be a dangerous, emotional backlash in the U.S. So Americans have to be woken up to a danger, posited by the revisionists, in order for those same Americans not to get emotional when they finally realize that the revisionists were right. If the shrill tone of fictional propaganda helps to wake them up, so be it. As James Fallows, a notable member of the revisionists, observed to the *Los Angeles Times:* "We [America and Japan] have serious conflicts and we need to resolve them. To the extent that fiction reveals them, it's having a useful effect."

This is how SCAP's censors argued too, except it was their business to avoid further conflict, and their fictions were more benign.

1993

WAKE UP, AMERICA

Once in a while—in America, perhaps more than once in a while—a book comes along whose interest is chiefly in the hype attending it. Michael Crichton's *Rising Sun* is such a book. The text of the publicity handout announced that this "explosive new thriller [was] rushed to publication one month earlier than previously announced because of its extraordinary timeliness with regard to U.S.–Japan relations"—at the height of the Japan-is-buying-up-the-U.S. hysteria in spring 1992.

This is unusual: thrillers are not generally rushed out to match political events. Odder still was the sheaf of newspaper clippings about the decline of American industries and the predatory methods of Japanese corporations stapled onto the advance reader's edition. Singular, too, is the bibliography at the end of the book, listing mostly academic works on Japan, but also, for example, Donald Richie's study of Kurosawa's movies. Strangest of all, however, is Crichton's afterword, which ends with a homily: "The Japanese are not our saviors. They are our competitors. We should not forget it."

With such a buildup, the literary press could not be left behind. On the front page of *The New York Times Book Review*, the thriller was compared to *Uncle Tom's Cabin* for stirring up "the volcanic subtexts of our daily life." *Kirkus Reviews* promised the return of the "Yellow Menace," only now "he wears a three-piece suit and aims to dominate America through force of finance, not arms."

Volcanic subtexts, Yellow Menace, Main Selection of the Book-of-the-Month club, first printing 225,000 copies, top of the best-seller lists, a Hollywood picture in the works—what exactly was going on here?

Michael Crichton clearly wanted to do more than entertain with a murder mystery. He wrote his book, so he told *The New York Times*, "to make America wake up." Now, on the whole, people who go around trying to wake us up, as though we were all asleep, oblivious of some apocalyptic Truth, tend to be boring, or mad—like those melancholy figures who wander about with signs announcing the end of the world.

Crichton's book isn't boring. He is good at snappy dialogue—though his copious use of Japanese is often incongruous and sometimes wrong—and he is a deft manipulator of suspense. He takes great pains to avoid giving the impression that he is mad. Indeed, the whole idea of the newspaper clippings, the bibliography, the afterword and so on, is to make sure we get the serious message buried in the "explosive new thriller." He dislikes the term "Japan-bashing," he says, because it threatens to move the U.S.–Japan debate into "an area of unreasonableness." The thriller, by implication, is reasonable.

Well, I wonder. But, before going on, perhaps I should mention the story, the vessel, at it were, for Crichton's awakening message to the American nation. In brief, it is this: a large Japanese corporation called Nakamoto is celebrating the opening of its new U.S. headquarters, the Nakamoto Tower in downtown L.A. A beautiful young American woman—Caucasian, naturally—is murdered during the party. Investigations follow. The Japanese obstruct, the American police bumble, the Japanese corrupt, the Americans are corrupted, and only through the brilliance of a semiretired detective called Connor, who speaks Japanese and knows the Japanese mind—who can see "behind the mask," so to speak—is the case more or less solved. Along the way, we have some kinky sex—the Japanese, unlike us, have no guilt, you see—and a couple of spectacular suicides: a U.S. senator, framed for the murder of the girl, shoots himself through the mouth, and a Japanese gets himself a concrete suit by jumping into wet cement from a considerable height.

Sex and violence aside, the story has two leitmotifs that are bound to appeal: the decline of America, our way of life, etc., and a clearly identifiable enemy. The first is constantly alluded to by characters in the story, as well as by the author himself. "Shit: we're *giving* this country away," says a crude cop. "They already own Los Angeles," says a woman at a party ("laughing"). "Our country's going to hell," says a television journalist. "They *own* the government," says the crude cop. "The end of America, buddy . . ."

"They" is, of course, the enemy: Japan. There is a great deal of talk about "they" in the book. The enemy is identified but it has no face. It is present everywhere, manipulating us, corrupting us, in our offices, our newspapers, our government, our universities and, who knows, perhaps soon on our beaches and our landing grounds. "They" have a mind, a mentality, but no characters, no ideas. The pervasive, manipulative, inscrutable, mysterious mind is never expressed openly or directly. It is masked by subterfuge. Nakamoto Corporation, we are told, "presents an impenetrable mask to the rest of the world." One of the few Japanese with a name, though without much in the way of human personality, Mr. Ishigura, has a face, but "His face was a mask."

Masked minds and inscrutable cultures need to be decoded, hence the stock character in many colonial and tropical fantasies: the expert, the man who has the lingo and knows the native mind, the white hero dancing dangerously on the edge of going native himself. This role is performed by Connor, who knows his way around sushi bars and knows when to be polite and when to be firm. Firmness, in his case, means breaking into the rough language of Japanese gangster movies. But in a good mood he will hold forth on the finer points of Japanese manners, why "they" behave as they do and so on. Connor likes Japan, but never forgets that we are at war.

The other stock figure in war propaganda is the good enemy, who has crossed over to the side of the angels. In Japanese wartime movies this role was often played by the Japanese actress Li Ko Ran, later known, during her brief Hollywood career, as Shirley Yamaguchi. She was the Chinese beauty who invariably fell in love with the dashing and sincere Japanese soldier—a love that symbolized the glorious future in Asia under Japanese tutelage. In nineteenth-century anti-Semitic fiction it is the "good Jew," such as the beautiful Miriam in Felix Dahn's *Fight for Rome* (1876), who identifies wholly with the German tribe and hates the rootless and treacherous Jews.

In *Rising Sun* we have the beautiful Theresa Asakuma. Theresa works in a high-tech research lab, one of the last not to fall into Japanese hands; hence, I suppose, its dilapidated state. Theresa is happy to help Connor and his wholesome American sidekick Lieutenant Pete Smith, the narrator, who plays Doctor Watson to Connor's Holmes. She is happy to help, because she hates the Japanese.

The beautiful Theresa is a useful character, because she represents the perfect target for Japanese bigotry. Her father was a black GI, and she has a crippled arm. She grew up in a small Japanese town, where the tolerance for blacks and cripples was low. Her story offers an opportunity to expound a little on Japanese racism—even the notorious treatment of polluted outcasts, the *burakumin,* many of whom work in the leather trade, gets an airing. Not that any of this is implausible or wrong—outsiders do have a hard time in Japan—but it functions as yet another stake driven through the heart of "they." It is a bit like European or Japanese descriptions of America, in which every American is either a gangster, a redneck or a poor black.

Uncle Tom's Cabin is actually the last book I would have thought of comparing to *Rising Sun.* I can think of two anti-Semitic works that are much closer in tone and imagery. One is *Jew Süss,* the German film, directed by Veit Harlan in 1940. The other is a Japanese pop best-seller by Uno Masami about the Jewish conspiracy to dominate the world. It is entitled *The Day the Dollar Becomes Paper: Why We Must Learn From Jewish Knowledge Now.*

Harlan's version of *Jew Süss* (there were many versions) shows how peaceful, prosperous eighteenth-century Württemberg is almost destroyed by letting in the Jews. The vain and gullible duke of Württemberg has virtually exhausted the state budget by indulging his taste for pomp and dancing girls. The Jew Süss Oppenheimer contrives, by oily flattery and promises of bottomless riches, to persuade the duke to let him take care of his finances. He also presses the duke to allow the Jews to settle in his city. Soon they control everything through their evil manipulation. As a symbol of German humiliation, the Jew has his wicked way with the county sheriff's daughter. She commits suicide, the good people of Württemberg at last rise up against the duke and his Jews. Oppenheimer is hanged, and the Jews are driven out of town. The message at the end of the film is that the burghers of Württemberg woke up to the danger in their midst and banished the Jews by law. This law should be upheld not only for the sake of our generation, but for our children, our grandchildren, and so on forever and ever.

Uno Masami's book is a collection of more or less mad conspiracy theories. Among the more outré ones is the notion that Roosevelt, scion of a well-known Jewish family, tricked Japan into going to war, so that the U.S., as a front for world Jewish interests, could save the Jews from Hitler. The basic premise of the book is a simple one: Jews control world public opinion by controlling the media. Jews have convinced the decent and gullible Japanese that Japan should be internationalist instead of looking after its national interests. Thus American Jews wrote the postwar Japanese constitution to make Japan impotent. Thus the Jewish-controlled press made the Japanese feel guilty about the war. Thus decent Japanese companies such as Mitsubishi or Fujitsu cannot compete with IBM, because IBM is controlled by Jewish interests which are out to dominate the world. One salient point about this lunacy is that, to the likes of Uno, Jewish and American interests are more or less interchangeable.

Michael Crichton's thriller is not quite as zany as Uno's tract, or quite as odious as Harlan's *Jew Süss*. And to call his book racist is perhaps to miss the point. After all, as he told *The New York Times,* he likes Japan very much. He may have painted a picture of the Japanese as liars and cheats, but as Connor, the expert on the native mind, points out, that is only from our point of view, not theirs. No, the problem with Crichton is that, like Uno and the makers of *Jew Süss,* he has conceived a paranoid world, in which sincere, decent folk are being manipulated by sinister forces. These forces need not be from a different race: in a different era, they might have been communist.

Paranoia can be based on half-truths. To say that the craziest red-baiters were paranoid is not to say that communism bore no threat. Just so, undeniable problems with Japan do not alter the fact that some of the wildest alarmists are a trifle unhinged. Crichton describes, again in Connor's words, how the Japanese in America are part of a "shadow world. . . . Most of the time you're never aware of it. We live in our regular American world, walking on our American streets, and we never notice that right alongside our world is a second world." Couple this to the refrain that "they own" our city, our government, our country, and one is not so very far removed from Veit Harlan's Württemberg.

The metaphors are remarkably similar. Masks are a key image both in *Rising Sun* and in *Jew Süss.* The idea in *Jew Süss* is to contrast an organic, decent, even somewhat slow-witted German community, rooted in its native clay, and the artificial, devious, clever floating world of the rootless Jews. The duke of Württemberg is warned by one of his courtiers that the Jew is always masked. In both Crichton and Harlan, the enemy is pictured as omnipresent, omnipotent and certainly more sophisticated. "The Jews are always so intelligent," says an exasperated Württemberger. "Not intelligent, just shrewd," answers another. As Richard Wagner liked to say, the Jew can only imitate, not create.

Connor, only a little ironically, calls America "an underdeveloped peasant country." Compared to the Japanese, he says, we are incompetent. But on the other hand, of course, "they" have bought our universities, because as an American scientist tells Connor, "they know—after all the bullshit stops—that they can't innovate as well as we can." Not intelligent, just shrewd.

In *Jew Süss* and in *Rising Sun,* we are shown how native institutions are slowly taken over by alien forces. Veit Harlan suggests this by using dissolves and music: the German motto on the Württemberg shield of arms dissolves into Hebrew; a Bach chorale gradually melts into the song of a cantor. In *Rising Sun,* as in Uno's book, "our" press is infiltrated; one of "their" people is "planted" at the *Los Angeles Times,* no less. Another *Los Angeles Times* reporter, one of "ours," explains the situation: "The American press reports the prevailing opinion. The prevailing opinion is the opinion of the group in power. The Japanese are now in power."

At the beginning of *Rising Sun,* Connor rides an elevator in the Nakamoto Tower with some American cops. An electronic voice announces the floors in Japanese. "Fuck," says the cop, "if an elevator is going to talk, it should be English. This is still America." "Just barely," says Connor.

This kind of paranoia is more complex than mere xenophobia. It suggests a deep frustration. Again, Harlan's film is instructive: the fiancé of the girl who falls prey to the wicked Jew's designs is shown as an impotent man—handsome in a blond, romantic, German sort of way, but incapable. In the beginning of the film, the girl makes advances to him, but he fails to respond. The Jew succeeds, albeit violently, where the decent German fails. The enemy as a potent stud: this is how an American floozy in Crichton's book describes her Japanese patrons: " 'A lot of them, they are so polite, so correct, but then they get turned on, they have this . . . this *way* . . . She broke off, shaking her head. 'They are a strange people.' "

There runs a streak of masochism through all this. And, to be sure, it wouldn't be the first time that American self-flagellation has sold many books. But there is also a hint of awe for the enemy, as though we would like to be more like "them." In 1942, Hitler quoted "the British Jew Lord Disraeli" as the source of the idea that the racial problem was the key to world history. The anti-Semitic jurist Carl Schmitt hung a picture of Disraeli above his desk. Uno Masami wants the Japanese to learn from the Jews, to learn how they maintained the purity, the virility and the independence of their race.

It is striking how often the fiercest Western critics of Japan are the ones who most want to emulate Japanese ways: protectionism, industrial policies, order, discipline. Crichton, or rather Connor, speaks about being at war with Japan, and at the same time repeats with admiration all the clichés of Japanese cultural chauvinists: how the Japanese people are "members of the same family, and they can communicate without words," or how good the Japanese police are, because "for major crimes, convictions run ninety-nine per cent." Connor forgets, perhaps, that confessions are enough to convict in Japan, and that the Japanese police are rather good at getting confessions.

Could it be, then, that some Americans are feeling frustrated with the messiness of American democracy, with its many competing interests and its lack of strong central power; that people are getting tired of freewheeling individualism and the hurly-burly marketplace; that they despair of all the immigrants, who barely speak English yet occupy

American cities in their expanding shadow worlds: that, in other words, many Americans would secretly like to feel part of one family, with order imposed from above? If so, it would be a sad thing. For America, thus awakened, would stop being the country to which millions came to escape from just such tribal orders. And those millions included quite a few Japanese.

1993

LOOKING EAST

A new phrase has recently come buzzing in: the Asianization of Asia. As in all such phrases, the concept is vague. Was Asia once less Asian? If Asia wasn't really Asian, what was it? How Asian does Asia have to be before it can be called truly Asian? And so on.

But a closer look at the kind of people who have taken up the slogan offers some clues to its meaning. At the 1993 Bangkok Declaration on human rights, politicians from various more or less repressive regimes in the region trumpeted what they called "the Asian Way." They meant a Way that stresses harmony, order and the collective good, as opposed to individualism and "human rights." (The frequent use of quotation marks around "human rights" by proponents of the Asian Way is meant to show that the idea is supposed to be not just alien to the Way, but rather distasteful too.) The Asian Way rests on the assumption that the government is benevolent and knows best what is good for the common weal. Those who beg to differ threaten that common good, and should be dealt with harshly. Human rights and democracy are dismissed as "Western values," the advocacy of which is a form of imperialist arrogance. And so, after decades of colonialism, neocolonalism and "Westernization," it is time for Asia to assert its own values. It is time to Asianize Asia.

That the Singaporean or Indonesian or Chinese government should take this line is understandable. Each profits from the Asian Way. It justifies their grip on power. If individual rights, the rule of law, and popular sovereignty are indeed no more than "Western values," why then should Asians not rule according to "Eastern values"? Who is to say which is better? If politics is a natural (or, if you prefer, organic) reflection of culture, then there can be no argument: the students in Tiananmen Square in 1989 were deluded by foreign values, and the Chinese government was upholding the Asian Way.

Spokesmen for the Asian Way are not lacking in allies in the West. Funnily enough, the people who come closest to their line of thinking are not authoritarian right-wingers, but often nice, liberal, anti-imperialists, who equate politics with cultures. These are the neo-Orientalists, who believe that Eastern people are fundamentally different from us. Their patron saint, in a way, is Johann Gottfried Herder, the eighteenth-century German philosopher of history, who believed that it was natural for Orientals to worship their kings. Herder deployed this argument against the universalism of Voltaire and other thinkers of the French Enlightenment, whom he regarded as arrogant imperialists.

Samuel P. Huntington, professor of the science of government at Harvard, though not a liberal, is a good example of a neo-Orientalist. The conflicts of the future, he wrote in *Foreign Affairs* in summer 1993, will happen along the "cultural fault lines" separating civilizations. This, he says, is because "differences between civilizations are not only real; they are basic." Following Huntington's somewhat arbitrary categories, differences between Arab, Confucian, Latin American, Japanese and Western civilizations are basic. Quite what is so basic about the differences between Latin American and Western, or Japanese and Confucian, civilization is unclear. But one thing is certain in the neo-Orientalist universe: East is East, and West is West, and never the twain shall meet.

James Fallows, the author of *Looking at the Sun,* is not a cultural expert. His main interest is in economics. But, like Huntington, he believes in basic differences. The subject of his book is the "Asian System." He means an economic system, based on the Japanese model, that fits the autocrats' description of the Asian Way. "The Chinese leadership," he writes, "is trying to demonstrate, that a country can have a powerful modern economy without allowing its people the individual freedoms that the Western world calls 'human rights.' [The quotation marks again.] The entire Asian model is based on a variant of this proposition: that it is possible to become as strong as the Western world without embracing its permissive ways."

That is indeed the proposition put forward by the autocrats and their allies, but does it fit the facts? Is the model specifically Asian? Is it culturally determined? Was it historically inevitable? And if it is true that the Asian System exists, what should we do about it? Should we admire and emulate it? Or must we fight it? Fallows does not seem entirely sure. There are strong hints in his book that he would like us to do both at the same time: fight it by learning from it. But the safest thing he can say with real conviction is "There is nothing inherently dangerous in the new social and economic models being developed in Asia. There is great danger in failing to see them for what they are."

Well, to be sure. But what exactly are they? Fallows approaches his Asian System in various ways, which don't always accord. He has assembled a ragbag of history, culture, *mentalités,* economics and travelers' tales, as experienced out East by the author and his family. And, since the model of the Asian System is Japan, most of the book is about Japan.

Fallows's description of postwar Japan rings true in some ways, but not in others. His analysis of the skewed relationship between Japan and the U.S. is reasonable enough. General MacArthur decided after the war that the Japanese Emperor should stay on his throne and be shielded from blame for the war. At the same time he had a new constitution drafted that made it illegal for Japan to maintain its own armed forces. The U.S. would take care of Japanese security, while Japan got on with building up its industrial power. Thus, as Fallows points out, "Japan's economic institutions grew stronger and stronger. Its political system atrophied. It was left with the ability to promote its industrial interests but to do very little else. This legacy of the Occupation is *the* fundamental source of the endless 'trade frictions' between Japan and the rest of the world."

Indeed. And Fallows's descriptions of bureaucratic battles, in Tokyo and Washington, between "pol-mil" types who did everything to keep Japan happy during the Cold War, and the commercial types who wanted more breaks for American businessmen, are interesting and to the point. But this perfectly rational explanation for Japan's present state is clearly not enough to sustain the idea of a peculiarly Japanese, let alone Asian, System. So Fallows looks back further, to the sixteenth century, when, in his opinion, many Japanese attitudes were shaped. In 1587 the strongman Toyotomi Hideyoshi expelled the Jesuits. Five years later he invaded Korea, where his bloody campaigns are still officially remembered with great bitterness. "In so doing," writes Fallows, "he underscored another of the constants in Japan's relations with outsiders: its own acute sense of vulnerability, which has affected its policies in profound ways."

This reading of Hideyoshi's motives is questionable. The "barbarian-slaying generalissimo" was driven less by fear of outsiders than by his obsession with personal power. The Jesuits were converting too many Japanese, which led to dangerous thoughts. Hideyoshi worried less about barbarian attacks than about subversion and social unrest at home. And his attempt to conquer Korea, and China too, is seen by most historians as the result of his megalomania and lust for power. These are not just pedantic points: Fallows's reading of history is typical of his tendency to confuse the politics of rulers with the alleged mentality of nations. "Japan" did not feel vulnerable (who was or is Japan?). Hideyoshi wanted to rule Japan, and Korea, and China. A considerable difference.

Fallows thinks that "Japan's" fear of barbarians then turned the country inward during the almost three centuries of virtual isolation, until the gates were blasted open in the 1860s. There is something to this, although again I would emphasize the desire of military strongmen to control Japan, more than their fear of foreign invasion. This period of isolation, he believes, produced some of the main elements of the Japanese/Asian System: among other things, suspicion of outsiders, cartel-mindedness, centralization and standardization. The last characteristic is illustrated by the observation that modern Japanese cities all look the same. This is, however, not so very surprising, since every city in Japan was reduced to charred splinters in World War II. Still, you get the drift.

Then, still following the course of history, Japan opened up in the Meiji period, and the Japanese became frantic learners, racing to catch up with the West. This national penchant for systematic learning, Fallows tells us, "leads to excesses," and there follows a charming traveler's tale to illustrate the point: "At the barber shop, individual strands of my hair were measured, and the lengths recorded, before and after the cut." I do not doubt his word. I'm sure he did meet such a barber. But I have had enough haircuts in Japan to know that either this barber was an eccentric or there must be something remarkable about Fallows's hair.

This anecdote leaves the reader with the impression that the Japanese are seriously weird. My objection to this line of reasoning is not that there are no seriously weird Japanese. The problem is that by conflating popular attitudes, cultural habits and the behavior of individuals with trade policies and official propaganda, and then calling it a System, you cannot escape from the conclusion that this System is both natural and immune to change. Fallows writes:

> Western ideas more generally are being called into question in Asia, ideas as basic as the primacy of free speech or individual rights. After centuries of having to listen to Western rulers and look up to Western technology, more and more Asian leaders— the politicians, scholars and business titans who would talk about such subjects—now say that the Western model is breaking down and that they have found a better way.

What he is referring to here, quite accurately, is the official propaganda, spouted by politicians, progovernment scholars and some business titans. Calling this an Asian System is to take the propaganda at face value, for there are very different views in Asia too. The people who died in Bangkok and Beijing (at the feet of a model of the Statue of Liberty), after demonstrating for free speech, human rights and popular sovereignty, had no truck with an authoritarian Asian System. Nor did the people who voted for Aung San Suu Kyi in Burma in 1989. The main reason Burmese students protested en masse in 1988 against the military dictatorship was not, as Fallows has it, "economic desperation." Yes, they were economically desperate, but they demanded a more democratic system, free speech, human rights. Large numbers of middle-class people in South Korea, who were not at all economically distressed, supported the student rebellion in 1986 for the same reason.

None of this means that these people wish to be just like Americans: they only wish to be free of despots. Only neo-Orientalists who cannot distinguish between politics and culture think otherwise. And, by the way, the 1948 UN Universal Declaration on Human Rights was signed by a committee, which included a Chinese. In the words of Dr. Nihal Jayawickrama, a law professor in Hong Kong, quoted in the London *Sunday Telegraph,* "The problem [with Asian countries] is that their *systems of government* are not compatible with their constitutions, not that their *cultures* are incompatible."

If the Asian System is so natural to Japan, because of "its" fear of outsiders, "its" cultural attitudes, and so on, why did a book entitled *Blueprint for a New Japan,* by the politician Ozawa Ichiro, become a huge best-seller in 1994? Ozawa is no student rebel, but a former chairman of the Liberal Democratic Party—the very heart of the Japanese/Asian System. He argues in his book for more open government, more popular sovereignty, laissez-faire economics, free trade and fewer social controls. And his main model is British parliamentary democracy. The book sold more than 600,000 copies in a matter of months.

To be sure, another book by a Japanese politician, Ishihara Shintaro, published in 1989, was also a best-seller. This book, *A Japan that Can Say "No,"* was a nationalist rant, and did indeed extol a superior Japanese Way. Japanese high technology had become vastly superior to anything produced in the U.S., Ishihara said, because of Japan's unique cultural tradition. Many a gratified reader presumably nodded in agreement. But all this shows is that public attitudes are fickle and thus an unreliable component of any purported System. Fallows moved to Japan just after a Japan Airlines Boeing crashed, and this was not long after the space shuttle *Challenger* crashed too. This, he says, reinforced the "general [Japanese] perception of shoddy American production." He quotes a Japanese pollster who said in 1992 that "the Japanese people think we should make ourselves whatever concerns human life."

No doubt this reflected polls taken then. In 1994, however, the Japanese papers were full of reports on the superiority of American high-tech products, particularly computer software. All of a sudden, America appeared insuperable. These moods, expressed in the mass media, of smug superiority or fear of failure, are whipped up by politicians, bureaucrats and businessmen in order to create or preserve the conditions that suit their interests. These interests can change as swiftly as public moods.

Fallows, like all neo-Orientalists, has much too mechanistic a view of the differences between East and West. Sometimes it results in utter incoherence. One of the basic differences between what he calls the "Anglo-American model" and the Asian System is the "view of power in setting economic policies." The "Anglo-American ideology," he writes, "views concentrated power as an evil ('power corrupts, and absolute power . . .'). Therefore it has developed elaborate schemes for dividing and breaking up power when it becomes concentrated. The Asian-style model views concentrated power as a fact of life. It has developed elaborate systems for ensuring that the power is used for the long-term national good."

I am uneasy about the idea of models and systems having "views," as though they were human beings. Still, I take his point. But, a few pages later, we learn that the "deepest critique of Japanese politics, made by the Dutch writer Karel van Wolferen, is that it lacks a centre of political accountability. In the French or American system, a president must finally make big choices, whereas in the Japanese system (in van Wolferen's terms) the buck keeps circulating and passing and never stops anywhere." Fallows does not express any disagreement with this. And it has become a commonplace in Japan too. Politicians and editorial writers are constantly pointing out that the sogginess of Japanese politics, with nobody apparently in charge, is causing political paralysis. It is precisely planning for the long-term good that is lacking in Japan, according to most experts and commentators.

What about this business, then, about the Asian model viewing "concentrated power as a fact of life"? Fallows has an answer: "whether the very centre of politics has been weak, as in Japan, or strong, as everywhere else, the political system as a whole has generally been authoritarian in Asia." Well, yes—and in Africa, much of South America, large parts of Europe and virtually all of the Middle East too. So what does this prove about the specificity of the Asian System? It is a little ironic that the model for this Asian System was supposedly developed in the least authoritarian country in Asia (with the exception, perhaps, of India). And one which lacks concentrated power to boot. If the buck keeps circulating in Japan, it is precisely because no one trusts any center of power: various centers—ministries, political factions, gangsters—circle one another like hawks.

About politics, culture and history, then, I find Fallows shallow and unconvincing. Perhaps economics provides him with firmer ground. He certainly knows his theory. The question is whether the application of economic theory strengthens his case. The case, as I understand it, is not just that Japan has practised mercantilism. Or that Japanese postwar mercantilism has been largely a legacy of the allied Occupation, which—remember—is *"the* fundamental source of the endless trade frictions between Japan and the rest of the world." No, the case is that Japan provided the model for the Asian System, which reflects deeply entrenched historical and political attitudes. Economically, so the thesis goes, the Asian System not only breaks all the rules of "Anglo-Saxon" free-market, free-trade theory, it also works better, in terms of building national strength. And, if we fail to understand it, the System might gobble up the West.

This makes slightly peculiar reading at a time of economic malaise in Japan, with banks sinking in bad debt, and government-led high-tech projects, such as high-definition TV, in tatters. And even as Japan is in recession, the U.S. economy is growing at a good clip. Still, a robust critique of neoclassical economics, or any other dogma, for that matter, can be a bracing exercise, and the growth of East Asian economics raises interesting questions.

As his paradigm for the basic difference between the "Anglo-Saxon model" and the Asian System, Fallows has chosen the rise and fall and rise of the semiconductor. First, American companies led the world in semiconductor technology. Then, in the 1960s, Japanese companies began to compete, and by the 1980s they led the world in some areas, notably DRAM chips. Some people—Fallows being one of them—began to worry that the U.S., and particularly its security, was becoming too dependent on Japanese technology. In 1986 Japan and the U.S. signed the Semiconductor Trade Agreement, forcing the Japanese to buy 20 percent of their semiconductors from U.S. companies. And within a few years some U.S. companies, notably Intel, did well, even in Japan. In fact, Intel does very well indeed: its X86 family of microprocessor chips has about 80 percent of the world market.

Fallows explains the Japanese success in terms of the Asian System: government support of Japanese corporations, a rigged domestic market, endless credit lines, business cartels and so on. In his words:

> If the American approach boiled down to "getting prices right," the Japanese approach boiled down to something different. Its essence was "getting enough money"—not worrying about theoretical efficiency, not being concerned about the best rules for competition, but focusing only on getting the nation's money into the hands of the big manufacturing firms. If companies could get *more money* to work with than their competitors, then in the long run they would prevail.

The Japanese approach, in other words, is akin to the Pentagon's support of certain American industries.

But does this really explain the ups and downs of the semiconductor story? And is the Japanese approach really always so formidable? For there is another version of the story. Japanese DRAMs did well because U.S. computer companies were happy to buy them. They were cheap, and of high quality. The Japanese are particularly good at manufacturing faultless products on a large scale. Producing memory chips is not a question of experimentation, but of perfectionism on the factory floor. This is a strength the Japanese have cultivated. The microprocessors produced by Intel—initially in response to a request from a Japanese customer—are a matter of design and imagination. And this is where the Americans—or, rather, the people of many nationalities, including many Asians, working in American labs—do better than the Japanese. Japanese companies now buy Intel's chips because they need them, and they would buy them even without a Semiconductor Agreement.

There are other examples of fruitful divisions of labor. The Japanese make the bulk of the world's fax machines, but the modern chips inside the machines are provided by an American company called Rockwell. Rockwell has kept its place in the Japanese market by better technology, good luck (during the 1980s, DRAMs kept Japanese chip factories running at full capacity) and a willingness to meet the demands of Japanese customers for high quality. It is not at all unusual for small American firms in Silicon Valley, which specialize in advanced design but lack their own manufacturing facilities, to have their chips made in Japan. This kind of interdependence is not dangerous: it is profitable to both sides. As for the virtues of government intervention (in R&D, for example), the Japanese have made terrible mistakes. MITI's $100 million Fifth Generation Computer Project is but one example.

This is not to say that mercantilism does not have its uses. As Fallows rightly points out, great powers (including Germany and the U.S.) have benefited in the past from protecting their own markets while exploiting the open markets elsewhere. This can be an effective way for developing countries to build an industrial base. As Fallows also points out, there is nothing Asian about this. Indeed, he stresses the influence of German nationalist economic thinking on Far Eastern economists. He quotes the theories of Friedrich List, as the antithesis of Adam Smith's *Wealth of Nations*. Adam Smith is set up as the Anglo-Saxon patriarch, as opposed to List, who is an honorary East Asian. List, like many Asian autocrats, believed in national economic power. Consumers were less important than producers. Getting the prices right was less important than boosting national industries.

This is, in effect, a case for authoritarianism. For, unless you believe that it is natural for non-Anglo-Saxons to sacrifice themselves for the nation, then they will have to be coerced through propaganda and, if necessary, by force. Propaganda extols the virtues of unity, discipline, self-sacrifice and patriotism. These can be virtues, to be sure. The question is whether authoritarianism—even the relatively soft kind—is the only, or indeed the best, route toward sustained economic success. It is possible that Fallows, dismayed by the messiness of American life, would like to feel the firm smack of discipline in his own country. He certainly thinks stern measures are effective elsewhere. One of the key sentences in his book is "The most successful Asian societies are, in different ways, fundamentally more repressive than America and most of Europe are, and their repression has so far been a key to their economic success." I'm not sure about "fundamentally," but the first half of the sentence is true. About the latter half, I have my doubts.

Fallows comes up with the Philippines as a negative example—an example, that is, of laxity, disunity, too much democracy. The Philippines, he says, imported from America a guiding theory of "rights and liberties first." The poverty and decay of the Philippines, he writes, no doubt correctly, fortified "Asian governments in the view that a 'rights-based' society represents a failed approach." The thing is, it also fortified Fallows's view of the same. For what "is it that 'authoritarianism' has given to many East Asian countries but that rights-based, 'American-style' democracy has denied to the Philippines? It can best be thought of as a useful kind of 'nationalism.' "

This is nonsense. Useful nationalism, in the sense of getting the best out of people, is not fostered by authoritarianism. Human behavior based on democratic participation tends to be more energetic and creative than the conformity imposed by autocrats. Open and free societies are also, on the whole, the richest. Japan is indeed in many ways a less liberal society than the U.S. or Britain, but it is freer than ever before. And its economic success probably has as much, if not more, to do with freedom of information, mobility of labor and freedom to travel as with nationalist propaganda. The decline of the Philippines, in any case, was largely the result of autocratic misrule. President Marcos's kleptocracy was both authoritarian and nationalistic, and his economic advisers believed in protected home markets and industries precisely because of that.

When Fallows turns to China to make his case, his reasoning is not just confusing, it appears to contradict everything he has said before. China, he says, might become richer and more powerful than Japan. But that would require "smart" economic management by the government, and "smart management, in turn, would mean continuing to give business—and technological development—primacy over everything else." Fallows thinks it would be smart for China's central government in Beijing to relax its control over the dynamic coastal regions of the south. Who could disagree with that? Well, the central government in Beijing. For Fallows goes on to explain that Chinese regimes, centered in Beijing, have not traditionally favored decentralization, since they "have consistently valued matters of national pride and political control over what the outside world might say is 'rational.' " This is puzzling, to say the least, for I thought that "useful nationalism," fostered by an authoritarian central government that believed in national pride and political control, was precisely what was supposed to have made the Asian System run.

Still, after hacking one's way through these knotty thickets, the least one can say is that Fallows is right about one thing: laissez-faire economics is not favored by most East Asian governments. But this still doesn't mean that an Asian System exists, except in the minds of Southeast Asian demagogues and Western commentators who think that they are on to something. However, even if we assume, for the sake of argument, that Fallows is right, that there is such a thing as a specifically Asian System combining mercantilism with authoritarian politics, does this disprove the main case for classical economics? Ricardo and Smith said that nations benefit from keeping their markets open, even if others keep their markets closed. Consumers benefit from cheaper products, and competition keeps producers efficient and quality-conscious. Fallows does not believe this. He thinks it is a dogma that blinds the Anglo-Saxon world to the reality of the East. This is why he thinks the U.S. should devise an industrial strategy, if it is not to follow Britain's giggling slide into the sea.

Britain is held up by Fallows as an example of neoclassical economic folly. In his reasoning, Britain benefited from mercantilism during its rise to preeminent power. But once it reached its place on top of the world, it began to preach the gospel of St. Adam, even as other nations, such as Germany and the U.S., broke St. Adam's rules to get ahead. It may be that some powers rose by breaking the rules of free trade: America yesterday, Japan today. But does sticking to those rules also explain the decline of others? I think not. Britain's decline was the result of many things. After the war, the statist, decidedly un-Adam Smithian Labour-government policy of choking the demand for automobiles at home in order to sell as many as possible abroad did not help. Here was an example of tightening people's belts for the nation, and it went wrong. Eventually, complacent management, bad labor relations and lack of quality and innovation almost killed the automobile industry in Britain. Only Japanese investment and expertise, invited by Mrs. Thatcher's dogmatically free-trading government, injected some flickers of life into the dying patient.

What, then, are Fallows's proposals to keep America alive and strong? He does not think the Asian System can be successfully emulated in the U.S., for, as he has pointed out, East and West do not share the same cultural principles. And besides, as Nakatani Iwao, a Japanese economics professor, told Fallows, "If the entire world were to adopt the Japanese system, the world's markets would be closed and Japan's economic expansion would be stopped right there." This, clearly, is not a price worth paying for the gratification of seeing the Japanese stopped in their tracks.

But what, then? According to Fallows, "the adaptability of Western societies will depend on whether they can bring themselves, as did the nineteenth-century Japanese, to learn everything they can about powerful new systems and change their own practices where necessary." Yes, but how? Well, by being "strong," by being "less dependent on Japan," by having an education system that helps to define "a national interest that is worth some sacrifice of immediate personal comfort or gain," by devising an industrial policy of "protection with conditions." This is perfectly feasible, he says, for in fact, throughout the 1980s, "the United States repeatedly 'broke' the rules of free trade by unilaterally imposing tariffs, under the dreaded Section 301 of its trade law, against nations whose markets it considered closed." So, if the answer is not to emulate his idea of an Asian System, the system Fallows proposes bears a striking resemblance to it. It is, if you like, an Anglo-Saxon version.

There is a more liberal alternative to this. Instead of the U.S. becoming less dependent on Japan, Japan should become less dependent, for its security, on America. For, to quote Fallows once more, this Japanese dependence is "*the* fundamental source of the endless 'trade frictions.'" As far as trade and industry are concerned, mutual dependence should be fostered, instead of being discouraged in the name of national strength. Imposing special tariffs, import quotas and other forms of bullying on Japan will only perpetuate the bureaucratic management of the Japanese economy, which harms consumers and hinders the efforts of Japanese politicians to liberalize their system. The way to deal with Japan, and other countries in East Asia, is to encourage open, liberal politics and free-market economies, not by confrontation and "protection with conditions," but by demonstrating that America's economy can still be the richest and most successful in the world, precisely by keeping its markets open.

But if one believes, with the neo-Orientalists, that authoritarianism and aggressive nationalism are natural and permanent features of East Asian societies, and if one believes that these are "Eastern values," and that to assume otherwise is to indulge in imperialist arrogance, well, then, I'm afraid the liberal alternative is not even an option.

1994

THE NANNY STATE OF ASIA

I'm no more a Chinese than President Kennedy was an Irishman.

Lee Kuan Yew in America, 1967

It could have ended like any number of squalid murder cases in Southeast Asia—with an execution and no fuss. In 1991 a Filipina maid called Mrs. Maga was found dead in Singapore with her ward, the small son of a Singaporean-Chinese family. Another Filipina maid was accused of the murders. She was arrested. She confessed. And in March 1995, she was hanged. So ended the life of Flor Contemplacion, one of 100,000 women and girls imported to Singapore from poor countries around the region. Some are sent by local contractors, others are attracted by ads like this, in the *Straits Times* of Singapore: "Filipino. Hardworking. No day off."

But the case turned out to be more complicated. Two weeks before Mrs. Contemplacion's execution, Filipinos protested against the verdict. There were rumors that she had been tortured by the police, that she might be innocent. Demonstrations were held in Manila. The Singaporean flag was burnt. The Philippine government asked for a stay of execution, so that possible new evidence could be examined. The request was dismissed, and the execution went ahead on schedule.

Protest escalated in the Philippines. President Ramos, who was running for election, had lost face, so he recalled his ambassador, and relations between the two countries went sour.

A Philippine commission was appointed to review the evidence. Mrs. Maga, it was alleged, had sustained injuries that a person of Mrs. Contemplacion's size could not have inflicted. The victim's body was dug up from its grave, and the commission concluded that she had been severely maltreated; bones appeared to be broken. Singaporean doctors, however, claimed that those injuries had been suffered long before the victim was strangled. Relations grew worse still. The Singapore Democratic Party, one of two tiny opposition parties, sent a letter to President Ramos, asking him to consider mediation. The other opposition party, the Workers' Party, stated that the commission's findings put the Singapore judicial system on trial.

In May I attended a session of the Singapore parliament. I had been told that questions would be asked about the handling of the Contemplacion case. Walking up the stairs to the main chamber, I noticed a piece of masonry (a rose) from the palace of Westminster hanging on the wall. It had been donated by the Queen. Like the fine old Singapore Cricket Club, the neoclassical law courts, and the statue of Singapore's British founder, Sir Stamford Raffles, all within five minutes' walk, the parliament showed a solid sense of tradition. The opposition, including members nominated by professional associations, sat on one side of the House, and members of the ruling People's Action Party (PAP) on the other. The language was in the best parliamentary tradition: "Mr. Speaker, a supplementary question, if you please, Sir . . ."

What followed, however, was not so much a debate as a piece of parliamentary theater. Two nominated MPs asked the government to explain its refusal to delay Mrs. Contemplacion's execution. The Foreign Affairs and Law Minister S. Jayakumar, who had been chatting with another minister all through the question, answered by giving a long speech about the excellence of Singapore's judiciary and the soundness of the government's decision. It was all done with the utmost decorum. If anything, there was a stale air of boredom in the House. There was not even a whisper of "hear, hear," let alone a throaty roar of dissent.

The next day, a Friday, things took a nastier turn. The members of the SDP and WP were taken to task by the Home Affairs Minister, Wong

Kan Seng, for aiding "an attempt by outsiders to undermine the Singapore judiciary." A former secretary general of the SDP, ousted by the present leader, Dr. Chee Soon Juan, expressed his disaffection with his old party by stating: "All Singaporeans, whether they are supporters of the ruling party or the opposition party, have to be loyal to Singapore. . . . And when there is a dispute with a foreign country, they must close ranks with the ruling party and all Singaporeans and stand united. This is the message that all Singaporeans must give to all the people of other countries."

These words were quoted with approval in the *Straits Times*. The banner headline in Saturday's paper read: JUDICIARY HERE CAN STAND UP TO SCRUTINY. Monday's headline said: MAID ISSUE: GOV'T THANKS S'POREANS. The acting Community Development Minister, Abdullah Tarmugi, expressed his gratitude for the public's support, and added that the "maid case" had made the nation "more cohesive."

Now, I do not know whether Mrs. Contemplacion was guilty or not. The reaction from the Philippines may simply have been an emotional outburst against the humiliation of being the main provider of cut-price maids for richer countries in the region. But there was something disturbing about these proceedings. Here was a British-style parliament, a democratic institution, being used to conflate patriotism with loyalty to a party which has never been out of power since independence in 1965. The merest hint of criticism was being treated as a kind of treason. The forms of Westminster, based on political contention, were made to serve the aim of authoritarian rule, to impose absolute unity. But what was most Singaporean of all was the sensitivity to any suggestion that the institutions left behind by the British Empire may now be in less than perfect order.

And such suggestions are being made, by Singaporean dissidents and, recently, by the Association of the Bar of the City of New York. Its report on international human rights concluded that "law no longer restrains [Singapore] government actions or protects individual rights." It went on to say that this "campaign against the rule of law is part of a broader effort by the current Singapore government to secure its hold on power. It parallels a similarly motivated effort to strangle the independent institutions of civil society and thus prevent the emergence of an effective and organized opposition."

Since the early 1990s Singaporean officials, especially the former prime minister, now Special Minister (SM), Lee Kuan Yew, have been promoting their brand of authoritarian politics as "the Asian Way." So-called Asian values, such as—to quote a 1991 Singapore government White Paper—"nation before community and society above self," and "consensus above contention," enforced by firm paternalistic government, have resulted in a vaunted combination of economic progress and social discipline. With its glittering high rise skyline, spotless streets, multinational high-tech industrial parks, rocketing GDP and obedient population, Singapore looks like the living proof that authoritarianism works, the dream of every strongman in Asia and beyond.

One might wonder why spokesmen from tiny Singapore, with its peculiar colonial history, have become the exponents of Asian values. Economic success is not the only explanation. Both the tinyness and the colonial background have much to do with it. It is in new, insecure, racially mixed states, such as Malaysia and Singapore, that you most often hear people talk about Asia, or Asian values, or the Asian Way. Indeed, the phrase "Asian values" only really makes sense in English. In Chinese, Malay or Hindi, it would sound odd. Chinese think of themselves as Chinese, and Indians as Indians (or Tamils, or Punjabis). Asia, as a cultural concept, is an official invention to bridge vastly different ethnic populations living in former British colonies. The "Asian" is a kind of sales gimmick, used for political and commercial public relations. The Japanese promoted a Pan-Asian identity during World War II in their effort to develop a broad front against the British, the Americans and the Dutch.

Promoters of the Asian Way blend culture and politics in a way that is most convenient for political propaganda. George Yeo, Singapore's Information Minister, explained why Singaporeans cannot be allowed to have satellite dishes, which would enable them to choose foreign cable television channels: "We must preserve our own sense of place, self and community." What did he mean, exactly? Was he worried that decadent Western values would corrupt an Asian sense of self, or that more choice of information would make it harder to impose political censorship? Of course, if he believes that Singapore's sense of self, place and community is embodied by the PAP government, the question becomes redundant, for then political and cultural identity are the same. This is the "core value," to use another favorite Singaporean government phrase, of every totalitarian system: you obey your leaders without question, because you are Chinese, or German, or Asian.

Last April a conference was held in Kuala Lumpur. The editors of English-language newspapers in East and Southeast Asia spoke about their common concerns. One of the speakers, Florian Coulmas, who teaches linguistics at Chuo University in Tokyo, pointed out that the desire for a common Asian perspective was "most popular among newspaper men from countries where the press is most firmly under government control." Coulmas also pointed out why: "Instead of allowing the issue of free speech to disturb the spirit of Asian community, the real or alleged differences between Western and Asian views of Asia are highlighted. Rather than decrying censorship, the dependence on the three big Western news agencies, AP, Reuters, and AFP, is portrayed as the greatest evil."

The first thing that strikes a visitor to Singapore is how Western it looks in comparison to most other cities in Asia. At the beginning of my stay, I had dinner with the son of a former Singapore government official. He was of Indian ancestry. His first language was English. And he was highly educated, partly in America. To save him from more trouble—he has already lost his job as a journalist for writing something mildly critical of the government; old friends no longer speak to him; he is a marked man—I shall not name him. We had Chinese noodles at an open-air restaurant. We gazed at the glass and chrome city across the bay, which could have been a picture on one of those visionary billboards you see in developing countries, showing the glorious future. "There is nothing Asian about Singapore," he sighed. "It is the most westernized country in Asia . . . but also the least free."

As is the case in all newly rich societies, culture in Singapore is less a matter of art than of lifestyle. The Singapore lifestyle is marked by Western and Japanese brand names: Swiss watches, Hollywood soap operas, American fast food, European fashions, Japanese cars, international Muzak. The ideal Singapore lifestyle can be discerned from newspaper advertisements for expensive real estate: "Gentle Villas: A Lifetime of Luxury . . . every inch a measure of the success you have earned." The bungalows in Gentle Villas are grand versions of European colonial architecture, with shades of southern California: "Finely proportioned windows and an exquisite Corinthian front door grace the elegant exterior. . . . The eternal beauty of marble in the master and guest bathrooms. Bedrooms and staircases furnished with parquet flooring. And kitchens which are tiled with top-quality Italian ceramics. . . . And a wireless remote control autogate guards your residence."

Singaporeans listen to Michael Jackson songs and read Sidney Sheldon novels or books on how to succeed in business. All this seems tame enough. Yet the government is worried. For Singaporeans, being highly computer literate, are also plugged into the Internet. Some have used this as an opportunity to express critical opinions. Some have even made abusive remarks about the SM. There is a group on the Internet known as "soc.culture.singapore," which provides a forum for uncensored information about Singapore. The Information Minister has voiced his alarm. The Singapore Broadcasting Authority (SBA) will be used to police the electronic airwaves, he promised. But he added that the "SBA cannot police on its own without the support and cooperation of members of the Singapore cyberspace community." He has told Singaporeans to alert "each other and the SBA" if they should come across "pornographic or incendiary broadcasts."

Self-censorship is part of the Singapore lifestyle. The National Arts Council is in charge of making sure that theater plays do not "erode the core moral values of society (that is, promote permissive lifestyles like homosexuality)" or "subvert national security and stability." Liew Chin Choy, the director of NAC, said that theater groups know "the onus is on them to exercise self-censorship responsibly." However, some theater groups have said they feel more comfortable leaving things to government censors. As the representative of one group called Sriwana put it: "If we go through them, they will take care of things. Then we can be on the safe side."

In 1987 a twenty-eight-year-old amateur dramatist called Wong Souk Yee found herself on the unsafe side. She had written satirical skits about the Singapore lifestyle, including the treatment of Filipina maids, for a theater group called Third Stage. She was jailed, together with a number of young lawyers and professionals, for being part of a "communist front" and trying "to reach out to and radicalize the public."

This summer Singapore CableVision (SCV) concluded a deal with CNN and the Turner Network Television & Cartoon Network. Henceforth Singaporeans will be able to watch CNN news, old Hollywood movies and Disney cartoons, as the SCV chairman put it, "in the comfort of their homes." I attended a party celebrating this event. It was held at the Hyatt Regency. CNN executives wearing Mickey Mouse ties paid tribute to their "Singaporean friends." Waitresses offered up glasses of Coca-Cola and 7UP on silver trays. I left early, but not before seeing the CNN representative and the SCV chairman waving at us in the company of two grown men dressed up as Tom and Jerry.

There is culture in Singapore with a more local color, but much of it has been destroyed, damaged or sanitized beyond recognition. Bugis Street, for example, used to be the center of an old Malay, or more precisely, Bugis cultural tradition: transvestism. This had its seamy side, to be sure, but it is a pity that the street had to be demolished, only to be re-created in a different location as a kind of tourist mall with food stalls, but without Bugis transvestites. They have not entirely disappeared, however. Some can still be seen lurking around the big hotels, making eyes at tourists. I asked one of them what life was like in Singapore. He slipped his arm into mine and sighed: "Sooo boooring!"

More serious is the linguistic poverty of Singapore. Seventy-six percent of the population is ethnically Chinese. The rest is either Indian or Malay. Most Chinese speak different southern Chinese dialects at home: Hokkien, Cantonese or Hakka. But this practice has been discouraged by the government since the late 1970s, when the Speak Mandarin Campaign was launched. Dialects were considered vulgar, the language of market hawkers; Mandarin was the official language of China. And a standard Chinese language was meant to unify the Chinese. So Mandarin was imposed on the mass media, and in public life. Cantonese soap operas from Hong Kong had to be dubbed. People who had never spoken Mandarin in their lives suddenly had to learn. Yet English is now the main medium of instruction in schools and universities. Chinese higher education was abolished in 1980, when Nanyang University was merged with the English-language University of Singapore. As a result of these measures, few Singaporeans speak any language well. Television announcers and government spokesmen speak painfully correct English or Mandarin in the manner of elocution teachers. But most Singaporeans speak a mixture of English and Chinese slang, or Chinese and English slang, or Malay and English slang, or all of the above.

A Chinese woman named Leena Lim, who runs one of the few decent bookshops in Singapore, lamented the disappearance of Chinese schools. She said nobody buys Chinese books anymore. Chinese bookshops have to survive by selling Sidney Sheldon novels, American how-to-succeed-in-business manuals and Ping-Pong bats. She said that the only people talking about Asian values are PAP politicians: "After breaking down communities, languages and cultures, they now want to re-create Asian culture artificially."

——

I'm told [repression] is like making love—it's always easier the second time.

Lee Kuan Yew, October, 1956

The story of Singapore is, in many ways, the story of Lee Kuan Yew himself. So much in the state was shaped in his image. One way of explaining Lee is to look at his enemies. He began his political career as a fighter against British colonialism. Yet he was very much a product of the British Empire. Born in 1923, Harry Lee Kuan Yew was educated in English. He took great care not to have a native accent. He refused to learn Mandarin (but spoke some Cantonese to his nanny). Harry went on to read law at Cambridge University, where he won two firsts, a feat of which he likes to boast, especially to British visitors. He returned to Malaya a believer in democracy and genteel socialism.

Those, indeed, were the principles on which he based his anticolonial politics. In 1955 he maintained that "If you believe in democracy, you must believe in it unconditionally. If you believe that men should be free, then, they should have the right of free association, of free speech, of free publication." He fought the British as an "Anglified Chinaman" (Lee's own words). But to mobilize the Chinese-speaking masses, the Anglified Chinaman had to speak to them in Chinese, so he began to learn Mandarin when he was about thirty years old.

His next enemy, after the British had gone, was the communists. In

1963 hundreds of dissidents, including members of parliament, were arrested and jailed for communist subversion. Most communists and leftists in Singapore were Chinese speakers: many of them graduates and students of Nanyang University. And now British antisubversion laws, British detention centers, and British methods of punishment were used against them. The oppressive apparatus left behind by the Raj—particularly the Internal Security Act—would henceforth be used to crush political opposition to Lee Kuan Yew's PAP government.

The most famous political prisoner is an academic and a former socialist MP called Chia Thye Poh. In 1966 he organized a demonstration against the Vietnam War, which was enough to detain him, but a better pretext had to be found. A few years later, while still in jail, Chia was accused of being a communist. No evidence was ever produced. And he would have been released, if only he had agreed to confess publicly to his alleged communism. But since he never agreed to do so, he is still confined to a room on Sentosa Island, a resort where mostly Japanese tourists come to admire the wax tableau of British generals signing Singapore's surrender to Japan in 1941. Chia is now allowed out during the day, but has to return to the island every night.

But even as the PAP struggled against communist subversion, Lee's party became an almost Leninist institution that gained more and more control over every aspect of Singaporean life, political, social and economic. PAP cadres keep a careful watch on housing estates, student organizations, trade unions and clan associations. It is impossible to start any private organization without government approval. Almost all local companies are linked to the government. For many years students could not enter a university in Singapore without a political Suitability Certificate. A Social Development Unit was set up to stimulate marriages between educated Singaporeans. Singapore, in short, is the epitome of the nanny state. But it is a peculiarly nosy and strict nanny. In 1987 the prime minister said,

I am often accused of interfering in the private lives of citizens. Yet, if I did not, had I not done that, we wouldn't be here today. And I say without the slightest remorse, that we wouldn't be here, we would not have made economic progress, if we had not intervened on very personal matters—who your neighbour is, how you live, the noise you make, how you spit, or what language you use. We decide what's right. Never mind what the people think.

The specter of communism was invoked again in 1987, when the dramatist Wong Souk Yee was detained without trial with a group of young lawyers and Catholic social workers. They were accused of organizing a conspiracy to overthrow the government and establish a Marxist state. In fact, no evidence ever emerged that they did more than speak up for the rights of Filipina maids and protest against the suffocating intrusiveness of PAP rule. But they were sufficiently frightened by their treatment in the Whitley Detention Center—interrogation without sleep, exposure to ice-cold temperatures, solitary confinement, threats and beatings—that they confessed their "crimes" on television. Three of them were represented by a lawyer named Francis T. Seow. His arrest brought a new enemy to the fore: the United States.

Seow's account of his problems with the PAP government has a typically Singaporean flavor. His book, *To Catch a Tartar: A Dissident in Lee Kuan Yew's Prison,* was published in the U.S. It cannot be bought in Singapore, even though it is not actually banned. It is merely "undesirable." As with smoking marijuana in Britain or the U.S., one can get away with reading undesirable books in private, but booksellers would be unwise to stock them. Seow's prose style, larded with quotations from Shakespeare, Oscar Wilde and Lee Kuan Yew, is flowery and self-regarding: his rise as a barrister was "meteoric," his speeches "won thunderous ovation." But the book is also a devastating account of the destruction of the rule of law.

Seow started off as a young star on the Singapore bench, educated in London and trusted by Lee Kuan Yew himself—hence the "meteoric rise." In the 1960s he helped to expose communists in Chinese schools. He became a feared prosecutor, then Solicitor General, and then president of the Law Society. And then, around about 1986, things began to go wrong.

Seow, as well as other members of the bar, felt that the Law Society should not only be consulted on promotions in the judiciary, but also make its views known on legislation. In early 1986 the Council of the Law Society issued a critical report on a new bill, which would enable any government minister to restrict the circulation of foreign publications at will. The tax authorities began to harass Seow. His bank loans were suddenly called in. His accountants, sensing trouble, wanted to be discharged from handling his affairs.

Lee Kuan Yew decided to curb the Law Society's public activities by staging a televised Parliamentary Committee hearing. This was meant to discredit the critical lawyers. Instead, it made rebel heroes out of them. Francis Seow and two young woman lawyers, Teo So Lung and Tang Fong Har, stood up to the PM's harangues. The PM flew into such a rage that technicians had to be brought in to tone down his skin color for the television broadcast. Eight months later, Teo and Tang were among the detainees, arrested for engaging in the Marxist plot. The PM declared that one of the ringleaders of the plot was a Catholic lay worker named Vincent Cheng. When the Singaporean Archibishop Yong asked him for proof of this allegation, Lee said he would not "allow subversives to get away by insisting that I [have] got to prove everything against them in a court of law . . ."

The plight of the political detainees became an international cause célèbre. Seow met American diplomats, representatives from law societies and human rights groups, and was asked to run as an opposition MP in Singapore. He was arrested while waiting to see one of his clients, Teo So Lung, in the detention center. The accusation: plotting with Americans to interfere in Singapore's internal affairs. American diplomats allegedly had paid him to oppose the PAP government. The proof: his dinners at Singapore restaurants with E. Mason Hendrickson, first secretary of the U.S. embassy. To force a confession, Seow was subjected to the usual treatment: seventeen hours of continuous interrogation (his clients endured seventy-two hours) while standing half-naked under a freezing air conditioner, threats, abuse and so on.

Seow remained in detention for more than two months. Officers of the Internal Security Department did their best to write a statement of Seow's guilt that would be ambiguous enough to enable Seow to sign it without losing too much face, while also satisfying the government. The allegations were so far-fetched, however, and so lacking in evidence, that Seow's case became an embarrassment. Yet, this being Singapore, the forms of due process and parliamentary rule had to be upheld. A parliamentary debate was staged to pass a government motion supporting the use of the Internal Security Act to prevent imaginary foreign interest groups from subverting Singapore. The *Straits Times* wrote that the PM had no choice but to keep Seow in detention: "To release the man would be an admission that it had been wrong to arrest him, and such an admission would confuse all those who have believed in the government."

Seow was released in the end, but was warned not to get involved in politics. He ignored the warning, won a nonconstituency parliamentary seat, and the government started proceedings against him for tax evasion. While visiting New York to see a doctor, he was convicted in absentia, and without the presence of his lawyer in court. The fine was high enough to block any further political aspirations in Singapore. He now lives in Arlington, Massachusetts.

Seow's clients got off less easily. And the way they were treated is the perfect example of Singapore's peculiar use of due process—not to protect individual rights, but to deny them. First, Teo So Lung and eight others were forced to confess publicly to their alleged Marxist plot. After being released, they complained in private that the confessions had been exacted under duress. When the stories came out in the foreign press, the Singapore government said no credence would be given to these allegations unless they were stated in public. The challenge was met, and the former detainees spoke at a press conference about being physically and mentally abused by ISD officers. Whereupon the government announced a formal inquiry into the allegations. But Teo and the others were quickly rearrested and sent into the custody of the very officers they had accused of mistreatment. After several days of interrogation by these same officers, the detainees signed a Statutory Declaration that their allegations had been "a political propaganda ploy to discredit the government." It is an offense to claim that a Statutory Declaration was made falsely. So the government could now announce with great satisfaction that the formal inquiry into alleged abuses would be abandoned forthwith.

Lee Kuan Yew likes to invoke the Confucian tradition in his political speeches. The insistence on public confessions is indeed modern Singaporean Confucianism in action. The law, under authoritarian regimes in China, South Korea and even sometimes in Japan, is not used to protect individual rights, but as an instrument of government power. Confessions are exacted to frighten people into submission. This is what is meant by "society above self" and "consensus above contention": consensus is what the government wants people to think. And the law is used to make sure that they do.

By and large, and especially in a tiny, rich state like Singapore, it works. People are frightened away from politics. They develop sensitive antennae for potential trouble. And if they are prosperous as well, they will do anything to stay out of harm's way, for they have too much to lose. A British academic at the National University of Singapore told me how he was sent an article from a Western newspaper which was critical of the Singapore government. He tried to show it to a Singaporean colleague. The man had a fit of hysterical blindness. He was unable to read it. He ran off in terror.

Singaporeans become very good at judging "tone," at knowing just what to say, when, and to whom. Some regard this heightened sensitivity as a sign of Oriental refinement, of superior culture. I went to see a highly successful Singaporean property developer called Ho Kwon Ping. He is chairman of the Speak Mandarin Campaign, tipped to be a pillar of the PAP. He is the embodiment of Singaporean success. But he, too, used to be a bit of a rebel, many years ago. He, too, was once detained for being a "Marxist." And he, too, made a public confession. I saw him at his plush modern office. In impeccable English, he drawled: "You know, I only feel comfortable talking about Asian values with my fellow Asians. For, you see, I think Westerners are so prejudiced."

> *My colleagues and I have been personal friends and political*
> *colleagues for fifteen, twenty years now, and we have been*
> *through fire together. . . . And you build a camaraderie that*
> *these little things [split or disagreement] cannot break . . .*
>
> Lee Kuan Yew, 1965

Some of the most embittered men in Singapore are Lee Kuan Yew's former colleagues, men of his own generation who helped him to fight British colonialism and build a free and independent nation. The former president, Devan Nair, now living in exile in the U.S., was for many years one of Lee's closest friends, and is now among his fiercest critics. He wrote the foreword to Francis Seow's book, comparing Lee's oppressive measures unfavorably to the treatment he received from the British as a young, communist, anticolonial rebel: "It surely cannot be termed progress in freedom and humanity to arrest and treat his own political prisoners so brutally, and with far less reason than the British had to detain me and my revolutionary comrades."

The founding chairman of the PAP and former deputy prime minister, Dr. Toh Chin Chye, accused the government of "administration by intimidation." He said, "People abroad say to me: 'You Singaporeans seem to be nervous, always looking over your shoulders.' And it's true, Singaporeans are so bloody scared. Nobody wants to say anything. It's always: 'Don't quote me.' . . . They're scared of losing a license or their jobs. . . . Here we're all ball bearings produced by quality control."

David Marshall, the chief minister in 1955, was never a close friend, and for much of his life has been a vocal critic. Marshall, a Baghdadi Jew born in Singapore, founded the left-wing Workers' Party in 1957. He beat the PAP in an election in 1961. He could have been a contender. Instead, he accepted Lee's offer to become ambassador to Paris. Marshall is an expansive figure, a bon vivant, a ladies' man, with cream and white hair, bushy eyebrows and soulful eyes. Singaporean liberals say that if Marshall had become prime minister instead of Lee, Singapore would have been poorer but freer, and certainly more fun. I went to see him at his law firm in the center of town.

"Could I have achieved what Lee did? The answer is no. I don't have the iron in my soul to have achieved it." This was in answer to my question whether Singapore's prosperity could have been achieved without Lee's authoritarianism. Then the conversation turned to Asian values. He called it "phony baloney." He did not see Asian values of being of any value. In Lee's case, he said, "lust for domination came with power."

And yet Marshall, the Oriental Jew, despised by British colonialists and Chinese chauvinists in equal measure, was curiously like Lee in his stress on culture as the basis of politics. There is no understanding of democracy in Asia, he said. There is just a brutal Asian approach. You kill your enemies. This, he feared, was the "movement of the future. With the ebbing of American influence, and the flowing of Chinese influence, we see an extension of nails in our coffin, and an expansion of our ruthlessness."

David Marshall did not seem bitter, just tired, old. Before parting, I asked whether he felt closer to the West, even though he was born and bred in the East. His eyes opened wide, owl-like. "Of course," he said. "The brotherhood of man, equality, what a wonderful concept! What a beautiful thing: a religion that makes brothers of all people."

The world would be simpler if Marshall and many others of his persuasion were right: that politics is mainly a reflection of culture; that liberal democracy is a matter of Judeo-Christian values; that despotism, enlightened or not, is destined to thrive in Asia, because of Confucius, or Shintoism, or whatever. But the example of Singapore shows that the world is not that simple. Underneath the rhetoric of Asian values lies a fear of not being equal to the West, of not living up to those Cambridge law degrees.

A Singaporean writer named Gopal Baratham told me that "the most ferociously anticolonial, anti-Western Singaporeans are those in the Westernized, English-speaking elite." They are sensitive to any suggestion that they might not be as good as their former masters. Of all the criticism leveled at Singapore, and Lee Kuan Yew in particular, two have caused more pain, more censorship, and more lawsuits than any other: the suggestion that political leadership is subject to nepotism, and that the judiciary is less than impartial.

In 1994 a Hong Kong journalist named Philip Bowring expressed the opinion on the op-ed page of the *International Herald Tribune* that "Dynastic politics is evident in Communist China already, as in Singapore, despite official commitments to bureaucratic meritocracy." He was hinting at the position of Lee's son, Brigadier General (BG) Lee Hsien Loong, who is serving as deputy prime minister and is groomed to be the next PM. The *IHT*, whose Asian edition is printed in Singapore, immediately published an apology, "undertaking not to make further allegations to the same or similar effect." Nonetheless, Lee brought a libel suit for £427,000 in damages. The Singapore Supreme Court duly awarded the damages to Lee, father and son, as well as the prime minister, Goh Chok Tong.

Two months after the *IHT*'s apology, another article appeared on its opinion page, this time by an American academic called Christopher

Lingle, who analyzed various types of political oppression in Asia without naming any country. Some governments, he wrote, use tanks to crush dissent, but others "are more subtle: relying upon a compliant judiciary to bankrupt opposition politicians . . ." Again the *IHT* apologized profusely. Again the Singapore government insisted on a trial for "criminal defamation and contempt of court." The Singapore High Court fined the paper, its printer and the Asian editor. Still Lee Kuan Yew was not happy. He filed another lawsuit, demanding an admission that the article was part of a concerted effort to undermine him.

This all sounds like an advanced stage of paranoia. But how to explain its particular nature? Why should Lee be so hurt by the allegation of dynastic politics? After all, if anything is in the Confucian tradition, dynastic politics is. And why should he use his country's law courts to stop accusations that these courts are sometimes used to stifle political dissent? After all, that is precisely how courts in China, and other parts of East Asia, have traditionally been used. The logical explanation is that Asian values are not really the point but, on the contrary, that Lee is terrified of what the British used to call "going native." There are hints of this fear of vanishing into the Oriental swamp, of being swallowed up by the Southeast Asian jungle, in some of the former PM's speeches: "My deepest concern is how to make the young more conscious of security. By security I mean defense against threats to our survival, whether the threats are external or internal. . . . Civilization is fragile. It is especially so for an island city-state." (Lee Kuan Yew, National Day, 1982.)

The BG once warned that without faith in Singapore, "we would vanish without trace, submerged into the mud of history." The only serious confrontations the state of Singapore has had in its short history were with Malaysia and Indonesia. Security, then, can only be seen in this regional context: security from the Malay world. But the Lees' paranoia is more complicated even than that. In fact, it is shared by the prime minister of Malaysia. Prime Minister Mahathir's anti-Western diatribes, like Lee Kuan Yew's, are not so distant echoes of their British colonial education. The White Man's Burden was justified by claims of European discipline (as opposed to native idleness), of European vigor (as opposed to native decadence), of tight ships and stiff upper lips. Lee

Kuan Yew's preoccupation with genes and his horror of decadence are the burning embers of nineteenth-century social Darwinism. Singapore is the last bastion of the hang 'em and flog 'em brigade. Lee and Mahathir still claim to uphold the old standards, even as the West goes to the dogs. They will stick to the forms of British rule, even as they destroy the content.

Once again it is instructive to see who Lee Kuan Yew's opponents are. For in fact the political contest in Asia is not between Asian and Western values. Dissidents in Singapore, Taiwan, Thailand or China are not Westernizers. The most trenchant critique of Lee's Asian Way came from the South Korean opposition leader Kim Dae Jung. Kim is a populist politician from South Korea's most rebellious province, the rural southwest. He is hardly a proponent of Western values (whatever they may be). Kim argued, in *Foreign Affairs,* that there was nothing in East Asian culture incompatible with democracy. On the contrary, he said, "Asia has democratic philosophies as profound as those of the West." He quoted Mencius to make this point. This might be a case of over-egging the pudding. But Kim made another observation, which is surely true:

> Asian authoritarians misunderstand the relationship between the rules of effective governance and the concept of legitimacy. Policies that try to protect people from the bad elements of economic and social change will never be effective if imposed without consent; the same policies, arrived at through public debate, will have the strength of Asia's proud and self-reliant people.

This is also the gist of a small book on Singapore politics written by Dr. Chee Soon Juan, the leader of the Singapore Democratic Party. His book *Dare To Change: An Alternative Vision For Singapore,* is "undesirable." Dr. Chee has to sell his book on street corners. The content, in any democratic society, would be banal. In the U.S., Dr. Chee would fit into the mainstream of the Democratic Party. What is interesting about his book is that, unlike Western democrats, he has to argue just why democracy is not just a "value," Western or Eastern, but a system that works better than other systems. He writes, "With man's corruptible nature, democracy ensures that no individual is able to abuse the powers entrusted upon him. It is exactly the same system that enables the citizens to remove a bad leader from office." This, in Singapore, constitutes rebellion.

He has other, more pointed things to say about Singapore, which apply to other countries in East Asia. By controlling much of the economy through so-called government-linked companies, the PAP has stifled private enterprise. He thinks an overregulated, overprotected economy will gradually stop being competitive. He argues that "authoritarianism is the one biggest obstacle to Singapore's growth as an international city of high-technology, business and commerce."

I met Dr. Chee in the lobby of an American hotel. We sat in soft leather chairs and drank cappuccinos, Muzak tinkling through the palm fronds. Large men with leather bags under their arms hovered around between the white grand piano and the front desk. They were watching our every move. Dr. Chee pointed to one of the bags. It had a little hole punched in it. "A camera," he said.

Chee is used to being followed. He has been hounded ever since he decided to run for a parliamentary seat in 1992. The usual things happened: libel suits, harassment by the tax department and trouble finding a job—he is one of the few neuropsychologists in Singapore. Businessmen who back him or his party financially are questioned by the ISD. "Enough," according to Chee, "to frighten them off." These and other pressures make it hard to find suitable opposition candidates. A person with ambition will get on better with the PAP. Nonetheless, in 1994 the SDP won 47 percent of the votes in constituencies it decided to contest.

The typical SDP voter is not a Westernized member of the elite. The prosperous English-speaking middle-class tends to be conservative, afraid of disorder, happy to be well-off. The typical opposition voter is more likely to be a Chinese-speaking market hawker, a taxi driver or a small Indian businessman, the sort of person who might have been a leftist in the 1950s. Culturally, the opposition voter is likely to be more traditionally "Asian" than most PAP supporters. Such a person will vote for the opposition not because of a superior understanding of John Locke or Western values, but because he or she does not feel represented by the oligarchy that runs the country.

Dr. Chee is a young man, Chinese, highly educated. He could lead a good life in Singapore if only he kept quiet, minded his business, accommodated himself to PAP rule. I wondered what possessed him to go against his own interests, against the wishes of his family, against all the advantages of conformity. So I asked him. He gave a vague answer about wanting to change the heavy-handed way things are done. He said that professionals don't want to join the opposition, yet always grumble that the opposition parties are not effective. "That is why I wanted to join."

To be an opposition leader in a system that does not recognize loyal opposition takes a steeliness, a fearlessness, a ruthlessness that very few people possess. Lee Kuan Yew had it. David Marshall, by his own account, did not. It is hard to tell whether Dr. Chee has it. His ideas are good, but then so were Lee's when he began his struggle against British rule.

I spent my last night in Singapore in the reconstructed Bugis Street. On the second floor of a café, on the corner of the street, is a place called the Boom Boom Club. I was taken there by a Singaporean woman who said she felt better about her city whenever she went there. That night was ASEAN night, the night of Southeast Asian nations. The star of the show was a Singaporean Indian drag artist called Kumar.

The place was packed and smoky. The decor was stripped down, deliberately shabby. "Young Singaporeans like to go down," explained the owner. "They're bored with marble floors and chandeliers." There were flamboyant Chinese and Malay homosexuals in the club, but most of the audience looked like well-scrubbed Singaporean yuppies, men in striped shirts, women in expensive dresses. The curtain lifted, the show began.

Dancers in outrageous costumes from the different Southeast Asian nations shimmied across the stage to Hong Kong disco music. They sang a song about being part of one big Asian family, singing one Asian song, in one Asian voice. The audience loved it. Then came Kumar, an apparition dressed in a cross between an Indian sari and a Western evening gown. He spoke in the Singlish patois: English with Chinese and Malay slang. "We're supposed to be one Asian family," he screeched, "but we don't care about that, la! I'm going to talk about something else . . . I'm going to talk about cock, very much la!"

The audience hooted and hollered. I had never seen Singaporeans in such a state. There is hope for Singapore yet. Then Kumar dropped his voice and said, "The trouble with Singapore is there are too many Indian chiefs telling us what to do. Too many politicians, la." A hush swept the room. Not even a titter was heard. The audience was too frightened to laugh.

1995

BIBLIOGRAPHY

Akutagawa Ryunosuke, *Hell Screen,* trans. Kojima Takashi, *Cogwheels,* trans. Susumu Kamaike, and *A Fool's Life,* trans. Will Petersen; foreword Jorge Luis Borges, intro. Sakai Kasuya (New York: Eridanos, 1987)

Allen, Thomas B., and Norman Polmar, *Code-Name Downfall: The Secret Plan to Invade Japan—And Why Truman Dropped the Bomb* (New York: Simon & Schuster, 1995).

Ali, Tariq, *Can Pakistan Survive: The Death of a State* (Harmondsworth, U.K.: Penguin, 1983)

Alperovitz, Gar, *The Decision to Use the Atomic Bomb and the Architecture of an American Myth* (New York: Knopf, 1995).

Bacarr, Jina, *How to Work for a Japanese Boss* (New York: Birch Lane Press, 1993)

Balke, Gerd (ed.), *Hongkong Voices* (Hong Kong: Longman, 1989)

Bhutto, Benazir, *Daughter of the East* (London: Hamish Hamilton, 1989)

———, *The Way Out: Interviews, Impressions, Statements and Messages* (Karachi: Mahmood Publications, 1988)

Burki, Shahid Javed, *Pakistan under Bhutto, 1971–1977* (London: Macmillan, 1980)

Burnstein, Daniel, *Yen!* (New York: Simon & Schuster, 1988)

Bywater, Hector C., *The Great Pacific War: A History of the American–Japanese Campaign of 1931–33* (London: Constable, 1925)

———, *Sea-Power in the Pacific: A Study of the American–Japanese Problem* (London: Constable, 1921)

Chaudhuri, Nirad C., *The Autobiography of an Unknown Indian* (London: Macmillan, 1951; Hogarth Press, 1987)

———, *Thy Hand, Great Anarch! India 1921–1952* (London: Chatto & Windus, 1987)

Chee Soon Juan, *Dare to Change: An Alternative Vision for Singapore* (Singapore: Singapore Democratic Party, 1994)

Chinnock, Frank, *Nagasaki: The Forgotten Bomb* (London: Allen and Unwin, 1970).

Clarke, Thurston, *Pearl Harbor Ghosts: A Journey to Hawaii Then and Now* (New York: Morrow, 1991)

Couperus, Louis, *The Hidden Force,* trans. Alexander Teixera de Mattos, intro. E. M. Beekman (London: Quartet, 1992)

Craig, Gordon, *The Germans* (Harmondsworth, U.K.: Penguin, 1982)

Crichton, Michael, *Rising Sun* (London: Century, 1992)

Cromartie, Warren, with Robert Whiting, *Slugging It Out in Japan: An American Major Leaguer in the Tokyo Outfield* (Tokyo: Kodansha, 1991)

Cussler, Clive, *Dragon* (London: Grafton, 1990)

Devi, Maitreyi, *It Does Not Die: A Romance* (Chicago: University of Chicago Press, 1976)

Dougherty, Andrew J., *Japan 2000* (Rochester, NY: Rochester Institute of Technology, 1991)

Eliade, Mircea, *Autobiography,* trans. M. L. Ricketts (New York: Harper & Row, 2 vols., 1981)

———, *Bengal Nights,* trans. C. Spencer (Manchester: Carcarnet, 1993)

Fairbank, John K., Edwin O. Reischauer and Albert M. Craig, *East Asia: The Modern Transformation* (London: Allen & Unwin, 1965)

Fallows, James, *Looking at the Sun* (New York: Pantheon, 1994)

Fest, Joachim, *The Face of the Third Reich,* trans. Michael Bullock (London: Weidenfeld & Nicolson, 1970)

Gluck, Carol, *Japan's Modern Myths: Ideology in the Late Meiji Period* (Princeton: Princeton University Press, 1985)

Hart-Davis, Duff, *Hitler's Games* (London: Century, 1986)

Hayashi Fusao, *Daitowa Senso Koteiron* ("A Positive Evaluation of the Great East Asian War") (Tokyo: Miki Shobo, 1984)

Hibino Yutaka, *Nippon Shindo Ron, or the National Ideals of the Japanese People* (Cambridge: Cambridge University Press, 1928)

Hicks, George, *Hongkong Countdown* (Detroit: Cellar Bookstore, 1990)

Higuchi Ichiyo, *Growing Up,* trans. Edward Seidensticker and Donald Keene, in *Modern Japanese Literature,* (New York: Grove Press, 1956)

Hirano Kyoko, *Mr. Smith Goes to Tokyo: Japanese Cinema Under the American Occupation, 1945–1952* (Washington, D.C.: Smithsonian Institute Press, 1992)

Holstein, William J., *Japanese Power Game: What It Means for America* (New York: Macmillan, 1990)

Honan, William H., *Visions of Infamy: The Untold Story of How Journalist Hector C. Bywater Devised the Plans That Led to Pearl Harbor* (New York: St. Martin's Press, 1991)

Hosoe Eikoh, *Barakei: Ordeal by Roses—Photographs of Yukio Mishima* (New York: Aperture Press, 1985)

Howe, Russell Warren, *The Koreans* (San Diego: Harcourt Brace Jovanovich, 1988)

Ienago Saburo, *The Pacific War, 1931–1945* (New York: Random House, 1978)

Ishihara Shintaro, *Danko NO to Ieru Nippon* ("The Japan That Can Firmly Say NO") (Tokyo: Kobunsha, 1991)

———, *NO to Ieru Nippon* ("The Japan that can say NO") (Tokyo: Kobunsha, 1989)

James, Clive, *Flying Visits: Postcards from* The Observer, *1976–83* (London: Jonathan Cape, 1984)

Jeal, Tim, *Baden-Powell* (London: Hutchinson, 1989)

Jenkins, Rupert (ed.), *Nagasaki Journey: The Photographs of Yosuke Yamahata, August 10, 1945* (San Francisco: IDG Films/Pomegranate Artbooks, 1995).

Joaquin, Nick, *The Aquinos of Tarlac: An Essay on History as Three Generations* (Manila: Cacho Hermanos, 1983)

José, F. Sionil, *Ermita: A Filipino Novel* (Manila: Solidaridad Publishing House, 1988)

Karnow, Stanley, *In Our Image: America's Empire in the Philippines* (London: Century, 1990)

Katzenstein, Gary, *Funny Business: An Outsider's Year in Japan* (Englewood Cliffs, N.J.: Prentice-Hall, 1990)

Keene, Donald, *Dawn to the West* (New York: Henry Holt, 1984)

Kennan, George F., *American Diplomacy: 1900–1950* (London: Secker & Warburg, 1952)

Koestler, Arthur, *The Lotus and the Robot* (London: Hutchinson, 1966)

Komisar, Lucy, *Cory Aquino: The Story of a Revolution* (New York: George Braziller, 1987)

Kousbroek, Rudy, *Het Oostindisch kampsyndroom* (Amsterdam: Meulenhoff, 1992)

Kripalani, Krishna, *Rabindranath Tagore: A Biography* (Oxford: Oxford University Press, 1962; rev. ed. Calcutta: Visva-Bharati, 1980)

Laurie, Dennis, *Yankee Samurai: American Managers Speak Out About What It's Like to Work for Japanese Companies in the U.S.* (New York: Harper Business Books, 1992)

Lifton, Robert Jay, and Greg Mitchell, *Hiroshima in America: Fifty Years of Denial* (New York: Grosset/Putnam, 1995).

List, Herbert, *Herbert List: Junge Männer,* intro. Stephen Spender (London: Thames and Hudson, 1988)

MacAloon, John J., *This Great Symbol: Pierre de Coubertin and the Origins of the Modern Olympic Games* (Chicago: University of Chicago Press, 1981)

Mandell, Richard D., *The First Modern Olympics* (Berkeley: University of California Press, 1976)

Manea, Norman, *On Clowns: The Dictator and the West* (London: Weidenfeld & Nicolson, 1992)

Mars-Jones, Adam, *Venus Envy* (London: Chatto & Windus [Chatto Counterblasts no. 14], 1990)

Maruyama Masao, *Thought and Behaviour in Modern Japanese Politics,* trans. and ed. Ivan Morris (Oxford: Oxford University Press, 2nd ed. 1969)

Mishima Yukio, *Naked Festival* (Tokyo and New York: Walker/Weatherhill, 1968)

Mohammad, Mahathir, *The Challenge* (Kuala Lumpur: Pelanduk Publications, 1986)

Morishima Michio, *Why Has Japan "Succeeded": Western Technology and the Japanese Ethos* (Cambridge: Cambridge University Press, 1984)

Morita Akio, with Edwin M. Reingold and Shimomura Mitsuko, *Made in Japan: Akio Morita and Sony* (London: Collins, 1987)

Mumford, Lewis, *The Culture of Cities* (London: Secker & Warburg, 1938)

Murata Kiyoaki, *An Enemy Among Friends* (Tokyo and New York: Kodansha International, 1991)

Nagai Takashi, *The Bells of Nagasaki,* trans. William Johnston (Tokyo: Kodansha International, 1984).

Naipaul, V. S., *An Area of Darkness* (London: André Deutsch, 1964)

———, *The Enigma of Arrival* (London: Viking, 1987)

———, *Finding the Centre: Two Narratives* (London: André Deutsch, 1984)

———, *Guerrillas* (London: André Deutsch, 1975)

———, *India: A Million Mutinies Now* (London: Heinemann, 1990)

———, *The Overcrowded Barracoon, and Other Articles* (London: André Deutsch, 1972)

———, *The Return of Eva Perón; with The Killings in Trinidad* (London: André Deutsch, 1980)

———, *A Turn in the South* (London: Viking, 1989)

Nathan, John, *Mishima: A Biography* (London: Hamish Hamilton, 1975)

Nobile, Philip, ed., *Judgment at the Smithsonian: The Uncensored Script of the Smithsonian's 50th Anniversary Exhibit of the Enola Gay* (New York: Marlowe and Company, 1995).

Nosaka Akiyuki, *Amerika Hijiki* (1972), trans. J. Rubin, in *Contemporary Japanese Literature* (New York: Knopf, 1977)

Oshima Nagisa, *Cinema, Censorship and the State: The Writings of Nagisa Oshima* (Cambridge, Mass.: MIT Press, 1992)

———, *Taikenteki Sengo Eizoron* ("Experiential Postwar Film Theory") (Tokyo: Asahi Shimbunsha, 1975)

Ozawa Ichiro, *Blueprint for a New Japan* (Tokyo and New York: Kodansha International, 1994)

Pater, Walter, *Plato and the Platonists* (London: Macmillan, 1893)

Pedrosa, Carmen Navarro, *Imelda Marcos* (London: Weidenfeld & Nicolson, 1987)

Pieczenik, Steve, *Blood Heat* (San Diego: Harcourt Brace, 1988)

Pons, Philippe, *D'Edo à Tokyo: Mémoires et modernités* (Paris: Gallimard, 1988)

Quijano de Manila [Nick Joaquin], *Reportage on the Marcoses* (Manila: National Book Store, 1979)

Randall, John D., *The Tojo Virus* (New York: Zebra, 1991)

Ray, Satyajit, *Our Films, Their Films* (Calcutta: Orient Longman, 1976)

———, *Satyajit Ray: An Anthology of Statements on Ray and by Ray* (New Delhi: Directorate of Film Festivals, 1981)

———, *The Unicorn Expedition and Other Fantastic Tales of India* (New York: Dutton, 1987)

Reischauer, Edwin O., *My Life Between Japan and America* (New York: Harper & Row, 1986)

Richie, Donald, *The Inland Sea* (Tokyo and New York: Weatherhill, 1971)

Rosenthal, Michael, *The Character Factory: Baden-Powell and the Origins of the Boy Scout Movement* (London: Collins, 1986)

Rubinfien, Leo, and Donald Richie, *A Map of the East* (London: Thames and Hudson, 1992)

Rusbridger, James, and Eric Nave, *Betrayal at Pearl Harbor: How Churchill Lured Roosevelt Into World War II* (London: Michael O'Mara, 1991)

Said, Edward W., *Orientalism* (London: Routledge & Kegan Paul, 1978)

Seidensticker, Edward, *Kafu the Scribbler: The Life and Writings of Nagai Kafu, 1879–1959* (Stanford: Stanford University Press, 1965)

———, *Low City, High City: Tokyo from Edo to the Earthquake* (London: Allen Lane, 1983)

———, *This Country Japan* (Tokyo and New York: Kodansha International, 1979)

———, *Tokyo Rising: The City Since the Great Earthquake* (New York: Knopf, 1990)

Scott Stokes, Henry, *The Life and Death of Yukio Mishima* (London: Peter Owen, 1975)

Seow, Francis T., *To Catch a Tartar: A Dissident in Lee Kuan Yew's Prison* (New Haven: Yale Center for Southeast Asian Studies, 1994)

Shawcross, William, *Kowtow!* (London: Chatto & Windus [Chatto Counterblasts no. 6], 1989)

Skinner, William (ed.), *The City in Late Imperial China* (Stanford: Stanford University Press, 1977)

Tagore, Rabindranath, *The Home and the World* (Harmondsworth, U.K.: Penguin, 1985)

Tanizaki Junichiro, *Childhood Years: A Memoir,* trans. Paul McCarthy (London: Collins, 1990)

———, *Naomi,* trans. John Chambers (New York: Knopf, 1985)

———, *Renai oyobi Shikijo* ("Romantic Love and Sex") (Tokyo: Chuo Koronsha, 1932)

Theognis, *Theogony and Works and Days by Hesiod and Elegies of Theognis,* trans. Dorothea Wender (Harmondsworth, U.K.: Penguin, 1973)

Thesiger, Wilfred, *The Life of My Choice* (London: Collins, 1985)

———, *The Marsh Arabs* (London: Collins, 1964)

———, *Visions of a Nomad* (London: Collins, 1987)

Thompson, Robert Smith, *A Time for War: Franklin Delano Roosevelt and the Path to Pearl Harbor* (Englewood Cliffs, N.J.: Prentice-Hall, 1991)

Tobin, Joseph J. (ed.), *Re-Made in Japan: Everyday Life and Consumer Taste in a Changing Society* (New Haven and London: Yale University Press, 1992)

Treat, John Whittier, *Writing Ground Zero: Japanese Literature and the Atomic Bomb* (University of Chicago Press, 1995).

Uno Masami, *Doru ga Kami ni Naru Hi: Ima Koso Yudaya no Chisei ni Manabe* ("The Day the Dollar Becomes Paper: Why We Must Learn from Jewish Knowledge Now") (Tokyo: Bungei Shunju, 1987)

Vat, Dan van der, *The Pacific Campaign in World War II: The US-Japanese Naval War 1941–1945* (London: Hodder & Stoughton, 1992)

Wakabayashi, Bob Tadashi, *Anti-Foreignism and Western Learning in Early-Modern Japan: The New Theses of 1825* (Cambridge, Mass., Harvard University Press, 1986)

Watanabe Tsuneo and Iwata Jun'ichi, *The Love of the Samurai: A Thousand Years of Japanese Homosexuality* (London: GMP Publishers, 1989)

Whiting, Robert, *The Chrysanthemum and the Bat* (New York: Dodd, Mead, 1977)

———, *You Gotta Have Wa* (New York: Macmillan, 1989)

Wolferen, Karel van, *The Enigma of Japanese Power: People and Politics in a Stateless Nation* (London: Macmillan, 1989)

Yoshimoto Banana, *Kitchen,* trans. Megan Backus (London: Faber, 1993)

Yourcenar, Marguerite, *Mishima ou la vision de la vide* (Paris: Gallimard, 1985); trans. as *Mishima: A Vision of the Void* (Henley-on-Thames: Aidan Ellis, 1986)

Zaide, Gregorio F., *José Rizal: Asia's First Apostle of Nationalism* (Manila: FNB, 1970)

IAN BURUMA was educated in Holland and Japan, and has spent many years in Asia, which he has written about in such books as *God's Dust* and *Behind the Mask*. He has also written a novel, *Playing the Game*, a fictional biography of K. S. Ranjitsinhij, the Indian prince who played cricket for England in Edwardian Britain. *The Wages of Guilt*, an exploration of how Germany and Japan have come to terms with their aggressive pasts, was published in 1994. His most recent book is *Anglomania*, an exploration of the unique love-hate relationship between Britain and the rest of Europe. Buruma lives in London.

ABOUT THE TYPE

This book was set in Bembo, a typeface based on an old-style Roman face that was used for Cardinal Bembo's tract *De Aetna* in 1495. Bembo was cut by Francisco Griffo in the early sixteenth century. The Lanston Monotype Machine Company of Philadelphia brought the well-proportioned letter forms of Bembo to the United States in the 1930s.